To Brian,

with very best

wishes from

Malcolm

СЛАВЯНСКИЙ МИР
SLAVIANSKII MIR

СЛАВЯНСКИЙ МИР
SLAVIANSKII MIR

The Story of Slavonic Studies at The
University of Nottingham in the
Twentieth Century

MALCOLM V. JONES

BRAMCOTE PRESS
ILKESTON, DERBYSHIRE
2009

First published 2009 by
BRAMCOTE PRESS,
81 RAYNEHAM ROAD,
ILKESTON DE7 8RJ,
UNITED KINGDOM

Printed in Great Britain by
the MPG Books Group

ISBN 978-1-900405-16-4

CONTENTS

ILLUSTRATIONS

Page 1
Heads of Department in the twentieth century
Janko Lavrin (1918-52), John Fennell (1952-56), Frank Seeley (1957-67). Monica Partridge (1967-80), Malcolm Jones (1980-97), Peter Herrity (1997-2001)

Page 2
Staff and graduands 1968, Staff 1997

Page 3
Locations of the Department
The University College, Shakespeare Street; Trent Building; The Orchards

Page 4
Locations of the Department
Cherry Tree Buildings ('the cowsheds'), Trent Building (quadrangle on the occasion of the Jubilee Reunion in 1999)

Page 5
Russian Visitors to the Department
A group with the Soviet film star Elina Bystritskaia (early 1960s), The writer Vladimir Lidin with Soviet Lecturer Irina Kireeva (1969), G.M. Fridlender after receiving an honorary doctorate (1990), Lesley Milne bids farewell to St Petersburg scholar Marietta Tourian at the Graduands' party (1994)

Page 6
Teaching in a new language laboratory in the Trent Building (late 1960s), The newly installed satellite dish on the roof of the Trent Building (1986),

Page 7
The Coffee Room
The Room, Memo on the use of the Coffee Room (1968), Washing up the cups

Page 8
The Departmental Russian Play
Three Sisters (1989), *Zoia's Apartment* (1990), *Enemies* (1991),

The cover design is by Sarah Keeling, and incorporates a photograph taken of current and former members of the Department of Slavonic Studies at the Jubilee Reunion in 1999

Prologue

WRITING this book was in many respects an unusual personal pleasure, and I hope that it may bring equal enjoyment to its readers. Even if the opportunity had not presented itself, I should have wished one day to commit to writing some of my impressions of my long association with the department and the University, and to trace the ways in which the student experience has changed over the years. Whatever our different reasons for undertaking the study of Russian—and most of us will at some time or another have been asked for an explanation by bewildered friends and relatives—I suspect that most will share my lifelong fascination with a country and a culture that seem so like our own on the surface and so unlike our own deep down, or perhaps the reverse.

Having joined the Department of Slavonic Languages at The University of Nottingham as an undergraduate in 1958, I was later to study for a doctorate under Frank Seeley. Then, after a break of two years at The University of Sussex, I was to lecture in the Department of Slavonic Studies under Monica Partridge from 1967 to 1980, eventually serving as professor of Slavonic Studies myself from 1980 to 1997. For most of that time I was head of department as well. Moreover, I came to know personally both Janko Lavrin (the department's first professor) and John Fennell (its second head), not to mention almost all the other academic staff who lectured in Slavonic Studies at Nottingham in the twentieth century, its undergraduates and postgraduates, and the sequence of professors and lecturers who taught, taught with, and succeeded me.

This range of perspectives is rivalled, I think, only by that of Cynthia Marsh, professor and head of department at the present time.

The fortunes of the department have of course fluctuated over the years (though not as much as those of some of its distinguished rivals), but it has endured and has entered the twenty-first century as one of the strongest Russian and Slavonic departments in the country. That alone merits attention. Nottingham began teaching Russian as early as 1915 and no less a figure than Janko Lavrin (whose small books on Russian literature in at least fifteen languages have been avidly read by many generations of undergraduates in virtually every country where Russian literature has been taught and studied) was lecturer and then professor of Russian at Nottingham from 1918 to 1952, with only a short break for the Second World War. Rather surprisingly, this remarkable association seems to have escaped the notice of some chroniclers of Russian Studies in the United Kingdom, but Lavrin is now once again coming into his own, with the publication of his correspondence and a recent television documentary on him in his native Slovenia, and a panel on him planned for a major academic convention in the United States.

Until 1928, Russian was taught from the Nottingham University College in Shakespeare Street. When, in 1928, the Trent Building was opened by King George V on the Highfields site, the Arts and Pure Science departments of The University

College transferred there.[1] In 1948, it received its Royal Charter and became an independent university, and soon after that it acquired 'The Orchards', a private house behind the present Social Sciences Building, which was initially adapted for use by the departments of Law and Slavonic Languages.[2] Towards the end of the 1950s, however, the department moved to the temporary buildings (popularly known as the cowsheds, later rechristened Cherry Tree Buildings, and now demolished) behind the new Portland Building. It moved once while there and then, in 1968, it took up residence on the ground floor of the Trent Building (Floor A) next to the English Department. There it remained until the end of the century, since which it has moved twice within the Trent Building, firstly to the first floor (Floor B) and subsequently to the top floor (Floor C). During these moves, many relics of the department's history were at risk of being destroyed or lost and, with the department's approval, I began to collect material that might one day be of interest. Sue Taplin (née West), now a lecturer in Social Work at Nottingham, recalls a visit to the departmental store room on floor A in the late 1980s where, she says, 'I shall never forget the discovery of a packet of ready-salted crisps which were probably about twenty years old but which Malcolm nevertheless felt should be kept as an archive.' That was a joke—I promise—but it did prove possible to begin to assemble an archive at that time.

Not only the location of the department, but also its name, has changed several times over the years. Until 1932, sub-degree courses in Russian were listed in the Calendar under the Department of Modern Languages. From 1931 to 1933, Russian and Slavonic Languages was listed as a separate department, and for the first time General and Honours courses in Russian were offered at BA level. Then, in 1933, the word 'Russian' was dropped from the department's title: it was evidently realised that, being itself a Slavonic language, Russian did not need to be named separately. The Department of Slavonic Languages continued under that name for nearly thirty years until, in 1962, it was changed to the Department of Slavonic Studies, to indicate clearly that its courses were not limited to the study of language. So it remained until the end of the twentieth century when the word 'Russian' was reintroduced to ensure that Nottingham could easily be found by potential students searching the Internet for Russian courses. So now it is the Department of Russian and Slavonic Studies. However, on the assumption that my readers will need no such prompting, I have reverted to 'Slavonic Studies' in the title of this book.

In writing the book, I might have assumed the position of an outside observer and confined myself to a dry chronicle of names, events, publications, statistics, and facts like those presented in the previous three paragraphs. I soon realised however that this would have produced a book that, while it might have been factually reliable, would have been devoid of the human warmth and colour that most graduates associate with their period of study at Nottingham, and would have failed to convey to other readers the character of life there in bygone days. So I decided unashamedly to adopt for each chapter a perspective that reflected my own position

[1] The Applied Science departments remained at Shakespeare Street for the time being. In 1945, a decision was taken to separate the technical instruction given in the old building from The University College and to establish a new independent Technical College there. In due course, this developed into the present Nottingham Trent University. See A. C. Wood (1953), pp. 98 and 148.
[2] See Frank Barnes (1993), p. 431. Both Barnes and Fawcett (1998) refer to the house as 'The Orchard' (singular). This may be correct, but it has certainly been known as 'The Orchards' (plural) since the 1950s. It still is, as the sign at its entrance today confirms.

in relation to it. The perspectives of the various chapters are not of course even, or entirely objective. I have tried to make them as accurate as possible, drawing both on the reminiscences of graduates and colleagues, and on written records, as well as on my own fallible memory.

For the research on the first chapter, which covers the period during which Boris Slepchenko lectured in Russian at the then Nottingham University College, I am indebted to Professor James Muckle who has been working simultaneously on a history of the teaching of Russian in the United Kingdom.[3] He has also kept an eye on the succeeding chapters and raised pertinent questions about the national context in which Nottingham was operating.

The second chapter, on the lengthy period during which Janko Lavrin conducted courses in Russian and other Slavonic languages, including Serbo-Croat, Czech and Polish, draws on my personal acquaintanceship with the Lavrins when they were already advanced in years, but also on published materials; on the Lavrin archive held in the Department of Manuscripts and Special Collections at The University of Nottingham; and on the kind assistance of his two sons, John and David.[4] I am also indebted to the testimony of others who contributed to the documentary broadcast by Slovene TV in February 2007 (to which I also contributed myself). Like every chapter from here on, this one has also benefited from the recorded memories of students of the time. In one important respect, it is different in conception from all the other chapters. If it had been limited to Lavrin's Nottingham connections, it would have been very short, for we know little about his courses and even less about all but a handful of his students. So far as we know, only one student graduated with a BA honours degree before his last two years at Nottingham, when ten more names can be added to the list. However, Lavrin's life and career was in many ways so extraordinary that the temptation to tell the whole story, or as much of it as I have been able to retrieve and make room for, proved irresistible.

I also knew John Fennell, though less well. As I say in the relevant chapter, he turned up repeatedly at crucial junctures in my own career, but, apart from student recollections and the printed record, the chapter benefited from the scrutiny of his widow Marina and son Nicholas and from the help of Dr Harold Shukman, a Nottingham graduate and Fellow of St Antony's College, Oxford, who kept in touch with the department for many years, and served as external examiner from 1976 to 1981.

I was myself an undergraduate and postgraduate during the Frank Seeley years (1957-67) and I continued to correspond with him, meeting him occasionally on both sides of the Atlantic, until his death in 2000. My memories of his Nottingham period have been moderated by those of some of my contemporaries, by those who came just before and after, and by one of his colleagues, the late Dr Bernard Johnson, himself an undergraduate and postgraduate student at Nottingham, who lectured in the department from 1960 to 1965, before taking up a position at the London School of Economics where he remained until retirement.

Monica Partridge taught in the department from 1948 to 1980, a period of service rivalled only by Lavrin's, and was professor and head of department from 1967 to 1980; I accordingly knew her both as a student (1958-62) and as a colleague (1967-80), eventually succeeding her as professor and head of department on her

---

[3] J. Y. Muckle, *The Russian Language in Britain* (2008).
[4] I was sad to learn of the death of David Lavrin in January 2008.

retirement. Here again, I write from a position of involvement, moderated by the assistance of others, but my viewpoint inevitably shifts from that of a student to that of a member of the academic staff. It was while I was putting the finishing touches to this book that news arrived of Monica's death, aged ninety-two, at the Queen's Medical Centre in Nottingham. Towards the end of her long life, she had lived in a residential care home in the county.

Those who knew these heads of department and their colleagues will be aware that they were all, in different ways, complex personalities, and were capable of evoking varying impressions in those who worked with them and studied under them. Such variations are reflected in the responses that I have received from graduates. All of them had their warm supporters among students, and admirers among fellow-Slavists. Where memories are less warm, I have tried to give some hint of it without digging deeper or giving unnecessary offence. In most cases, this objective has been easily achieved.

It will be understood in the light of this last comment that the most difficult chapter for me to write was the one on the period when I was sole professor myself (1980-97). This is not just a question of giving an unbiased account of the successes and disappointments of the period over which I presided and of my own role in them. It is also because my own view inevitably diverged more and more from that of the student body and to some extent even from that of my colleagues. As I became convinced that the problems of Slavonic Studies in UK universities could be successfully addressed only from outside the department (both within the University and on a national level), it increasingly became a view from outside as well. I am therefore more than ever grateful to those graduates and colleagues whose own impressions of the period have helped to restore the balance.

It has been fascinating trying to match graduate memories with my own, and with the documentary evidence. While most correspondents welcomed the opportunity to relive what one of them called their 'fragrant memories' of Nottingham, and nearly all remembered it with great fondness and gratitude, others had difficulty in retrieving more than a few sketchy details, but these were no less welcome. Of those who replied to the circular from the Alumni Office sent out in the autumn of 2007, only one had been disappointed in the course. No doubt this was also true of some who did not respond, or whose contact details were unavailable when the circular went out. On their behalf, I have tried to indicate some of the weaknesses as well as the strengths of the course as it evolved over time. Inevitably, each part of it appealed to some more than to others. It would be strange if it were otherwise.

More amusingly, quite a number of the hazy recollections that surfaced showed how unreliable the human memory can be. Favourite pubs, buildings on campus, even the location of the department, were at times transposed to other places and even names and titles of appointments were remembered wrongly. None of us is immune to this sort of distorted memory and sometimes, on checking, we find that our most vivid recollections are inconsistent with established facts. This will not be news to the historian (including the amateur family historian) who makes frequent use of oral evidence, or who has multiple sources at his or her disposal, but it runs against the common assumption that the witness 'who was there at the time' will necessarily be the most dependable. Nor will the historian be surprised to find that information that one might have supposed to be in the public domain is often untraceable and apparently irretrievable. This was a particular problem in the early chapters, but not exclusively in them. It is relevant to the list of members of staff that I have provided in the Appendix. Here and there data have been lost, particularly the identity and periods of service of visiting or temporary lecturers who filled in during staff vacancies or were at Nottingham for only a short period, and these I have regretfully omitted. I have tried to check the dates of service of lectors and lectrices from the former USSR and Yugoslavia, but University Calendars (in which complete staff lists used to be published) are of uncertain help here, especially for the period during which Monica Partridge was head of department. This is because the Calendar often went to press before the identity of the following year's lector or lectrice was known, and Monica preferred to repeat the name of the current incumbent rather than leave a blank. As for the University's own staff records, I understand that these are now destroyed within a few years of the member of staff's departure. It is possible that the publication of this book will prompt corrections. I hope so.

Behind this narrative, of course, lurk other possible narratives, only hinted at. There are the stories of individual graduates and their passage into the world beyond the University. There are the personal stories of members of the academic staff, only developed to any extent in the chapter on Lavrin. There is the broader history of Slavonic Studies in the United Kingdom, which is taken up only in the first chapter, in setting the scene. And there is the whole history of Eurasia in the twentieth century, of the rise and fall of the Soviet Union and its sphere of influence, with the attendant story of relations between these countries and the United Kingdom in peace and war. Some of our undergraduates and postgraduates were brought into contact with these other stories, before, during or after their period of study at Nottingham, and here and there I have alluded to them by way of illustration.

And finally, there is the history of the development of the University itself. The experience of life at today's University with its 34,000 students, on its four Nottingham and two overseas campuses, would have been literally unrecognisable, and probably unimaginable, to the handful of locally based students learning Russian under Janko Lavrin in the 1920s on Shakespeare Street. But it is not simply a question of size and location, or even of the transformation of a provincial University College into a major international institution, appearing in the league tables among the top ten UK universities, and the top seventy in the world. There are also, of course, the changes in the international status of the United Kingdom over that period, together with those wrought by the irresistible march of technology and the globalisation of the student body.

Our conception of the University as such has changed as well, along with its articulation of its mission, and students' perception of their relationship to the institution and its courses. When I arrived at Nottingham in 1958, it was, in common with other UK universities, seen first and foremost as a community of scholars, seeking through research and publication to deepen human knowledge and understanding, and admitting successive generations of students to temporary membership. Moreover, the five per cent of the age group who gained admission were normally supported by generous grants from the state or a local authority. Though the majority of graduates would move into other fields of employment, where they might never use the subject they had studied, it was assumed that their intellectual skills would have benefited from systematic training in discrete fields of academic study and the rich experience of living at a university, where they could also develop their own life skills in traditional student activities. All would have developed such values as intellectual integrity, respect for the balance of evidence, the free exchange of ideas and the importance of aiming for high professional standards.

Nobody sought to measure the University's success in developing these qualities: the evidence would lie in the contribution that graduates would make to the world beyond the confines of academe. As the century wore on, universities were progressively made to recognise that they were also publicly accountable institutions, whose activities are roughly divided between research and teaching and that both should be subject to robust outside assessment. This viewpoint merged into that of the general public which, particularly as cohorts of first generation students overwhelmed those whose parents had received higher education, saw universities as higher-level colleges, and regarded the research function, if they were aware of it at all, as a sort of optional extra, which should not be allowed to interfere with the institution's teaching mission. From this point of view, universities had to adjust their academic mission to the requirements of their stakeholders, which included funding agencies, students and their parents: high among these priorities would be good grades and transferable skills for future employment. As governments set targets for higher proportions of the age group (not to mention other age groups) to go into higher education, and grants gave way to student loans, these pressures became irresistible.

Modularisation, with more focussed teaching, was one response to these pressures, but that came within an ethos that was more and more influenced (as changes in the language show) by business culture: public accountability, monitoring, assessment, audit, training, cost-effectiveness, targeting of resources, a less generous staff-student ratio, and a heightened awareness of the importance of public relations, of raising financial support from outside sources and, not least, of doing well in all the league tables.

Inevitably, there have been major losses as well as major gains in this process, but this is not the place to discuss them or to draw up a balance sheet. To judge from the responses that I have received from graduates, it would seem that the Department of Russian and Slavonic Studies has succeeded in preserving the best of the traditional ethos while making the most of the innovations. May it long continue to be so.

As for the chapter headings, I apologise to those who think that publications from or about universities should be humourless. In my first draft, I divided the text into chapters, according to who was head of department at the time, and named them accordingly. However, although the head of department—especially if the department is a small one and its head has a forceful personality—may have a powerful effect on its atmosphere and development, I by no means wished to imply that the head of department is the only person who really matters, or that this is a book chiefly about heads of department. In any case, the picture was complicated by the fact that Peter Herrity served as head of department for several years when I was the sole professor. Preserving my original divisions, I then turned to descriptive chapter headings, such as 'Modest Beginnings', 'Pioneering Years', and 'Expansion and Crisis', but decided that they were as dull as they were uninformative.

So I finally opted for the titles of well-known Russian works of literature. I have tried to capture something of the character of life during the relevant period in my choice of titles, but they should not be taken too literally, and no attempt should be made to dig for deeper meanings. I take full responsibility for the title of Chapter 3, though I cannot claim authorship of the joke. In order not to cause embarrassment, I shall allow the author to remain anonymous.

Acknowledgements

It would have been impossible to write this book without the assistance of the many graduates, former colleagues and others who have generously shared their memories, background knowledge and personal experience. I have mentioned many of these above or in the text that follows, but a further word of thanks will not be superfluous. Dates in brackets below indicate, where relevant, the year of graduation.

For assistance with the second chapter concerning Janko Lavrin and his Nottingham associations, I am particularly grateful to John Lavrin and the late David Lavrin (his sons); to Mitja Meršol (who knew the Lavrins when he worked as a journalist in London), Ana Nuša Dragan and other contributors to the Slovene TV programme on Janko Lavrin broadcast in February 2007; and also to Nancy Binyon (an occasional student, 1945-6), Herbert Brookes (one of the first cohort of Russian graduates from the new University of Nottingham in 1951) and Marion Uglow (née Hopkins, a subsidiary student of Russian, 1950-2). I am also very grateful to Peter Hoare, formerly Chief Librarian at the University, for giving me access to his notes on Lavrin and the Lavrin archive at an early stage of my research. My thanks also go to Richard Davies, of the Leeds Russian Archive, for allowing me to consult the transcript of an interview with Janko Lavrin conducted some years ago by Professor Gerald Smith, then working on his biography of D. S. Mirsky. Gerry has kindly agreed to my quoting it. He was of course himself a lecturer at Nottingham from 1964 to 1971 and became professor of Russian at Oxford in 1986.

The third chapter, covering the period when John Fennell was head of department, has benefited from the help of Dr Harold Shukman (1956) and from the scrutiny of Marina Fennell (John's widow) and Dr Nicholas Fennell (his son). For help with the period of transition from John Fennell's to Frank Seeley's headship, I am particularly grateful to Robert B. Wood and John Gowling (1958); and Joan Newiss (1959).

For the period when Frank Seeley was head of department, I gratefully acknowledge the assistance of the late Dr Bernard Johnson (1957); Arthur Mayer (1961); Joanna Hughes, née Penny, John Edwards and Gerry May (all of whom, as I did, graduated in 1962); Sasha Gillett, née Lubetkin (1964); Peter Hammond, Kate Hudspith, née Sheaf, Professor Cynthia Marsh, née Ball, Ruth Morgan, née Fisher, Kate Ray, née Jackson, and Peter Ray (1967). For help with the period of transition from the headship of Frank Seeley to that of Monica Partridge, my thanks go to Dr Robert Owen, Rita Price, née Pildins and the Revd Roger Stubbings (1968); and Sandra Kent, née Suter (1969).

Thanks for help with the period during which Monica Partridge was head of department are due to Julian Nundy and Terry Sandell (1970); Brenda Charlwood, Tina Pamplin, Sheila Sarkar, née Christopherson and Nancy Taplin, née Cunningham (1971); Charlotte Sing and Lawrence Weldon (1972); Heather Haslett, née Birch (1973); Roman Iwaskow, Graham Johnston and Jovan Marcetić (1975); Dr Della Thompson (subsidiary, 1975); Elaine Thawley, née Watkins (1976); Susan Coatman, née Bennett and Dorothy Strickland (1977); Elizabeth Masterman (1978) and John Culley (1979). Similar thanks for memories of the period of transition from Monica Partridge's headship to my own are due to Dr David Denton (1980, PhD 1984); and Lucyna Peracchi Cavendish, née Makuch and Paul Szyszczak (1982).

For the period of my own headship, shared latterly with Peter Herrity, I should like to express my gratitude to Stephanie Briggs, née Batty and Fiona Woodings, née Murdoch (1988); Julia Garrett, née Glover (1989); Robert Davison, Gina Mance and Sue Taplin, née West (1990); Justine Colley (1992); David Gatenby and Dan Vowles (1993); John Butler, James Tyrrell and Dr Alex Harrington (1995, PhD 2002); and Marcus Richardson (1996).

For the last three years of the century, during which Peter Herrity assumed the headship, valuable assistance was received from Corinne Redwood (1999) and Kate Curran, née Murphy (2000). I must also acknowledge with thanks similar assistance from Michael Snook (2007) who shared his reflections on the department in the twenty-first century.

Most of these memoirs would have been unavailable to me without the willingness of Katrine Scott-Mitchell of the Alumni Office to circulate those graduates on her data base with a request for their assistance: to her and to her colleagues in the Development Office I give my particular thanks; and also to Ann Howe, current Secretary to the Department of Russian and Slavonic Studies, who received them and forwarded them to me so efficiently.

I am also grateful to all those who have supplied photographs (whether I have used them or not); to Dr Dorothy Johnston, Caroline Kelly and Jayne Amat of the University's Department of Manuscripts and Special Collections for help in locating images of The University College, Shakespeare Street and the Temporary Buildings and for permission on behalf of the University to use them; to Martin Kirk and Lisa Gilligan of the Media and Public Relations Office for permission on behalf of the University to use the photographs of Professor G. M. Fridlender receiving his honorary doctorate in 1990, of the departmental staff in 1997, and the cover photograph; and to the Language Centre for the photograph of Gerald Smith at work with students. The photographs of the Trent Building, The Orchards and the Coffee Room are my own, as are the images of Lesley Milne with Marietta Tourian and the group photographs of staff and graduands in 1968, and of the Alumni Reunion in 1999. Cynthia Marsh took the photograph of me washing up cups in the coffee room because, she explains, it was such a rare event. Thanks are also due to her for permission to use three images of departmental plays found in the departmental archive, although it has unfortunately proved impossible to identify the original photographers. The image of Vladmir Lidin was also in the departmental archive, its origin unknown. Gerry May provided the group photograph taken on the occasion of the visit of Elina Bystritskaia. Permission to use portrait photographs of former heads of department was kindly given by the late David Lavrin (Janko Lavrin), Mrs Marina Fennell (John Fennell), Mrs Maria Seeley (Frank Seeley) and Simon Collins (Malcolm Jones and Peter Herrity). Permission to use the portrait photograph of Monica Partridge was given by the Manuscripts Department at The University of Nottingham. However, it proved impossible to contact the original photographer, Albert Towlson of Long Eaton, to whom we are ultimately indebted. The photograph of the group with the satellite dish on the roof of the Trent Building was taken by the University Library's Photographic and Printing Unit.

Needless to say, I also benefited enormously from conversations and correspondence with members of staff past and present, including former Serbo-Croat lectors and lectrices (Dora Maček (1982-3), Damir Kalogjera (1983-4 and 1993-4) and Marka Filipović (1986-7), and the present Slovene lectrice Ivana Petric Lasnik, who very kindly translated some of Lavrin's correspondence for me and provided me with information about Nottingham's Slovene courses. Among other past members of the lecturing staff whose help I gratefully acknowledge are Professor Gerald Smith, Dr Gerald Stone, Professor Peter Herrity, Professor Wendy Rosslyn and Sabina Grahek. Among existing members: Professor Cynthia Marsh, Professor Lesley Milne and Dr David Norris. I am also very grateful to Dr Derek Spring, formerly of the Department of History, for information about the Soviet Studies course and the Institute for Russian and Central and East European Studies (IRSCEES), and to Deirdre Evans for conversations relating to the Faculty of Arts. Helpful advice was also received from Professor John Beckett, John Massey Stewart and Brian Tolley. By no means least, I should like to express my very warm thanks to Jane Dewick, for providing me with otherwise irretrievable information about the department, and for her unique perspective on its affairs as its secretary for fifteen years.

Finally, a special word of thanks to Dr Della Thompson whose willingness to proof read, copy-edit and perform other editorial tasks was so generously given at a crucial stage in the writing; and to Professor James Muckle, to whom I am exceedingly grateful for his enthusiastic encouragement throughout this project—especially at moments when I was about to give it up—and for undertaking to publish the book under the imprint of the Bramcote Press, which already has to its credit many other important publications in the field. I am also grateful to Sarah Keeling of the Nottingham University Press for valuable professional assistance in preparing the illustrations and the cover design.

Malcolm V. Jones
Nottingham 2008

On the Eve

(1915-1918)

THE first person to lecture in Russian at The Nottingham University College was Basil Slepchenko, of whom no living memory remains. He was, nevertheless, in some sense the founder of the present Department of Russian and Slavonic Studies, and for that reason alone he deserves to be remembered, and the circumstances of his appointment deserve to be examined afresh. As indicated in the Introduction, the research for this short chapter was conducted by James Muckle, and the following account, slightly modified to conform to the style of the rest of the book, is essentially his.[1]

The idea of introducing the study of Russian to Nottingham's University College was first floated in 1915 by Arthur Durose, Chairman of the Nottingham Chamber of Commerce, on behalf of the Principal of The University College, William H. Heaton. At the time, The University College was situated on Shakespeare Street in the city centre. Its stately Victorian Gothic building[2] had been opened by Prince Leopold, Duke of Albany, in 1881, and it was still a fairly young, provincial institution, now feeling the effects of the First World War on its recruitment.

The initial response will be familiar to all pioneers in the teaching of Russian from that day to this. 'I met with a certain amount of opposition,' Heaton says, 'perhaps it would be more correct to say criticism, as to the possibility of English students acquiring the Russian language.'[3]

Why Russian, why Nottingham, and why 1915? In retrospect, it is clear that a number of factors led to the introduction of Russian at Nottingham at the time: commercial, political, military and, it has to be admitted, emotional. The College made use of all these arguments in support of its conviction that an institution of higher education that took itself and the modern world seriously had an intellectual obligation to include Russian in its curriculum.

Before the outbreak of war in 1914, Russia, its people and government, had on the whole had a bad image in Britain. Russia was widely perceived as the 'bear', an authoritarian, brutal regime of prisons and Siberian exile, where human rights were not respected and where free speech was denied. Disaffected émigrés disseminated a picture of the regime which was distasteful to the average British reader. The two nations had come to blows over the Crimea in the 1850s, and nearly did so again over the Balkans in 1878. Russia was seen as a threat to British imperial interests in

---

[1] For an account that sets this episode in a wider context, see James Muckle, 'Russian in the University Curriculum' (2008), pp. 359-81.
[2] Known as the Arkwright Building, it now belongs to the Nottingham Trent University.
[3] *Minutes of the Nottingham Chamber of Commerce Council Meeting*, 13 April 1915, pp. 19-21. Two bound volumes of printed minutes dated 1915-1918 are held in the Hallward Library, University of Nottingham, uncatalogued.

Asia, especially with respect to its ambitions in India. Russian terrorists and revolutionary activists in British exile, like Stepniak-Kravchinsky, even acquired a certain popularity in Britain for a while, being seen as heroic opponents of an oppressive government.

The British government itself was ambivalent. On the one hand, it was necessary to have smooth diplomatic relations with Russia. On the other, Russia was seen as a threat: Britain was suspected—probably correctly—of having supplied Japan with military intelligence in the Russo-Japanese War of 1904-5.

In the early years of the twentieth century, the British foreign secretary in the Liberal Government, Sir Edward Grey, sought to improve relations through the Anglo-Russian Convention of 1907. The Government, however, was split between those who took Grey's view and 'those in his own party who disliked Russia on principle'—like Lord Curzon, who saw Russian diplomacy as 'one long and manifold lie', and his successor as Viceroy of India, Lord Minto, who had 'a pathological distrust of Russia'.[4]

Far from high politics, the pulp literature of the time often cast Russia, along with France, as the bogeyman. One popular novel of 1911[5] portrays an invasion of the South coast of England by an evil alliance of French and Russian soldiers, who brutally and mercilessly kill, rape and pillage. Though people who read literature of this kind were scarcely likely to influence the introduction of Russian into universities, it must be said that more serious novelists too were apt to paint a distasteful picture: Joseph Conrad in his 1911 novel *Under Western Eyes*, which portrays both oppressive and sinister Russian officialdom and unprincipled, unrealistic and ineffective resistance to it by incompetent émigrés, wrote of 'hate and fear, the inseparable companions of an uneasy despotism'.

Happily, this was not the whole story. In spite of the political antipathy, a more favourable view of Russia was to become fashionable. In the 1890s, an Anglo-Russian Literary Society had been set up to promote all things Russian—not just literature—and did so with great energy and enthusiasm. There had always been enthusiasts for Russia and her culture and literature; Turgenev's major works had been translated into English during his lifetime (he died in 1883), and several dozen volumes of Tolstoy and Dostoevsky appeared before 1914. Dostoevsky's novels were taken as reinforcing the 'depressing' image of life in Russia, but all this literature had a striking effect upon the intellectual life of Britain. One of the literary elite captivated by the Russians at this time was Nottingham's most famous literary alumnus D.H. Lawrence, who, as early as 1911, had read Tolstoy's *War and Peace* and *Anna Karenina*, and Dostoevsky's *Crime and Punishment*.[6] In fact there is a further link with the teaching of Russian at Nottingham here, for although, so far as we know, Lawrence never met Janko Lavrin, Nottingham's first professor of Russian, Janko and his wife Nora became close friends of Jessie Chambers, the Miriam of *Sons and Lovers*.

In one of his stories, Somerset Maugham captured the new spirit:

---

[4] Keith Neilson (1995), pp. 12 and 16-17.
[5] Neilson, pp. 85-89.
[6] See George J. Zytaruk (1971).

It was at the time when Europe discovered Russia. Everyone was reading the Russian novelists, the Russian dancers captivated the civilised world, and the Russian composers set shivering the sensibility of persons who were beginning to want a change from Wagner. Russian art seized upon Europe with the virulence of an epidemic of influenza. New phrases became the fashion, new colours, new emotions, and the highbrows described themselves without a moment's hesitation as members of the intelligentsia. It was a difficult word to spell, but an easy one to say. Ashenden [Maugham's protagonist] fell like the rest, changed the cushions of his sitting-room, hung an ikon on the wall, read Chekoff and went to the ballet.[7]

A Russo-British Chamber of Commerce was founded in St Petersburg on 21 June 1916 and later extended to London. A few individual businessmen knew Russia well and spoke its language; some of them gave both moral and substantial financial support to further the cause of Russian studies.

Then, in 1914, Russia the bogeyman became our 'glorious ally'. When Russia and Germany went to war with each other, trading relations between them collapsed. The Nottingham Chamber of Commerce, along with very many of its counterparts in other cities, saw its opportunity. If only we had learned Russian during the past twenty years, as the Germans had, and set about exploiting the market, like the Germans, we should have been in a stronger position to exploit the situation now. Nevertheless, Nottingham could find new markets in Russia, provided people could be trained to seize the opportunity.

Before Nottingham, the teaching of Russian had been introduced at five English universities. Oxford and Cambridge had established Russian in the late nineteenth century. It was taught in the English Department at Manchester from 1904, while at Liverpool the redoubtable Bernard Pares began his lifelong crusade for Russian and East European Studies in 1908. London introduced Russian in the autumn of 1915, at the same time as Nottingham.

By comparison, there were four chairs of Slavonic languages in Germany before the War, three of them in Berlin.[8] In the USA, Russian was taught by 1913-14 at Harvard, California, Yale, Wisconsin and Chicago.[9] There were two chairs of Russian in France: Lille (founded 1892) and the Sorbonne (founded 1902).[10] Other West-European countries where Slavonic languages and culture were already studied and taught included Switzerland, Sweden and Denmark.

In Britain, universities were not alone in responding to the imperatives of international wartime trade. By 1916, Russian was appearing on the curriculum of several secondary schools, both state and 'public'; chambers of commerce all over the country were pressing county and municipal authorities to start Russian in their technical colleges. In addition to those already mentioned, Russian courses were being planned by 1916 at Birmingham, Sheffield, Leeds, Glasgow, Edinburgh,

---

[7] Somerset Maugham (1951), vol. 2, pp. 864-65.
[8] Anton Palme (1914?), pp. 131-36 (pp. 133-34).
[9] C. D. Meader (1913?), pp. 194-196. Meader was in charge at Michigan. See also W. B. Edgerton (1985), pp. 491-528. Edgerton regards only the first two as 'significant' departments at this time.
[10] J.Hamm (1985), pp. 245-303.

Southampton, Bristol and Armstrong College (University of Durham) at Newcastle. Industry and commerce were closely involved in the initiation of Russian courses in most of these places.

The minutes of the Nottingham Chamber of Commerce show that the first move came from the Principal of the College. We do not know, however, whether the letter he addressed to the Chamber followed informal contacts with its chairman or whether it was entirely his own initiative. At a meeting of 2 March 1915, a letter was read from the Principal seeking advice from the Chamber as to the necessity of providing classes in Russian and as to the 'probable response [...] by those engaged in commercial pursuits in the City if classes were started.'

The apparently cordial relationship between Principal W. H. Heaton and Chairman Arthur Durose is surprising in view of a major rumpus which had occurred in 1908. The Chamber of Commerce (of which Durose was not yet Chairman, but to which he belonged) had published a damning but—so the local press said—ill-informed report on the College, criticizing it for the low level of the teaching in some technical subjects, the small amount of higher-level studies, and its high running costs. This had provoked much wrath, correspondence and press comment, much of it to the detriment of the Chamber rather than the College. The *Nottingham Guardian*, while robustly defending the College, hinted at a more general dissatisfaction in the city, and commented that the population was neither particularly interested in education nor willing to pay much for it. Heaton had taken up office in 1911 and was involved neither in this controversy, nor in the scandal just before his appointment when the College had—inadvertently, says its official historian—falsified its returns of student numbers to the Board of Education, forcing the resignation of the former Principal.[11] It seems that the dust had settled by 1915, and that in the new wartime conditions College and Chamber were friends again.

The Chamber of Commerce took steps to explore the likelihood of young men from business houses in Nottingham being willing to join Russian courses, and to establish whether it was likely that a teacher could be found. It was estimated that fifty students were likely to present themselves. A teacher of Russian origin was found and appointed. In a very short space of time, the College prospectus offered instruction, both day and evening, and Russian classes were accordingly started in autumn 1915.

The fifty students hoped for did not quite materialize: the 1915 report to the Governors of The University College claimed a total of 'more than 40' day and evening students. The Chamber of Commerce was involved in the appointment of the teacher and contributed fifty pounds a year for two years to assist with the expense. They endowed a prize for excellence and they sought and obtained donations of 200 books from the Russian Ministry of Education on behalf of the College. The Ministry donated books to several English universities at this time.

Nottingham University College was untypical in that for nearly forty years Russian was taught not by British teachers, but entirely by Slavs. The first holder of a teaching post in Russian at Nottingham was Vasilii Semenovich Slepchenko, known in Britain as Basil Slepchenko, who served from 1915 to 1918.

---

[11]For a fuller account of these events and controversies, see A. C. Wood (1953), pp. 51-54.

The College archives tell us little about Mr Slepchenko, but materials have come to light[12] showing that he was a Kuban' Cossack from Ekaterinodar, born at Stanitsa Pereiaslavska on 27 February (old style) 1887. He had financed his studies at the Commercial Institute in Moscow by teaching in schools. His trip to England a few weeks before war broke out had been intended to improve his English as well as to investigate the possibility of exchanges between England and the Institute. He volunteered for service in H.M. forces in 1914, but was rejected as physically unfit, as were 27% of applicants at that time. Later in the war he was placed in the Army Reserve, but was exempted from military service by reason of being 'indispensable at [his] position'— presumably at the College. He found employment first as secretary to the Imperial Russian Consulate in Liverpool. Unexpectedly stranded in England by the outbreak of war, and presumably reluctant to return home after the Revolution, he was to make this country his home, becoming a naturalised British citizen in 1930.

The salary offered to Basil Slepchenko by the College is not known, but it cannot have been princely. His successor, Janko Lavrin, was awarded less than £200 a year, and whatever he and Slepchenko were receiving was almost certainly regarded as a part-time salary. While at the Nottingham College he taught also at technical schools in Derby and Leicester. Leicester budgeted for no more than £60 a year including travel expenses, and Derby paid him 12s. 6d. per evening in February 1917; in November, however, this was raised to 10s. 0d. per hour. At this period, full-time salaries at the Technical College ranged from £180 to £535 per annum. Even though the 10s. 0d. per hour was more than most lecturers received, and some received only 8s. 0d. an evening, Mr Slepchenko must have found it hard to make a living wage, though it was customary in those days, before nationally-negotiated salaries, for lecturers to receive a generous proportion of the fees paid by students to the University.

Slepchenko claimed to have had as many as 150 students in total at his peak, though this may be a slight exaggeration.[13] The Derby Municipal College of Commerce, where he taught for one year, 1917-18, was very highly regarded,[14] as were many such institutions at the time. The Leicester Technical School claimed to 'rank as one of the best in the country.'[15] Slepchenko taught there from 1916 to 1918. Though the teaching of Russian at Derby and Leicester is not the theme of this work, Mr Slepchenko's activity in those places is worthy of note. It may be thought curious, for example, that both institutions attracted significantly more Russian students than

---

[12]Basil Slepchenko: curriculum vitae of 1931 (typescript, 1 p.); Testimonial by A. Bruce Boswell, Professor of Russian, dated 28 Nov. 31 (typescript, 1 p.); Grant of British nationality by naturalisation, 28 June 1930. National Archives, Kew, certificate 18419, HO 144/11688, disclosed by request under Freedom of Information Act.

[13]Records of the Derby College do not show numbers of students studying Russian while Slepchenko was teaching there: there were 24 recorded by a Modern Language Association survey published in December 1917. He was apparently teaching 73 students at Leicester at that time: Modern Language Association, 'Memorandum on the Teaching of Russian' (adopted by the General Committee), *Modern Language Teaching*, xiii, 3-4, 1917 (pp. 75-85), p. 84.

[14]B. H. Tolley (2001), vol. 1, p. 9. Named the Derby Municipal Technical College, this institution was formed in 1891 from the former School of Art and the former School of Science.

[15]Kelly's *Leicestershire and Rutland Directory*, [title page and verso missing, date assumed to be 1916], p. 530.

Nottingham University College. It may be that the type of working- and lower-middle-class young man (and most of the students were male) who sought to learn Russian for commercial purposes was intimidated by a university-level establishment, even if the teaching of elementary language was little different from that at the technical and commercial colleges. It is also clear that Leicester Chamber of Commerce, as we shall see later, showed a good deal of initiative in exploiting the talents and experience of Slepchenko; Derby and Nottingham did not, apparently, do that.

The few scraps of evidence that we have help to build up a sketch of Slepchenko's character as a teacher. He played a prominent part in a 1917 conference of teachers of Russian, delivering a short paper on the assessment of students, which showed a strong awareness that enthusiasm for the subject could diminish if students were not assessed fairly.[16] Slepchenko also reminded participants at that conference of the importance of commercial Russian, which he seems at the time to have made his speciality, particularly in view of his fruitful link with the Chamber of Commerce at Leicester. The Chamber invited him to tour various Leicester industries in order to learn the appropriate terminology, find Russian terms for it and pass them on to his students. At the same time, the possibility was mooted of holding a small exhibition of Leicester goods in Moscow, at which some of Slepchenko's students would be present.[17] Political turmoil in Russia must have put an end to this imaginative suggestion, which may have been Slepchenko's idea.

A Board of Education report on Russian at Nottingham University College when Slepchenko was in charge in 1917 has not survived, but it was reportedly glowing—to such an extent that the Principal circulated it in bids for funding for the continuation of Russian teaching.[18] The Principal was a referee on Slepchenko's application for naturalisation much later, in 1930, and stated that he had remained on good terms with him for many years after his departure from Nottingham. In an academic testimonial of 1931, Professor Bruce Boswell of Liverpool praised Slepchenko's skill as a teacher, his experience and his zeal. This testimonial was written because Slepchenko had lost his job at Liverpool at that economically very difficult time. Boswell described his departure as 'disastrous to Russian studies and to me personally': it was due to financial stringency and no other cause. The (British) secret police described him as 'a person of splendid character and undoubted loyalty'.[19] We do not know if Slepchenko ever found another teaching post, but he may of course have returned to the business world. His name appeared as a visiting lecturer at Liverpool University until 1951, which may be the date of his death.

It should be remembered that colleges such as Nottingham saw it as their function to run courses of all types, not exclusively directed to degree-level study. Russian began in the commercial section, and degree qualifications were doubtless not sought by many students. This was by no means unusual for the time: even the School of Slavonic Studies at London University taught far more external students—as many as a hundred at one time—in contrast with the one or two who might have been presenting themselves for first or further degrees. Any who did seek a degree at

---

[16]B. Slepchenko (1917), pp. 163-64.
[17]*Minutes of the Leicester Chamber of Commerce*, 1915-20, held at Record Office for Leicestershire, Leicester and Rutland.
[18]*Council Minutes* 27.3.17.
[19]Papers relating to his grant of British citizenship.

Nottingham were prepared for The University of London external examinations. It was many years before Nottingham presented candidates for degrees in Russian.

We know little of the curriculum offered to the first Russian students at Nottingham, but it can be assumed that Mr Slepchenko gave them a good grounding in commercial language. Teaching materials at the time were very limited in scope, and dreary in appearance. They were not few in number, as one can see from the many advertisements in the *Times Russian Supplement*, a regular publication distributed gratis with *The Times* newspaper from 1914 to 1917, but most of them made little mark and are long-forgotten. Classes used Bondar's *Simplified Russian Method*, which contained an extensive commercial section. Bondar, an enterprising teacher at a commercial college in Manchester, also produced and sold magazine-type publications for learners of different standards of knowledge. In Nottingham, a course in Russian history was taught alongside the language classes. Public lectures on such topics as Anglo-Russian relations and the industrial resources of Russia were free to students of Russian. The link with London University suggests that Nottingham University College followed the tradition being established at London, what its proponent, Sir Bernard Pares, called 'nation study'. This meant attention to the history, culture, society and customs of a nation alongside the language. A much more recent generation of Russian teachers called it *stranovedenie*.

The optimism with which Russian was introduced was soon replaced by a sense of disappointment, reflected in the College's annual reports. Shortly after courses started in 1915 we read: 'In Russian a satisfactory start has been made, and the day and evening classes are being attended by more than 40 students.' A year later: 'Russian classes, day and evening, are being held, both for beginners and those who have completed one year's study, and there is a fair attendance.' It is also noted that German has almost disappeared. In December 1917 we learn: 'The day classes in Russian cannot be considered satisfactory: the number of students is at present—first year, ten; second year, two; third year, three. The attendance at evening Russian classes was fair last Session, but nothing to what it should be in a commercial community. At present the number attending is—first year, ten; second year, six; third year, two.' One must, of course, remember that it was precisely the young men who sought to learn Russian for commercial purposes who were being called up into the armed forces in large numbers and at short notice. This must have constantly disrupted classes.

Meanwhile, the minutes of the Council of the Nottingham Chamber of Commerce show no diminution of interest in matters Russian. The Minutes throughout 1915 and beyond refer regularly to Russian at the College. They also contain frequent references to trading conditions with Russia: a 'new Russian tariff' (13 April 1915) and in the same minutes, the 'formation of a Russian Chamber of Commerce in London on 25 March'. This body had been founded in Russia in 1908. Later in the year (5 October 1915) concern was voiced at the effect on Nottingham industry of increases in Russian customs duty, and a letter was read from the Russo-British Chamber of Commerce in Petrograd urging firms to explore the Russian market. In 1916, the Chamber resolved to 'facilitate the interchange between English and Russian families of the Commercial Classes for the purpose of learning the language vis-à-vis their own' (9 November 1916). This highly imaginative suggestion, a minute of 5 December 1916 noted, had been accepted with great enthusiasm by the Russo-British Chamber of Commerce. We have no evidence as to whether these exchanges (or any others proposed in many cities) ever took place. In 1917 the Chamber responded in detail to a government inquiry into modern languages in the education system. This was the report of one of the four committees set up by the Prime Minister, Herbert Asquith, in response to widespread wartime public disquiet about schools; the 'Modern Studies' committee was chaired by Sir Stanley Leathes.[20] The Chamber also pressed for the appointment of a Russian Consul or Vice-Consul in Nottingham 'having regard to the considerable commercial interests of Nottingham with Russia' (1 May 1917).

College minutes refer, we think not ironically, though we may be wrong, to 'the liberality of the Chamber of Commerce'. This 'liberality' amounted to £50 a year for two years. In addition Mr Durose personally had offered £20 for a prize 'in connexion with the teaching of Russian', but the Chamber thought they should more appropriately offer this sum in their own name. While all contributions were doubtless very gratefully received, it should be noted that the Birmingham Chamber of Commerce gave £10,000 and more to their civic university to establish Russian; similar sums were presented by businessmen and commercial enterprises to Leeds, Glasgow, Sheffield and Manchester Universities for Russian departments. The chair at Liverpool had been established with gifts and legacies of between six and seven thousand pounds in 1908.

In fact, the honeymoon with the businessmen of Nottingham was soon over. When invited to continue its subvention in May 1917, the Chamber of Commerce refused. It had been presented with details of the social and professional background of the forty-two students, both day and evening, and recorded in the minutes:

> The Chamber of Commerce had supported the initiative as a means to extending the trade between Nottingham and Russia at the end of the war. They had no interest in providing with tuition ladies intending to travel, foreigners and gentlemen of position. The majority of the young men whom the Chamber desired to assist have joined the army, whilst certain aliens are learning the language with the avowed intent of capturing the trade with Russia at the end of the war. Your committee is of opinion that some consideration should be given by the military authorities to youths who have made good progress with and are still studying the language with a view to going to Russia to represent Nottingham houses.
>
> Having regard to the above the Committee cannot recommend the Council to make a further unconditional grant, but suggests that the Chamber should offer to make a grant of £1.1s in respect of each student approved by the Foreign Trade Committee.[21]

The Chamber therefore took a myopic view. Russian was to be learned for purely commercial purposes: any money from the business world not spent on that was wasted. They could apparently not conceive that women might have reasons for

---

[20]*Report of the Committee appointed by the Prime Minister to enquire into the position of modern languages in the educational system of Great Britain*, HMSO, London, 1918. Command paper 9036
[21] Nottingham Chamber of Commerce Council Minutes, 1.5.17.

language study except for travel. This attitude was outmoded even in 1917: many women had known for twenty years that a knowledge of Russian provided opportunities for 'remunerative women's work' in translation and journalism, for example. Blinkered attitudes among some business people persist to this day, when business representatives on national consultative committees on education are known to declare that business has no interest in culture, but only in the mechanical aspect of interpretership. Happily for other universities, the business benefactors elsewhere did not take the view held in Nottingham. In Birmingham, for example, they specifically stated that they had no desire to manipulate the University, and they did not do so.

The information to which the Nottingham Chamber of Commerce reacted in this way concerned the social provenance of the students. This was:

Day students: 2 lace manufacturers; 5 no occupation; 3 students, (six of these ten were women) ,
Evening students: 1 lace manufacturer; 1 hosiery manufacturer; 1 solicitor; 4 teachers; 1 clerk of works; 3 no occupation; 2 managers; 3 warehousemen; 14 clerks; 1 agent; 1 apprentice hosier[22]

On the face of it, it is hard to see why the Chamber of Commerce felt it was not getting value for its niggardly £50.

Maybe it was this lack of support that caused Basil Slepchenko to seek a move. In 1918, he offered his resignation in order to take up a joint lectureship at Liverpool University and Liverpool College of Commerce.[23] This cooperation in Russian-teaching appointments had been in force in Liverpool for ten years already; in practice it probably resembled the arrangement he had set up for himself by teaching at Derby and Leicester. Slepchenko was replaced by Janko Lavrin, who was to stay and run Russian single-handedly for nearly thirty-five years. He is the subject of the next chapter.

College reports continued: in 1918 'German and Russian [may be described] as under an eclipse.' The Report for 1919 is worth quoting in detail:

During the early part of the Session 1918-19 war-weariness made itself felt [...] Evening classes were well attended as far as numbers go, without any great enthusiasm for real work being discernible. It is pleasing to note that peace has wrought a complete change in this respect [...] German is reviving [...] Russian showed some revival after Mr Lavrin's appointment and a respectable start has also been made with Serbian.

Many demobilized officers are taking courses in economics and commerce. Classes in Russian are offered to them along with French, German, Italian and Portuguese.

As far as Russian was concerned, external factors were again influencing events. The February Revolution of 1917 was not the issue: it was the October Bolshevik

---

[22] Ibid.
[23] Bernard Pares (1939), pp. 55-72 (p. 58).

Revolution that entirely changed the situation. Russia was no longer willing to continue the struggle against Germany; the Western allies were to fight on alone. The essayist Max Beerbohm amusingly expressed the feeling of the time:

> There was, at the outbreak of the War, a great impulse towards Russian. All sorts of people wanted their children to be taught Russian without a moment's delay. I do not remember that they wanted to learn it themselves; but they felt an extreme need that their offspring should hereafter be able to converse with moujiks about ikons and the Little Father and anything else—if there were anything else—that moujiks cared about. This need, however, is not felt now. When, so soon after his début in high politics, M. Kerensky was superseded by M. Lenin, Russian was forthwith deemed a not quite nice language, even for children. Russia's alphabet was withdrawn from the nurseries as abruptly as it had been brought in, and le chapeau de la cousine du jardinier was re-indued with its old importance.[24]

There is an essential truth behind the flippant style of this passage. Just as war and all the emotional pressure which went along with the knowledge that Britain was allied with Russia brought about the institution of Russian studies, it might have been expected that Russia's withdrawal from the War in 1918 would put this process into reverse. The failure of Britain and the West to understand the situation in Russia has been incisively chronicled by George F. Kennan.[25] The Western allies were desperate to ensure that Russia stayed in the War but, if they had had any ability to judge rationally, they would have perceived that Russia could not do so.

The consequent disillusionment with our once 'glorious ally' did not, however, undermine the establishment of Russian Studies in British higher education. This is a credit to the teachers and professors who tirelessly promoted the subject. One writer commented at the time of the October Revolution: 'The test of their ability [that is, of teachers of Russian] will be their success or failure in maintaining the newly founded study of Russian in spite of the complete collapse of popular enthusiasm for the subject.[26] This refrain might have been heard the length of the twentieth century, for the subject, as we shall see, has been notoriously susceptible to swings in public opinion, quite outside the control of teachers and academics.

What with war-weariness, a totally new political situation in Russia, a change in fashion, and the collapse of popular enthusiasm, it is perhaps a wonder that Russian studies survived at all. In the institutions where the only motivation had been commercial, it did not survive to any great extent: it suffered a steep decline in the technical colleges. In schools too enthusiasm waned. In the universities, however, intellectual and academic reasons for supporting Russian departments had been well accepted, and sudden post-war change was not sufficient to undermine that position. In some universities, plans to start Russian departments got under way only after the War. True, in Belfast, money allocated to Russian was quickly switched to Spanish. In Edinburgh, Bristol, Armstrong College, Newcastle, and Southampton, the mainly part-time courses in Russian petered out after a few years. At Birmingham,

---

[24] Max Beerbohm (1920).
[25] G. F. Kennan (1960, 1961). He writes of 'the myopia of the Western capitals in the face of Russia's growing agony' (p. 19.)
[26] G. Waterhouse (1917), pp. 219-221.

Cambridge, Leeds, Liverpool, London, Manchester, Oxford and Sheffield, however, Russian survived for many years. Of these universities, only Liverpool has now closed its Russian department: the remainder continue to flourish. The fact that more than 90 years later Nottingham has one of the strongest Departments of Russian and Slavonic Studies in the country, despite the minimal financial support it received at the beginning, is a testimony to the strength of the foundations laid by Basil Slepchenko, and subsequently by Janko Lavrin, and to the moral support that the subject received from colleagues in other subjects and from the College and University authorities.

In the chapters that follow, I shall attempt to place developments at Nottingham in the wider, national context only when they seem to demand it. However, those interested in this background may find it in articles by two Slavists with Nottingham connections.[27]

---

[27] Gerald Stone (1985); Malcolm V. Jones (2005).

Virgin Soil Upturned

(1918-1952)

Introduction

WHEN I was appointed to the Chair of Slavonic Studies in 1980, I realised that I already knew all my predecessors as professor and head of department personally, apart from Janko Lavrin himself, who had occupied that position, with a break for the Second World War from 1918 to 1952. I did of course know his books (like many others all over the Western world, I had benefited from them as a student) and I had heard that he could hold an audience spellbound. I had also read his recollections of his period at Nottingham, written for the departmental journal *Slavonica*[1] in celebration of its sixtieth birthday in 1977. I realised that he was now in his nineties and I immediately wrote to him to introduce myself and to ask if we might meet. The very next day, he contacted me by phone and invited me to the flat he shared with his wife Nora in London, at 28 Lower Addison Gardens.

I made haste to visit them and to make their acquaintance. Janko indicated to me that he would like to donate some books to the University Library. These were busy times in my professional life—I was soon to become Dean of the Arts Faculty—and it was very difficult to find free days to visit Shepherd's Bush. So I suggested that Peter Hoare, then Chief Librarian at the University, accompany me on my next visit. From then on, Peter called on the Lavrins more often than I did, and it was thus that not only gifts of books, but the entire Lavrin archive came to Nottingham University, including some paintings, drawings and lino-cuts by Nora.[2] Peter was so fascinated that, on top of his other duties, he began to research the materials himself.

We got to know the Lavrins quite well as a result of these visits. They were now a charming and agreeable elderly couple, both still very active in spite of advancing years. Janko delighted in recalling his past but, sadly, it was now often impossible to pin his recollections down to exact times and places. I was later to learn that his family had encountered similar problems. Nora had been an accomplished professional artist and book illustrator. More than once, they sent me postcards, which she had designed herself using scraper boards, and which showed Addison Gardens with the back of their flat just visible at the left-hand side. In their spacious, old-fashioned flat, full of atmosphere, they would treat us to coffee and banana custard in sundae glasses, and Janko would regale us with his recollections.

---

[1] Janko Lavrin (1977). *Slavonica* was a journal published by students of Nottingham's Slavonic Studies department for many years. It had no connection with the present-day academic journal published at the University of Manchester, which adopted the same name some years later.
[2] Nora's illustrations of their 1928 honeymoon in Slovenia were deposited in the Ashmolean Museum, Oxford, and recently published as Nora Lavrin (2004).

The University, where he had worked for so long, began to take notice of him again. By way of acknowledgement of his generous gifts, the University Library planned an exhibition to mark his centenary in 1987; in recognition of his contribution to the study of Dostoevsky, Garth Terry and I, as co-editors of *New Essays on Dostoyevsky,*[3] dedicated the volume to him when it was published in 1983; Monica Partridge, my predecessor as head of department and a protégée of Lavrin, arranged for a book on D. H. Lawrence, illustrated and written by Nora, to be published in 1986 by Astra Press[4]; and, on the eve of his death in 1987, the University was belatedly exploring the possibility of awarding him an honorary doctorate. Unhappily, the proposal to award the honorary degree came too late, though it would have given him great satisfaction, and the exhibition, of necessity, became a memorial one. In the course of time, Janko and Nora's elder son, John, himself an artist, made further valuable deposits of correspondence, and I myself began to explore the Lavrin archive, to accumulate materials for a biography and to publish the occasional article on his legacy.[5]

Fragmentary information about Janko's long and eventful life soon began to accumulate; indeed we were not the first in the field; there were already encyclopaedia articles and other publications devoted wholly or partly to him. But it was from David, the Lavrins' second son, that I first obtained details of Janko's Slovene origins.

Childhood and Youth

His father, David said, was born on 10 February 1887 in the village of Krupa in Bela Krajina, then a part of the Austro-Hungarian Empire. He had one sister, Anka, who was a year or so younger than him. His parents died before he was 5, possibly of tuberculosis, and he was looked after initially by his grandparents, then by an uncle who was a priest in a nearby village. He was regarded as very bright, and a promising future priest; so he was sent away to a seminary school in Novo Mesto. He disliked it very much, and found the teachers dictatorial and oppressive, but benefited greatly from the rigorous instruction that they gave. Apart from Slovene, Serbo-Croatian and German, which he grew up with, he also learnt Latin and Greek, which gave him a basis for most European languages. He also learned Italian at an early age. In subsequent visits to Krupa he enjoyed the ceremonies associated with the local church, but the seminary seems to have completely turned him off religion: he was well versed in theology, but neither David nor John could ever remember him expressing any religious belief. According to information gathered by Janja Žitnik[6], Lavrin was born on a wealthy farm, and on the death of his parents 'by the age of 6', his guardians found tenants for the farm he inherited. But the young heir received no share of the income; his relatives exploited him and he had a difficult childhood. She adds that he attended grammar schools from 1899 to 1907, first in Novo Mesto, and then, from 1905, in Sušak. Even at school, she says, he suffered financial hardship and had to support himself by giving lessons.[7] According to

---

[3] Malcolm V. Jones and Garth M. Terry, eds. (1983).
[4] Nora Lavrin (1986). Astra Press was (and still is) owned by Garth Terry, a graduate of the department and former Slavonic Librarian.
[5] Malcolm V. Jones (1996); Malcolm V. Jones (2001).
[6] Janja Žitnik (1996).
[7] Žitnik, p. 4.

Lavrin's niece, his sister Anka eventually proposed giving him her dowry in exchange for his rights to the farm. He agreed to this, signed the papers, and the very next day he left the village for good.[8]

St Petersburg

Before he turned eighteen, the young Lavrin left Austria-Hungary to avoid military conscription or state service and travelled across Europe, picking up languages as he went, following literary and artistic trails. For example, his liking for Ibsen took him to Norway; he was in Paris for a while, then in Prague, where he followed courses at the University and finally ended up in St Petersburg in 1908, where he enrolled in the Archaeological Institute. Although he seems to have followed a number of University courses in European universities, Lavrin never, so far as we know, pursued them to the point of obtaining an academic qualification. His subsequent MA was awarded to him ex officio by The University of Nottingham when it became an independent University in 1948, presumably because it was embarrassed to have a professor without a degree. All his life, Lavrin was an intellectual and a creative thinker, rather than an academic in the traditional sense. What mattered to him was the free life of the mind and spirit, not paper qualifications or dull documentation, and, once in St Petersburg, he swiftly gained entrée into the intellectual and cultural life of the Russian capital.

The speed and ease with which he apparently became an active part of this life is still a cause for amazement. He must have had introductions. His contacts were already sufficient by 1909 for the promising young artist Boris Kustodiev (1878-1927) to paint him in oils. The portrait is now in the keeping of the Russian Museum in St Petersburg and was recently on display there[9]. Kustodiev, who, like Lavrin, had been educated in a seminary, had been attracted by the life of the artist, and had also studied in Paris. By 1809, he had achieved a considerable reputation as a portraitist and painter with a special interest in folk traditions, so he was not short of willing sitters. There must have been something that drew the two men together.

Slavianskii mir

It may have been a common interest in Slav folk traditions for, as early as December 1908, we find Lavrin publishing and co-editing a new journal called *Slavianskii mir* (*The Slavonic World*), a St Petersburg publication that was to endure until May 1911. There had, of course, been such journals before, dedicated to the dissemination and mutual knowledge of Slav cultures, but what was new about this one was its left-wing tendency and its commitment to Slav unity. Its appearance in 1908 was not a matter of pure chance: it was the year of the Austro-Hungarian annexation of Bosnia and Herzegovina and of the Slav Congress in Prague. It is even possible, though we do not know this for certain[10], that Lavrin was in some way involved in the Prague

---

[8] As recorded in a television programme on Janko Lavrin broadcast by Slovene TV in February 2007.

[9] It was spotted by my colleague James Muckle. Contact was subsequently made with the Russian Museum and a photographic reproduction obtained through the good offices of Sarah Young on a visit there in 2004. The young Lavrin sports long black hair and the then fashionable goatee beard and moustache.

[10] Although we at present have no evidence one way or the other, it is rather difficult to imagine Lavrin not getting involved in the Slav Congress if he was in Prague at the time.

Congress and, enthused by the launch of a new form of Panslavism to be known as Neoslavism, hurried to St Petersburg with the establishment of a new journal in mind.

In 1981, the Soviet scholar O.V. Mudrova published a fascinating article on *Slavianskii mir* and on Lavrin's involvement with it.[11] As well as being co-editor with M.V. Shil'der until 1909, and M. I. Khrutskaia thereafter, Lavrin published in it a large number of his own articles and translations under the pseudonym Lev Savin (sometimes contracted to L. S. or just L.). Work on the journal brought Lavrin into contact with many distinguished Russian writers and academics.[12]

The journal did of course print material on modern Russian poets and writers (including Lermontov, Tolstoi and Andreev), but its pages were principally dedicated to translations from other Slavonic languages, particularly those of the future Yugoslavia, among which were the first Russian translations of the prose works of Ivan Cankar, the poems of Prešeren and works by a large number of prominent Serbian and Croatian writers. 'Lev Savin' also wrote articles about Cankar, who was accorded greater prominence in the pages of *Slavianskii mir* than any other Slavonic writer, and drew attention to the influence of modernism on his work. According to Lev Savin, the motifs of death, suffering and futility stalk the works of Cankar and other Yugoslav writers, but the fact that one lives in a fog does not mean that there is no sunshine beyond. It is the task of literature to create new men, new forces and new hopes, characteristics that he saw in the poetry of Anton Aškerc.

The journal did not restrict its coverage to purely literary matters. Among the ideas promoted by Lavrin and the journal were the development of national Slav cultures; the superiority of the Slav world over that of Europe and its potential for bringing new life to European culture; the unity of the Slav nations (in which context Lavrin commended the unification of Serbian and Croatian literatures); and the importance of bringing the intelligentsia and the people into closer contact. The journal discussed the possibility of a common Slavonic language, but reported a general preference for the adoption of the mother tongue of Turgenev, Tolstoi and Dostoevsky as a lingua franca. Underlying everything was the then fashionable debate about the opposition between civilisation and culture, to which Lavrin brought his own ideas. In such ways, democratic ideals were combined with some of the ideas preached by the Slavophiles.

When the journal closed in 1911, Lavrin was still only 24, and his contributions already testify to that irrepressible energy and enthusiasm, intellectual as well as physical, that characterised him in later years. He mopped up ideas, made them his own and propagated them with immense enthusiasm, sweeping others along in his wake and overcoming his organisational inexperience by the force of his personality. When this enthusiast for the superiority of all things Slav found himself making his

---

[11] O. V. Mudrova (1981).

[12] Among the academics who wrote for *Slavianskii mir*, and listed by Mudrova, were the Slavonic philologist Aleksandr Ivanovich Iatsimirsky; the historian, philologist and linguist Aleksandr L'vovich Pogodin; professor of St Petersburg University and corresponding member of the Academy of Sciences, Petr Alekseevich Lavrov; Academician Vladimir Mikhailovich Bekhterev, at that time much involved in the promotion of cooperation between scientists and medical specialists from the Slavonic countries. The journal also enlisted the support of first-rate translators from the Slavonic languages, such as N. N. Bakhtin (pseudonym N. Novich), A. N. Sirotinin, S. V. Stein and V. N. Korabl'ev. Mudrova also lists a number of contributors from other Slavonic countries resident in St Petersburg.

home in England for the last 70 years of his life, some temporising would be necessary. But he never lost his love of his native country and, for that matter, never concealed his reservations about his adoptive homeland. He was in his element among groups of intellectuals, afire with ideas and artistic promise. It hardly mattered whether it was Oslo, Paris, St Petersburg or London. For Lavrin, it was culture and thought that gave life its meaning and no other pursuit would be truly worthy of his attention.

St Petersburg Literary Circles

During his stay in St Petersburg, Lavrin mixed in a number of literary circles and made the acquaintance of many prominent Russian writers. These included Vladimir Maiakovsky, whom he knew well, but did not much like, Sergei Gorodetsky, with whom he worked on *Veles* and who was a great friend, Fedor Sologub, Osip Mandel'stam, Anna Akhmatova, Nikolai Gumilev and Velimir Khlebnikov. Khlebnikov actually lived in his flat for five or six weeks.[13]

In his reminiscences of Velimir Khlebnikov, published in 1985,[14] Lavrin recalled how, in December 1912 or January 1913, he sought out Khlebnikov's home in downtown Moscow, and how disenchanted he was at first by the impression of poverty and chaos: papers, books, pieces of linen and clothing, even unwashed plates, strewn everywhere.

At first, Khlebnikov was cautious in his welcome, and looked perplexed on hearing that Lavrin had come on the recommendation of Burliuk and Maiakovsky.[15] But his face lit up on learning that his visitor was a South Slav and the acquaintance-ship that followed was evidently of considerable value to the poet in further developing his knowledge of non-Russian Slav cultures.[16]

The 26-year-old Lavrin was at this time Secretary of the *Obshchestvo slavianskogo nauchnogo edineniia* (*The Society for Slav Scientific and Scholarly Unification*).[17] He recalls that at some time Khlebnikov had changed his name from Viktor to the South Slav Velimir and that they conversed about folklore and the work of Vuk Karadzić in collecting Serbian epic folk songs. Three weeks later, Khlebnikov visited Lavrin in St Petersburg on the Ofitserskaia ulitsa. At that time, Lavrin was working on the journal *Argus* in the centre of town. Having no means of support, Khlebnikov stayed with him for at least a month.

While Khlebnikov was staying with him, Lavrin tried, with little apparent success, to introduce him to the artistic circles in which he was moving. He recalls:

---

[13] This information is taken from the transcript of an interview by Professor Gerald Smith with Emeritus Professor Janko Lavrin at 28 Lower Addison Gardens, on 30 January 1974, at present in the possession of the Leeds Russian Archive (Ms 400/3). Elsewhere in the interview Lavrin comments on his acquaintanceship with Rozanov in London and Remizov in Paris. However, the main focus of the interview is not Janko Lavrin himself, but D.S. Mirsky, on whom Smith was at that time preparing a book.

[14] Janko Lavrin (1985).

[15] See A. E. Parnis (1992).

[16] Parnis, p. 139.

[17] Parnis, p. 138. The Society published a collection of essays entitled *Slavianskii vopros v ego sovremennom znachenii: rechi i stat'i A. M. Aleksandrova, V. M. Bekhterova, M. M. Kovalevskogo, Ianko Lavrina, D. I. Semiza i M. P. Chubinskogo*, Obshchestvo slavianskogo edineniia, St Petersburg, 1913.

Even at the home of Ol'ga Ivanovna Leshkova, the high-spirited and witty friend of the artist Le-Dantiu, in whose flat young artists and writers such as Mikhail Le-Dantiu, Nikolai Lapshin, Il'ia Zdanevich and others would assemble, he would sit engrossed in his own thoughts and make little effort to strike up new acquaintanceships.[18]

Lavrin also introduced Khlebnikov to Boris Kustodiev, who lived close by, and subsequently obtained a commission for him on the newspaper *Slavianin*, whose editor he knew slightly.

On one occasion, Khlebnikov read him his poem 'Mariia Vechora' and asked if Lavrin could provide any further information about the subject of his work, to which Lavrin disconcertingly (and not necessarily correctly) replied that his heroine's name was probably of Greek origin.[19] On other occasions, he attempted to put him right about the derivation of words that took Khlebnikov's fancy owing to their phonic resemblance to other Slav words. The Slovene word 'zemlja' (bread roll), he told him, was cognate with the German 'Semmel', not as Khlebnikov would have liked to think, the Russian 'zemlia' (earth). He comments on the 'unscientific' character of Khlebnikov's approach to etymology.[20]

However this may be, there seems little doubt of the importance to Khlebnikov's poetic development of the encounter with Lavrin at a vital moment in his life. Lavrin's Slav programme perfectly complemented and augmented Khlebnikov's cultural and linguistic programme. Bearing in mind that Lavrin's reminiscences were penned more than seventy years after the events they describe, and that he was then approaching his nineties, the detail in which he recalls their exchanges is remarkable. By contrast with his account of the Khlebnikov episode, Lavrin was not very forthcoming in his later years about his other acquaintances among the literary elite of St Petersburg.

For someone who was interested in avant-garde literature, it is striking that Lavrin makes no mention of an epoch-making cultural event involving Khlebnikov that took place in St Petersburg in December 1912, namely the promulgation of the Futurist Manifesto, *Poshchechina obshchestvennomu vkusu* (*A slap in the face of public taste*), jointly signed by Khlebnikov, Maiakovsky, Burliuk and Kruchenykh. Since two of these (Burliuk and Maiakovsky) had originally despatched Lavrin to Khlebnikov's flat in Moscow, there can be little doubt that Lavrin knew of it, but it seems that his interest in such avant-garde developments was not always matched by sympathy and understanding. The omission perhaps echoes the preference for the style of old-fashioned realism, which Mudrova sees as a feature of Lavrin's contributions to *Slavianskii mir* and which is evident in his own writing of the period.

Perhaps this also explains why he was not always taken as seriously as he would have liked in avant-garde circles. Mudrova gives a hint of this, recalling that in the

---

[18] Lavrin (1985), p. 98.

[19] Other authorities hold that she was of Rumanian or Hungarian extraction. Cf. footnote 4 to Lavrin, p. 98.

[20] For Khlebnikov's own reflections (1915) on 'z' as the initial letter of words referring to reflecting surfaces and reflected rays, see 'Z i ego okolitsa', in N. Khardziev and T. Grits, eds, *Velimir Khlebnikov, neizdannye proizvedeniia*, Khudozhestvennaia literatura, Moscow, 1940, pp. 346-8; or, on 'z' as the resonant vibration of distant strings, see 'Perechen'. Azbuka uma', in Iu. Tynianov and N. Stepanov, eds., *Sobranie proizvedenii Velimira Khlebnikova* (5 Vols.), Izdatel'stvo pisatelei v Leningrade, 1928-33, 5, pp. 207-9.

years 1915 to 1916 one of the literary circles that he frequented—the one he had tried to introduce Khlebnikov to—circulated among its members a duplicated journal entitled *Beskrovnoe ubiistvo* (*Bloodless Murder*), one of whose numbers was devoted to a humorous description of him by O.I. Leshkova, a member of the group.

Leshkova explained that, while the young Lavrin was always a great favourite with the company, they were also inclined to tease and make fun of him. For example, it was customary to use the neuter form of the pronoun in referring to him because his name ended in an 'o'. It is also a well-known fact, adds Mudrova tantalizingly, that the poet Il'ia Zdanevich based his 'transrational' play *Ianko Krul' Albanskii* (Janko, *King of Albania*), published in Tiflis in 1918, on the 'Albanian' number of *Beskrovnoe ubiistvo* devoted to Lavrin.

Janko, King of Albania

This episode is further explored in an article of 1991 by Marzio Marzaduri, based on previously unpublished correspondence between Leshkova and the artist M.V. Le-Dantiu.

Evidently, Lavrin's unflagging youthful energy and enthusiasm among the avant-garde literary elite had struck some of the company as slightly ridiculous, and his book on Albania had finally offered them an irresistible opportunity for lampooning him. Marzaduri tells us that Lavrin was constantly being ridiculed in *Bezkrovnoe ubiistvo*, and that its 'Albanian number', which came out in October 1916, contained a highly entertaining satire on his *V strane vechnoi voiny: albanskie eskizy*, in which he was depicted as 'His Highness the ex-King of Albania Janko Lavrin', elected sovereign by the Albanian people. After ludicrous attempts to 'lavrinise' the population, the new king is eventually driven out with the throne still stuck to his trousers. The satire was accompanied by drawings by Le-Dantiu and Vera Ermolaeva.

Zdanevich was so amused by this when he read it in November 1916 that he instantly composed his first transrational drama on the subject. Drawing on unpublished correspondence, Marzaduri gives a highly amusing account of the play and also of its performance in the studio of the artist M. D. Bernstein. A full discussion of the drama and its language, together with a reproduction of its opening three pages, is given in Gerald Janecek's fascinating book *The Look of Russian Literature*.[21]

Personal quirks apart, the fact that Lavrin's enthusiasm for the avant-garde was not always matched by understanding of or sympathy for its more subtle or revolutionary aspects, especially its theoretical side and its experiments with language, seems to have been his Achilles heel so far as its exponents were concerned. He is the author of some well-crafted short stories himself, but none of them displays anything that could be remotely described as avant-garde features.[22] His preference was evidently for 'good, lucid prose'[23] and romanticised topics, of exactly the kind that the Futurists were determined to consign to the scrap heap.

---

[21] Gerald Janecek (1984), pp. 164 ff.

[22] Janko Lavrin (1987).

[23] See Malcolm V. Jones (2001), p. 75.

War Correspondent for *Novoe Vremia* (*New Time*)

According to David Lavrin, his father travelled a lot in Russia, especially in south Russia and the Caucasus, ending up as Balkan correspondent for the Petrograd newspaper *Novoe vremia* in Serbia and the various Balkan kingdoms and principalities, taking the opportunity to spread the Neoslav gospel on his travels. On the outbreak of the First World War, he was already in the region and was appointed military correspondent to the newspaper. The Austrians immediately declared him a renegade and put a price on his head. David recalls his father telling of one occasion when he had to switch from one train to another heading in the opposite direction, in order to avoid being caught. But even more hair-raising was his retreat with the Serbian Army over the mountains into Albania, in which he took part in the winter of 1915-16. As a consequence, as we have seen, he was to publish his *Albanian sketches*, based on his reports for *Novoe vremia*. He crossed Albania, continued to the port of Salonica and, having retuned briefly to St Petersburg to consult his editor, Mikhail Suvorin, eventually arrived back in Corfu.

In 1978 Peter Liddle recorded an account of Lavrin's First World War experiences. Lavrin recorded his own reminiscences. Copies of both are at present held at the Brotherton Library at The University of Leeds and a copy of the latter, with manuscript corrections, is held in the Lavrin Archive at Nottingham University.[24] Apart from gruelling descriptions of the retreat itself, with accompanying suffering and atrocities, and assessments of the developing political and military situation, Lavrin tells of his encounters with prominent individuals in the theatre of war, including the Serb political leader Nikola Pašić, a Russian monk who had been involved in Karakozov's assassination attempt on Alexander II, Essad Pasha, the 'president' of Albania, General Vešović of Montenegro and Milan Ciganović, the mentor of Gavrilo Princip, whose assassin's bullet in Sarajevo had started the process that led to the outbreak of war in 1914.

After a period of recuperation in the South of France, he proceeded from Corfu via Paris to London, arriving there in the summer of 1917, en route to Petrograd. However, news from Russia was discouraging, his health had been badly affected by his experiences in Albania, *Novoe vremia* had ceased to publish and he had no source of income.

He decided to stay in England and look for work there. Within 6 months he had added English to his linguistic repertoire.

Arrival in England

In no time at all, Lavrin had made valuable contacts in the London literary and academic world, just as he had on his arrival in St Petersburg nearly ten years earlier. He soon found casual literary and teaching work, and made the acquaintance of A. R. Orage, the editor of the literary journal *The New Age*, who invited him to join its staff. It was Orage, David Lavrin thinks, who encouraged him to apply for a lectureship in Russian at Nottingham. Lavrin himself says that

---

[24] The Leeds documents are held under strict copyright restrictions and permission has to be obtained to quote from or to summarise them. I have here drawn on the Nottingham holdings, which are not subject to such restrictions.

it was Professor Sir Bernard Pares, the founder of the School of Slavonic and East European Studies, who advised him to apply.[25] Perhaps they both did. At all events, it was to be a turning point in his long life.

A glimpse of his contacts and an indication of the speed with which he integrated into English life are given in his letter of application to The University College , dated 6 September 1918. He writes that he has heard from M. Trofimov, Reader in Russian at King's College, London, and Mr Raffi, Lecturer in the same College, that a Russian lectureship has fallen vacant.[26] He goes on to say that he received his higher education at Petrograd, in the Archaeological Institute; that for upwards of two years he was chief editor of *Slavianskii mir*, during which time he wrote and translated several books; that for six years he was on the staff of *Novoe vremia*, to which he contributed several articles dealing with Slavonic politics and literature; that he served as special Russian correspondent of *Novoe vremia* with the Serbian Army, which he accompanied on its retreat through Albania, and that his articles had been republished as a volume in Petrograd two years previously; that on his recall to Petrograd in the previous summer he had broken his journey in London, owing to the institution of the Bolshevik regime; that during his year's stay in London, he has contributed several articles to *The New Age* on philosophy and literature, including a series on Dostoevsky which has been accepted by Allen and Unwin for publication as a book; and that he has been lecturing in Russian at the Serbian Theological College at its temporary quarters at Dorchester. He goes on to state his languages, curiously omitting Slovene from the list, claiming a perfect command of Russian, Serbian ('in which I have written several treatises'), Polish, Czech, English, French, Italian and German. 'Of course', he adds, 'I am a classical scholar'. He adds that he is 30 years of age, unmarried, and exempt from military service.

There is in this application an engaging mixture of self-confidence, breathtaking energy, genuine achievement and, here and there, a gift for self-promotion that leaves certain facts conveniently vague. Nowhere, for example, does he state his nationality, or say whose military service he is exempt from. He conveniently skates over the question of his lack of academic qualifications by saying that he 'received his higher education in Petrograd'. Whether he was pressed on these questions, or on references to his publications (his 'several treatises' in Serbian, for example) we do not know. But, these things apart, his curriculum vitae was mightily impressive, and he was appointed to the post. According to the minutes of the Council of The University College for 24 September 1918, it was 'resolved that Mr J. Lavrin be appointed lecturer in Russian at a salary of £150 plus 15% war bonus'.[27]

---

[25] Lavrin (1977), p. 12.

[26] A. Raffi lectured in Russian at King's College, London, and, from 1932, in the independent School of Slavonic and East European Studies within the University of London, from 1915 to 1944, while M. V. Trofimov did so only from 1915 to 1918. See I. W. Roberts (1991), pp. 122 and 123.

[27] The salary seems a fairly modest one, even by the standards of the times. *The Report of the Board of Education for 1916-1917*, HMSO, London, 1918, p. 77, records that 'At King's College, London [...] the salary of the Prof. of Russian has been secured by a grant of £600 a year from the L.C.C.' Of course, not all of this may have gone directly to the employee. There is further occasional information about Lavrin's classes at Nottingham, fluctuating numbers of students, lectures and publications in official University publications during the inter-war years. I am indebted to James Muckle for drawing my attention to all of this.

The Move to Nottingham and The University College
The Inter-war Period

Where Lavrin lodged on first arriving in Nottingham we do not know. According to the interview with Gerald Smith, he moved to the little village of Hathern, near Loughborough, from which he could commute to both Nottingham and London by train, but he did not like it there, finding the snobbery of the English village even more offensive than the snobbery of the town.[28] At first he found only a handful of students brave enough to tackle Russian: the only relevant book he found in the Library was an old-fashioned Russian grammar. But for the encouragement of Professors Weekley and Granger, he would have returned to London. However, a number of former soldiers joined his classes after the War, and a series of public lectures was unexpectedly successful. He invited colleagues from London to give lectures, including Pares himself and D. S. Mirsky. He also began to build up a respectable collection of Russian books in the College Library, including a number of rarities, published abroad, which are still part of the Library's holdings.

Somehow, in 1921, still aged only 34, he managed to persuade The University College to give him the title of professor,[29] apparently on the grounds that without such a title he would never be taken seriously in Europe, where his chief academic contacts lay.

Nevertheless, it can hardly be said that he liked Nottingham, or the Midlands weather, and he seems to have spent as much time as possible in London, where he continued to mix in academic, artistic, publishing and literary circles. His surviving correspondence over the years not only testifies to continuing contacts with compatriots but also contains letters from Edwin Muir, Edith Sitwell,[30] Sacheverell Sitwell, Herbert Read, Henry Miller, A. L. Rowse and many other leading figures on the English literary scene.

Lavrin, says his son John, attached himself not so much to the Bloomsbury group as to the Fitzrovians. Fitzrovia was the area north of Oxford Street, centring originally on the Fitzroy Tavern on Charlotte Street, and was at the time the artists' and writers' quarter, rivalled only by Chelsea. Dylan Thomas, William Empson and George Orwell were among those who frequented it, though it is not known whether Lavrin knew them personally. At all events, he must have made a beeline there on his arrival in London, where he may have made his first literary, artistic and academic contacts. He reportedly became one of the first members of the International PEN Club founded in London in 1921 under the inspiration of Mrs C.A. Dawson Scott and the founding presidency of the novelist John Galsworthy. The incomplete list of members in Mrs Dawson Scott's biography[31] does not include his name, but this may simply mean that nobody had yet taken him seriously enough. Lavrin is unlikely to have allowed this state of affairs to last very long. He is known to have been involved in setting up the PEN Centre in

---

[28] Interview with Gerald Smith.

[29] *Annual Report of the University College Council*, University College, Nottingham, 1921, p. 35.

[30] Edith and Osbert Sitwell lived at the sixteenth-century Renishaw Hall, two miles north of Staveley in Derbyshire, where Lavrin is presumed to have visited them.

[31] Marjorie Watts (1987). Names of English members are included in the index and of foreign members on pp. 208-9.

Ljubljana. Much later, in 1965, his efforts resulted in the PEN Congress at Bled, in which numerous international writers, including Arthur Miller, took part.[32]

It was in London that in 1928 he met the young artist Nora Fry, a member of the famous Quaker family. Nora records that they met at a party given by a young writer, Wilfred Hindle of *The Times*, at the Middle Temple, and were introduced by their host. Hindle invited her to join a party planning a trip to the mountains of Slovenia: a crowd was gathered round a professor of Russian, a certain Janko Lavrin, who was to lead them. Nora declined to join the group for financial reasons, but Janko had fallen for her; there was a whirlwind romance and they decided to marry and go off to Slovenia on their own, leaving the group to its own devices. Nora kept a diary of tinted drawings of their honeymoon, now in the Ashmolean Museum, recently published as a book in Slovenia.[33]

On returning to Nottingham, they moved into a large, semi-detached house that Lavrin had bought in the Mapperley district. Tired of living in furnished rooms year after year, he had bought a newly-built, red-brick, house, had it whitewashed, and named it the Villa Savva. Nora gives a delightfully humorous account of their moving in, how she found the kitchen barricaded by Janko's books, and how he had arranged for their meals to be provided on a regular basis by the next-door neighbour, Mrs Brown, who brought them through a hole in the hedge.[34]

It would seem that this was not the first such group excursion to Slovenia that Lavrin had offered to organise, for in 1927 there had appeared a satirical novel by the prolific journalist, novelist, friend of the great and professional tramp Stephen Graham, entitled *Midsummer Music*, whose main character is a Professor Spandin, 'a product of Austrian civilisation, educated at Zagreb and Vienna' who would have become a remarkable journalist had there been no war, who wrote on literature, politics and national customs in several different languages, who had been taken prisoner by Brusilov's army in 1916 and who on being set free, had begun to earn a living in Moscow from journalism. Arriving in England, he received an 'up-country' university chair in 1922, and so on, and so on. Although the concrete detail differs subtly from Lavrin's actual biography, there is no doubt that Spandin is a thinly veiled caricature.

If the circumstances are recognisable, the dialogue must have been taken from life. 'His impulses outshot his will, and his will outshot his act,' wrote Graham. 'Seeing a mountain by chance he would at once call out "Ah, let us climb it, let us go right to the top," but never got a quarter of the way up any mountain.' Or, 'in literary salons where Spandin was found, there were always explosions. If someone had mentioned Cubism, Spandin suddenly shewed Cubism in eruption, Cubism for a while became a volcano throwing up a hot lava of continental ideas. As may be imagined, Spandin was both an entertaining and brilliant talker, a genuine cosmopolitan; his speech coruscated with phrases derived from all sorts of cultures… This leaping about in the mind, this butterfly flight of statement, if bewildering to the pedestrian foot-at-a-time thinker, proved also attractive. In a big mixed company the tendency of other talkers was to break off conversation to

---

[32] Dušan Moravec, ed. (2002), p. xviii.

[33] Nora Lavrin (2004).

[34] It now seems impossible to locate the Villa Savva, which is unlikely to have retained this name and must have acquired a number. There are sketches of the house by Nora, but all from the back garden.

listen to what Spandin was saying. He was a valuable unifier. He could turn a frivolous tea-party into a lecture by himself.'[35]

Here the plot of the novel may remain untold, save to say that it revolves around the varying adventures and misunderstandings that arise as Spandin chaotically conducts his party across Europe on a trip to Dalmatia, where the spot he has chosen for their holiday turns out to be infested with flies and in all respects a disaster. 'For sheer impracticality,' writes Graham, 'he could not be matched—a man into whose care you must never trust yourself to take a bus or taxi, to find a book or a place, or get a hotel.'[36]

Lavrin was evidently quite upset by the novel and could see no resemblance at all between himself and the fictional Professor Spandin, never forgiving Graham for the libel; but his acquaintance, the sculptor Marin Studin (who also features in the novel as a character called Resić) reportedly laughed, and said that the portraits were actually quite true to life. How far this episode poisoned Lavrin's relationship with Graham is not clear, but it is certain that he held a very low opinion of Graham in later years, as a pen-portrait held in John Lavrin's private collection demonstrates.

It is clear that all his life Lavrin continued to evoke affection and admiration, while seeming at times to be so much larger than life as to be a caricature of himself. This is easily understood within the repressed culture of the English, who produce eccentrics enough on their own account, but it was an impression that he had left behind among the more expansive Slavs as well.

Between all these adventures he was, of course, still teaching students at Nottingham's University College. It cannot have been easy for Lavrin when he took over from Slepchenko in 1917. His predecessor had ridden on the crest of a wave of enthusiasm for the subject, even if young men had been called up into the forces, inevitably disrupting the classes, and if numbers had begun to drop before the end of the War. There were at this time few really good textbooks and teaching materials for Russian; for many years book reviewers continued to complain that there was no good translating dictionary, and even when Segal's eventually appeared many years later in 1948, its appearance was described as 'an opportunity missed'. Meanwhile, Mr Bondar of Manchester continued to issue edition after edition of his *Simplified Russian Method*, for which many a teacher must have been grateful. It is, however, scarcely the most inspiring of primers. Success must certainly have depended on a teacher with a lively personality and students who were keen to learn.

This indeed appeared to be the case. The Annual Reports of The University College in the 1920s say the same thing year after year in slightly different words. In 1920: 'For Italian, Portuguese, Russian and Serbian, the classes are comparatively small, but consist of serious students.' In 1921, the classes were small but composed of earnest students. In 1922 Serbian was not continued, but the small Russian classes were of 'satisfactory quality'. The 1923 report states: 'There was unfortunately very little enthusiasm for this language during the session. Students were easily repelled

---

[35] Stephen Graham (1927), pp. 13-18.

[36] Graham, p. 67. During the War, Graham was supervisor of Slav broadcasts at the BBC, so he must inevitably have come into contact with Lavrin again at this time (see brief account of Lavrin's wartime service with the BBC below), so it seems remarkable that in his autobiography he makes no mention of him.

by the initial difficulties, but those who persevered constituted very good small classes.' Early that year the College Council minutes recorded: 'The Principal reported that the number of students in the Russian classes had gradually declined and stated that he had seen Professor Lavrin who had suggested that he should teach for two terms only during the present session and that his salary should therefore be reduced by one third. RESOLVED that no alterations be made in this matter for the present year.' The message continued from year to year: small classes, but good and enthusiastic students for Russian. The Council minutes give absolutely no indication that continuation of the subject was under review.

On the contrary, Annual Reports contain some heartening remarks. Lavrin's 'stimulating' public lectures on Russian literature get reasonable audiences and are greatly prized. His publications continue to pour out: books on Tolstoi and Gogol, a History of Russian Literature, and over a dozen articles in a very few years. In 1926 a student is preparing for a PhD at London University, and another is 'reading for the higher branch of the Civil Service'. A non-recurrent Treasury grant in 1926 enabled the Library to 'form the nucleus of a real University Library in Modern Languages'.

Professor Ernest Weekley was the professor of Modern Languages at Nottingham to whom Lavrin was originally responsible, and Lavrin is known to have held him in high regard, looking on him as the quintessential English gentleman.[37] This was the same Professor Weekley whose wife, Frieda von Richthofen, had run off with the Eastwood novelist D.H. Lawrence.[38] The Lavrins also knew Jessie Chambers (Auntie Jessie to the boys), the model for Miriam in Lawrence's novel *Sons and Lovers* (1913), to whom Lawrence had once been engaged. Nora made a drawing of her that is in the Nottingham collection. But at Nottingham he seems at first to have found very little in the way of intellectual stimulation.

If 1928 had been a watershed (the marriage to Nora, the honeymoon, the opening of the grand new Trent Building in University Park[39] by King George V, followed the next year by the opening of the equally grand new Council House in Nottingham's Market Square), 1932-33 seems to have been another.

The Lavrins were living at the time at 10 Broadgate, Beeston ('beastly Beeston', as Lavrin called it), within easy walking distance of the Trent Building on the new University College campus, when they decided to purchase a picturesque late fifteenth-century house (Maltman's Hill House) in Smarden, near Ashford, in Kent, as a kind of holiday cottage. From then on, Lavrin could commute to both Nottingham and London from there, though to judge by the volume of correspondence between Janko and Nora in their son John's possession, Janko actually spent very little time at Smarden. 1932 was also the year in which London University's School of Slavonic and East European Studies

---

[37] Private conversation with John Lavrin, 2006.

[38] Professor Ernest Weekley has received a bad press among Lawrence scholars in general. For a more sympathetic and balanced view, see John Worthen (1995).

[39] Previously Lavrin would have had a room in the University College building in Shakespeare Street. This building now belongs to the Nottingham Trent University. From 1928, his room would have been in the Trent Building in the University Park. In 1950, The University purchased a private house called The Orchards behind the Trent Building, and the Department of Slavonic Languages moved there. It is not known for certain whether the move took place before or after Lavrin's retirement in 1952.

left King's College and was established as an independent institute within The University of London; Lavrin was appointed an Honorary Lecturer at the School.

But suddenly things at Nottingham began to look up as well. A surviving letter from Janko to Nora, of 20 January 1933, reads in part,

> I am feeling decidedly better, and yesterday I gave a lecture in the Large Theatre of The University College, arranged by the Cosmopolitan Debating Society. Can you imagine?—The entire hall ... was absolutely crowded with people so much so that quite a lot of them had to stand throughout the whole of the lecture and the discussion. A large audience always exhilarates me, and so I gave a d-d good lecture on the modern cultural crisis. It was so successful indeed that various questions and discussions lasted another hour and a half. This means that I spent on the platform two hours and a half and the hall remained full to the end. It was quite a delightful and original experience—original, because, together with the advanced, younger, 'intelligentsia', there came all the local communists and 'labour'. I never suspected I was so popular with them. Fortunately, they were extremely attentive, and all their questions were intelligent. Moreover, one decidedly felt a lot of vitality and good will in them. All the better! At the end they asked me again to give a series of lectures, which I shall do with pleasure. I prefer their zeal a thousand times to the deadening passivity of the usual university audience.
>
> However, I must not become garrulous or boastful. I just mentioned it, because in this direction there certainly is more life here in Nottingham than I ever suspected. I felt rather tired after the lecture, but today I am almost all right.
>
> Another pleasant news: my department (Russian language and literature) is going to become entirely independent of Weekley, or anyone, except the University Senate–which will give me a much freer hand in everything. My literary work too is progressing very satisfactorily.[40]

Strictly speaking, therefore, 1932 is when the department, as such, was founded and Nottingham first offered BA General and Honours courses in Russian. In the same letter, Lavrin refers to the prospect of getting out of their financial embarrassments, exacerbated no doubt by the purchase of the Smarden house.

Lavrin's literary work had certainly been progressing very satisfactorily. At Nottingham, he wrote a series of influential books and articles on Russian and Comparative Literature—some of which were later translated into several other languages – and continued his campaign of popularising European modernism in the literary reviews of his adoptive homeland. The book on Dostoevsky that he referred to in his letter of application to Nottingham was published in 1920, and was followed by a string of well-received books on other writers and movements.

He had found his own voice. The key word would be 'psychocritical', and his field was modern European literature. The fruits were to be such titles as *Dostoevsky and his Creation: a Psychocritical Study* (1920); *Ibsen and his Creation: a Psychocritical Study* (1922); *Nietzsche and Modern Consciousness* (1922); *Tolstoy: a Psychocritical Study* (1924); 'Dostoevsky and Modern Art' (1926); 'Dostoevsky and

---

[40] Letter from Janko Lavrin to Nora Lavrin, 30th January 1933, in the Lavrin Archive.

Proust' (1927); 'Knut Hamsun' (1930); *Aspects of Modernism from Wilde to Pirandello* (1935).

Among the other writers on whom he was writing at the time were Oscar Wilde, Anatole France, d'Annunzio, Rimbaud, Blok, Rozanov, Weininger, D.H. Lawrence, Rilke, Cankar, Esenin, Pirandello, Kafka, Maiakovsky and, of course, the other Russian classics.[41] Certainly he also wrote on and translated Slovene literature, but his interest in the great European modernists and in contemporary themes is already evident, as is the psychoanalytic tendency of his critical work.

Following his early meeting with Orage, he had been actively engaged in editing and writing for the literary journals.

The first of these, as we have noted, was *The New Age*, founded in 1907 by George Bernard Shaw. From 1908 to 1922, according to Wallace Martin, it would be an 'arena of cultural and political debate without parallel in the contemporary world'.[42] Among the debates to which Wallace alludes, one of the liveliest was that between Orage and Randall on the subject of psychoanalysis. Randall had championed Ernest Jones and his celebrated Freudian analysis of Shakespeare's Hamlet. Orage accepted the fundamental principles of psychoanalysis, but doubted whether they could be applied successfully to literature. All this had taken place in 1912.

Several years later, there were several psychoanalysts writing for the review and Lavrin himself contributed to the controversy with his book on Dostoevsky, in which he tried to show the value of a psychological approach to the Russian novelist. The expression 'Russian novelist' is used here advisedly, because Lavrin made no clear distinction between the author and his works. On the contrary, he confused them with an enviable self-confidence, which he justified by reference to his belief in an 'integral' approach to the study of literature. At the same time he was always careful to link Dostoevsky to the broader tradition of the European novel and to pin down his influence on other writers, such as Nietzsche, Bourget, Hauptmann, d'Annunzio, Gide and the German expressionists.

A revised and corrected edition of his book (under the title *Dostoevsky: a study by Janko Lavrin*) was published in 1943. It contains a discussion of Dostoevsky's influence in England, in which he makes some general observations on 'modernists' who have been influenced by him, among whom he makes explicit mention of Conrad's novel *Under Western Eyes* and Hugh Walpole's novels *The Dark Forest* and *The Secret City*. Dostoevsky was also, he reminds his readers, of some importance for D.H. Lawrence who was closer to him than other English novelists of his generation.[43]

In his books on Dostoevsky, Lavrin combined two major trends in contemporary English literary criticism—psychoanalysis and the cult of Russian literature. He also contributed to their development, by his collaboration on the journal which was their principal vehicle, and which put into circulation juxtapositions such as Dostoevsky and Freud, Nietzsche and Kafka, Ibsen and Nietzsche. Lavrin must have been in his element here. In fact the very word 'intelligentsia' had appeared for the first time in English in 1913 on the pages of *The New Age*, and was used to designate the journal's own readers.

---

[41] See, for example, Janko Lavrin (1935).
[42] See Wallace Martin (1967), p. 1.
[43] Janko Lavrin (1943), p. 37.

Like *Slavianskii mir*, *The New Age* leant to the left in politics, but its principal service to its readers was to introduce them to the buzz of contemporary modernist European literature and thought, and to exercise at the same time a formative influence on a new generation of English writers. Among contributors to the review were Ezra Pound, Katherine Mansfield, Herbert Read, Aylmer Maude (biographer and translator of Tolstoi) and Edwin Muir (translator of the novels of Kafka).

The New Age lasted until 1920. Then, in 1934, in collaboration with Edwin Muir, Lavrin founded a new literary journal, *The European Quarterly*. The enterprise was of short duration, but is said to have had considerable influence. For two years the journal published, among other things, essays on the contemporary novel, architecture and art, on Hitlerism and bolshevism; articles on D. H. Lawrence (by Jessie Chambers, under the nom de plume, E.T.), T. S. Eliot and Spengler; and translations of Dostoevsky, Blok and Kierkegaard.

Lavrin himself wrote on Rozanov, Weininger and D. H. Lawrence, Rimbaud and Sergei Esenin. But the review was a commercial failure, and was forced to close in 1935. Perhaps it was now preaching to the converted.

In 1931, the novelist William Gerhardie, at that time the most celebrated of the younger generation of English novelists, wrote that 'in our time every young writer aspires to combine the most varied and refined stylistic elements'. Among others, he mentions the influence of Bertrand Russell, Bernard Shaw, H. G. Wells, Proust, Lawrence, Chekhov, Goethe, Wordsworth, Shakespeare, Dostoevsky, Tolstoi, Turgenev, Pushkin, Lermontov, Gogol, Voltaire, Johnson, Flaubert....[44]

Gerhardie was himself born in St Petersburg in 1895 and one might therefore suspect him of an unusual bias in favour of Russian literature. But, on the contrary, his enthusiasm was shared by many of his contemporaries. Hogarth Press which, under the direction of Leonard and Virginia Woolf and with the collaboration of Koteliansky, Murry and Lawrence, specialised in Russian literature, was already up and running in 1916, just before Lavrin's arrival in England, and became commercially viable in 1920. During the 1920s, Lawrence made his translations of Shestov, Bunin, Dostoevsky and Gorky, and the cult of Dostoevsky, which went back to the Great War, became a passion for Russian literature in general.[45] At the time of his collaboration in *The New Age*, Lavrin was therefore at the very forefront of the development of English literary culture. But by the mid-thirties, the battle was already over and done with.

I am aware of two (accurate, but to my mind misguided) criticisms that have been made of Lavrin's literary critical work. One was that he wrote his books without any original research or direct reference to primary sources. The other, less kindly, was that he was no more than a journalist with academic pretensions, who soaked up other people's ideas and passed them off as his own. The former was passed on to me in private conversation by one of his former colleagues, who had seen him at work; the latter was the view of Professor Elizabeth Hill of Cambridge, who writes in her autobiography, in the course of describing her circle of London acquaintances, among whom were Stephen Graham and Dmitrije Mitrinović,

---

[44] William Gerhardie (1990), pp. 164-65.

[45] See Virginia Woolf (1948), p. 216, 'The most elementary remarks upon modern English fiction can hardly avoid some mention of the Russian influence, and if the Russians are mentioned one runs the risk of feeling that to write of any fiction save theirs is waste of time.'

and Janko Lavrin, a Slovene journalist, with academic pretensions. I learnt later that Valerie [Cooper] had been his flame. He had greatly impressed her by his illuminating tirades on Dostoievsky, about whom he was writing. But that only lasted until she met Mitrinović, who had sat down next to them by chance in the Underground. When he began to speak, Valerie suddenly realised that his sage remarks and ideas on Dostoievsky's genius Lavrin had borrowed from him, and that the book was really DM's sole inspiration. Did Lavrin ever acknowledge that debt to DM's fertile mind? In fact we are all DM's debtors.[46]

The perception of Lavrin as 'a journalist with academic pretensions' was probably quite widespread in academic circles at the time. He hardly gets his due in the history of Slavonic Studies and, of course, there is some truth in the accusation. Lavrin had never exposed himself to the rigours of academic training, and rarely if ever gives references to his quotations, or mentions the work of other scholars, but he thrived in an atmosphere where ideas were the currency of social exchange. Moreover, if he had indeed been inspired by Mitrinović, it is unlikely that, by the time he had made the ideas his own, he was still aware of their origin. The fact that the basic ideas for his 1920 book on Dostoevsky had already been formed by the time of his application to Nottingham in 1918 suggests that Elizabeth Hill was doing him an injustice. At all events he is known to have held her in high regard, a regard not extended to Mitrinović, whom he considered to be no more than a poseur and a charlatan.[47]

With respect to the other accusation, it is interesting to read Lavrin's own account, in his interview with Gerald Smith, of the way in which he wrote his books. He begins by describing how Dr Rose, the editor of a series called Benn's Sixpenny Library, had, with D. S. Mirsky, persuaded him to write a short history of Russian Literature.[48]

Well, I went to Paris, sat down, in about seven or eight weeks finished the whole book. I think I muddled a few dates only, you know, but at any rate it was one of the things with which I was very much grateful to Mirsky.[49]

And again, on his book on Tolstoi,

He [Mirsky] was very interested in my [...] English book on Tolstoy, because that was a new approach to Tolstoy there, and I had some very interesting letters, one of them from Aylmer Maude, very ... who was very enthusiastic letter, you know. And Mirsky was very much pleased with it, although I wrote it very quickly, you know. My usual method was, d'you know, when I had an idea, my method was to put it down as quickly as possible, and to leave it alone for about a year. After a year, I came back to it, as though it had been another person's book or another person's idea and so on, I went back to it critically, with a critical sense more or less...That was my method. But sometimes you know, that book about Tolstoy was taken immediately I think – oh yes, it was by Methuen, Methuen published it once, you know, and they –

---

[46] Elizabeth Hill (1999), p. 138.

[47] Private conversation with John Lavrin, 2006.

[48] Janko Lavrin (1927).

[49] Smith, p. 1.

was it Collins – I think it was Collins, sorry: Collins wrote to me: you must send us your book on Tolstoy right away, we cannot wait because, I don't know what happened, you know, they wanted it. And it came out, before it was really completed – I completed it later on, during the Second World War, you know.[50]

While it is possible to see from this description why academics sometimes expressed reservations about Lavrin's academic credentials, it is also possible to understand the freshness and appeal of his writing, which endures to the present day. His vast reading, his ability to keep so much information in his mind, to be able to order it and subject it to evaluation and critique in the context of modern European culture in general, is quite remarkable. Even after all this time, when research has forced us to modify many views that seemed fresh and unexceptionable in Lavrin's day, one is frequently struck by his ability to strike just the right note, and to say in a few well-chosen words what others who came later laboured over at length. And, as many testified, it was arguable that Lavrin's approach matched the needs of the day much more closely than conventional literary scholarship.

Apart from living in London, Nottingham and Smarden, the Lavrins went abroad in the interwar years as much as their finances would allow, especially to Yugoslavia (where they had an apartment at Piran) and to other parts of Europe. Nora pursued her artistic career and, of course, gave birth to two sons, John in 1930 and David in 1932. On the occasion of David's birth, Lavrin was presented with a cottage and garden by a relative in Krupa.

Although the successful lecture the following year temporarily lifted his gloom, the weather did not improve. In 1934, he wrote to Nora from Nottingham, 'My sweetheart, Just the few usual lines to send you my love from this foggy place, and together with my regrets to be so far away from you all. My stay in London yesterday was quite eventful.' And he goes on to describe an encounter with the Italian writer Pirandello, and an invitation by the PEN Club to go to Spain. He does not think that their finances would permit this on top of a trip to Russia. Sadly, no description of a trip to Russia in 1934 seems to have survived. In July 1936 we find him almost marooned in Spain by the events of the Civil War, but fortunately he has reached the French frontier in the nick of time.

By 1937, their Nottingham residence had moved once again, to 'The White House', Chilwell Lane, Bramcote, of which, once again, some of Nora's sketches survive, enabling us, this time, to identify the house with some certainty.

During the interwar years, Lavrin became personally acquainted with a wide variety of European and North American writers and scholars. His surviving correspondence adds colour and detail to some of these acquaintanceships. The Sitwells have already been mentioned. On 17 October 1941, Sacheverell Sitwell writes to him commending a young man (A. D. Poole) who, he believes, has just become one of Lavrin's pupils at Nottingham. At the same time, he recalls how long it is since Lavrin used to come to dinner with Osbert and himself; he also remembers Edith's parties.[51] And there is an undated letter from Edith herself,

---

[50] Smith, pp. 6-7.
[51] Janko Lavrin, Correspondence, 7.

saying that she is in London and hoping that they may meet.[52] There are a number of letters from Herbert Read and three from the American novelist Henry Miller, one of which acknowledges the writer's debt to Lavrin.[53] Another makes special reference to the book on Nietzsche[54] that had so impressed the philosopher Michael Oakeshott.[55] And, of course, there is a steady stream of letters from academics, admirers, publishers and friends.

During the thirties Lavrin also published quite extensively in Slovene, particularly for *Ljubljanski zvon* and *Modna ptica* and collaborated with W. K. Matthews, Harry Leeming, Vivian de Sola Pinto, Monica Partridge and others on translations of Slovene poetry into English. Pinto became well-known as the translator of Prešeren's *Sonetni venec* although, according to Lavrin, it would have been a disaster without his own unacknowledged help. His entry in the University College Calendar for 1937 indicates that he had been elected a Fellow of the Royal Society of Arts.

As we have seen, numbers of students fluctuated over the years, but Lavrin continued to attract enough to secure his position. Few of them advanced to degree level,[56] but there were two exceptional students who actually obtained PhDs for their work in the 1930s (Ina Beasley, for a thesis on 'The Dramatic Art of Ostrovsky', in 1931, and Richard Gill, for a thesis on 'The Poetry of Alexander Blok' in 1939). Lavrin records that he persuaded those who showed some literary talent to translate Russian short stories, essays, even poems, which were then printed in various periodicals with which he happened to be connected.[57]

He enjoyed the support of a number of colleagues, and that may have been crucial when numbers of students were low. One of these was Frank Granger, Vice-Principal of the University College. Another was Hugh Stewart, who occupied the office of Principal from 1930 to 1934, when he unexpectedly died. Like Lavrin, he had been in Russia in the years before the First World War. His Cambridge tutor and translator of Russian literature, Dr J. D. Duff, had been a friend of the wealthy and influential Pashkov family, who on Duff's recommendation, turned to Stewart as tutor for the young Alexander and Vasilii Pashkov.[58] He had also known Sir Bernard Pares, who founded the School of Russian Studies at Liverpool and became Director of the School of Slavonic and East European Studies at The University of London, even lecturing in Russian briefly at Liverpool. Stewart was the author or co-author of two books on Russia.[59] Moral and practical support was also forthcoming from two professors of English, Reginald M. Hewitt and Vivian de Sola Pinto. Like Pinto Hewitt

---

[52] Janko Lavrin, Correspondence, 68

[53] Janko Lavrin, Correspondence, 33.

[54] Janko Lavrin, Correspondence, 35.

[55] Michael Oakeshott (1947-48). Oakeshott concludes his review by saying, 'And if it is true (as I believe it is) that the most valuable sort of book on Nietzsche is not one *about* Nietzsche, but one which passes on what has been fired by Nietzsche in the writer's imagination, then this unpretentious book is certainly worth while. Indeed, I believe it to be the most enlightening brief treatment of its subject in English.'

[56] The first graduate was Richard Gill (1933), after which five students graduated in 1951, another five in 1952 and two in 1953. For complete lists of graduates of the department from 1933 to 1991, see Cynthia Marsh and Wendy Rosslyn, eds. (1991).

[57] Lavrin (1977), p. 13.

[58] The Pashkov papers are now held at the University of Birmingham.

[59] See John Massey Stewart (2007).

translated poetry from Russian. Pinto, as we have seen, collaborated with Lavrin in his translations from Slovene. He was to chair the first English summer school set up by Lavrin in Bohinj in 1955 and eventually donated a unique collection of Soviet war posters to the University, now held in the Department of Manuscripts and Special Collections.

From the sole report that seems to have survived, it would appear that Lavrin's teaching technique was as original and infectious as his writing. The following description from Nancy Binyon relates to the academic year 1945-6, but there is no reason to regard it as untypical. Mrs Binyon writes,

> I do not now remember how I heard of the class but it was certainly not part of any course. It was for beginners in Russian, though one was expected to have a knowledge of the Cyrillic alphabet.
> At the outset there were five of us, but one fell by the wayside almost immediately.
> That left a Mr Campbell, who was engaged in research into nucleic acids at the University, a priest (either High Anglican or Roman Catholic) who was always addressed as 'Father', Mrs Partridge and myself.
> I don't think we were given any grammatical instruction; we were left to acquire that on our own.
> We had a volume of poems and prose extracts which we tackled in class and towards the end of the period Professor Lavrin would dictate his thoughts on various authors which we were required to translate into Russian for the next session.
> It was quite hard work but I enjoyed it very much. Professor Lavrin was always so enthusiastic and the classes were very lively.
> At the end of the session it was suggested that I should take an examination, but I declined to do so. However, on the last morning I was ushered into a room and presented with the paper.
> It seemed churlish to make a fuss so I tackled it – happily successfully.
> On our return at the beginning of the 1946 session Russian was abandoned in favour of Serbo-Croat.
> …On leaving, Professor Lavrin presented us with a signed copy of his *Introduction to the Russian Novel*.[60]

The reference to Mrs Monica Partridge is important for Lavrin's legacy to Nottingham. It is slightly odd to find her in a beginners' class in 1945-46 since, from 1943 to 1947, she had herself been teaching at the Boyanus School of Russian in London, where she had studied with Boyanus from 1940 to 1943. However, it was certainly Lavrin who introduced her to Yugoslav Studies, and who later encouraged her to embark on a doctorate.[61] He appointed her as assistant lecturer in his department in 1950, and enlisted her to start up the English language summer schools at Koper, Piran and Ankaran (Slovenia) after the War.[62] Monica Partridge was to become professor and head of department

---

[60] Letter from Mrs Nancy Binyon to myself, 4th October, 1991, in my own possession.
[61] Peter Herrity et al., 'Monica Partridge', in Peter Herrity, ed. (1990), pp. xi-xiv.
[62] See Dušan Moravec (2002), p. xviii. A general impression of Monica Partridge's involvement in the summer schools may be gained from this correspondence.

from 1967 to 1980, during which time she fostered Yugoslav Studies at Nottingham, especially the study of the Serbo-Croatian and Slovene languages.[63]

Lavrin had started a Serbo-Croat class at Nottingham as early as 1919, though it lasted only until 1922. In 1935, a Polish class was started, followed a while later by a class in Czech and this was followed by the donation of a large collection of books to the Library by the Polish and Czechoslovak governments[64].

The Second World War

At the start of the War in September 1939, thinking that the house in Chilwell Lane, Bramcote was too close for comfort to the Chilwell Ordnance Depot, and that it was likely to be bombed, Lavrin moved the family into the centre of Nottingham, living first in a house on Park Row, on the line of the old city wall, with deep cellars and tunnels connecting all the houses, and then moving to 1 Clare Valley, in the Park, a handsome Victorian housing estate near the city centre, where they stayed until 1942.

In 1940-1, Lavrin broadcast once a week for the BBC. Then, in the 1941 session, he resigned his post at Nottingham to join the Editorial Board of European Broadcasts for the BBC at Bush House in London, and the family moved to Essex Court in the Inner Temple, a short distance from Bush House. David Lavrin remembers there being a barrage balloon in the garden, and their keeping rabbits. John and David were sent to school at Clayesmore in Dorset. At the BBC, Lavrin met many of the leading émigrés from Hitler's Europe, such as Beneš and Masaryk. He resisted the attempts of Yugoslav royalists to enlist his support, reportedly regarding King Peter as 'a silly person'. Apart from his Yugoslav broadcasts, he was also switch censor for the Rumanian programme, since the British were so short of Rumanian speakers that they used prisoners of war to read the news and it was necessary to monitor them with a hand on the switch[65]. Details of Lavrin's work with the BBC were incorporated in a recent Slovene television programme about the BBC World Service, called 'The BBC in Slovene', in which a Mrs Hirsch Houlton, the first Slovene speaker on BBC radio, who worked with Lavrin during the Second World War, was interviewed.

Drafts for some of Lavrin's wartime broadcasts are held in the Lavrin Archive at Nottingham; they contain up-to-the-minute commentary on current events and assessments of their likely development in the allies' favour. Beginning with the significance of the Anschluss (1938-9), Lavrin comments on France's betrayal of the allied cause; the miracle of Dunkirk (1940-1); Hitler's policy of expansion at the expense of small European nations and the significance of the Atlantic Charter for their morale (1941); the deterioration of relations between Germany and Italy and their treatment of the Slovenes (c. 1942); and many other topical issues. The tone combines the general thrust of British wartime propaganda with what seems to be a highly personal reading of current events.[66]

---

[63] A biographical sketch of Monica Partridge may be found in Peter Herrity (1990), pp. xi-xiv.

[64] Lavrin, pp. 13-14.

[65] Information provided in private correspondence by David Lavrin.

[66] Summaries of some of these drafts are included in the University of Nottingham's annotated catalogue to the Lavrin Archive.

Lavrin escaped the London blitz almost unscathed. David Lavrin recalls how one day a V-1 bomb landed in the Aldwych, right outside Bush House. Many people in the Air Ministry were killed and Bush House was also damaged. The large plate-glass window at the entrance was blown in and several people were blinded by glass fragments. Lavrin was cut badly in the foot, but went back on air shortly afterwards, still bleeding, and with the ambulance crew standing by. Afterwards, he went to recuperate in Leicester with some close friends.[67]

After the War, continues David, the lawyers wanted the Inner Temple back and the Lavrins moved back to Smarden for a while, and also to West Hill, in Putney. Then they sold the Kent house and bought a lovely Queen-Anne House in Thames Ditton, where the Lavrins lived until they moved to 28 Lower Addison Gardens in about 1968.

Russian did not lapse at Nottingham during the War. Vivian de Sola Pinto is said to have held the fort during Lavrin's absence[68]. Pinto's enthusiasm for the subject led him to chair the English summer schools in Slovenia after the war, together with Monica Partridge. Lavrin appears to have engaged the interest of a number of other Nottingham colleagues in the project. Among names mentioned in his correspondence are Professor J. D. Chambers (History) and Professor W. J. H. Sprott (Philosophy and Psychology).

Lavrin came back to Nottingham for three days a week in 1943-4 in order to take charge of the department again, returning to his work as part-time head of the Department of Slavonic Languages at the beginning of the 1944-5 session. He continued in post for a few years after the War, seeing the University College receive its Royal Charter and become an independent university in 1948, being awarded an MA ex officio, and seeing the first cohorts of graduates in Russian with Nottingham degrees. While in Nottingham, the Lavrins stayed in their old house in Clare Valley, then owned by Professor of Biology E. J. Barrington. Lavrin retired in 1952.

Herbert Brookes,[69] who graduated in 1951, remembers Lavrin as a brilliant and inspirational teacher, with a phenomenal memory: 'He both amused and confounded us,' he recalls, 'by his habit of continuing his discussion of a particular subject with an exact repetition of the last sentence of the previous week's lesson. This was made more remarkable by the fact that he never used any notes.' During the first two terms, lectures were partly in English and partly in Russian, thereafter solely in Russian. His assistant, Mrs Partridge, gave various tutorials. Marion Uglow (née Hopkins), who took Russian as her subsidiary subject from 1950-52, recalls that at the time Monica Partridge dealt with the language and Lavrin with the literature. For various reasons she struggled with the language and took private lessons during the vacation with someone at SSEES, but without

---

[67] This episode is also recalled by Mrs Hirsch Houlton in the broadcast on Slovene TV mentioned above. She refers to a pool of blood on the floor that was noticed by colleagues only when Lavrin finished his broadcast, which they were determined to complete so that the Germans would not know that they had hit Bush House.

[68] That Professor Reginald Hewitt assisted in the teaching of Russian during Lavrin's absence is attested by Vivian de Sola Pinto (1955), p. 41.

[69] Herbert Brookes also recalls that 'all three' on the honours course in his year were from the local High Pavement Grammar School. Since there were five graduates in 1951 (Herbert Brookes, Alan Collard, Paul Haslam, Roy Jones and Lawrence Joyce), the first cohort to receive degrees from the newly independent University of Nottingham, there seem also to have been two from elsewhere.

Monica Partridge's excellent language teaching, she remembers, she would never have known how to teach a foreign language herself. She especially recalls how very kind Professor Lavrin and his wife were to her during a period of serious illness and how he would discuss literature with great patience and good humour. She has never forgotten his exceptional help and kindness.

Retirement

On retirement in Thames Ditton and then in London, Lavrin certainly did not cease his scholarly activity. He continued to publish books in English[70] and he successfully promoted collaboration between Slovene and British Slavists in the publication of Slovene literature in English translation. He encouraged Monica Partridge and others in the activities of the English summer school at Piran, Kuper and Ankaran. He was elected a Corresponding Member of the Slovene Academy of Sciences, and he kept up an active correspondence with Slovene colleagues, some of which has fortunately survived. His standing in Slovenia has constantly risen, though he was often heard to complain during his lifetime that, owing to translations of his work, he was better known in Japan than in his native land. Moreover, he exercised an important influence on the development of Slavonic and Comparative Studies, especially between the wars, in every country where translations of his books appeared.

He was to die, aged ninety-nine, in London, on 13 August 1986.

Legacy

An important part of Lavrin's legacy is therefore his contribution, through his publications, to the development of Slavonic Studies, not only in the Western world, but also in the Far East. His books, while often stimulating to scholars, both in Slavonic Studies and in the field of Comparative Literature, were highly accessible to the general reader and to the university student, and being infectious in a way that Tolstoi would have understood, often excited a burgeoning interest in Russian Studies in those working in neighbouring fields. They are still capable of having this effect, and it is noteworthy that Slovene translations of some of his works are even now being published for the first time in Ljubljana.

Secondly, there was his contribution in the 1920s and early thirties to the English literary journals and the literary and philosophical debates of the day. His golden age was undoubtedly the period of his critical activity for the Russian and English literary reviews between 1908 and 1935. It was in reality a lengthy enough period, although it constituted only approximately a third of his natural life. From certain points of view, Lavrin was no doubt a man of his time. He was more of an essayist than a philologist. Born in a province of the Austro-Hungarian Empire, the very existence of which was perhaps unknown to the greater part of his English and even Russian contemporaries, he considered himself a Slav first of all and secondarily a European. In St Petersburg, he had taken upon himself the mission of introducing the Slav cultures to each other. Later he adopted a more ambitious mission, to diffuse the conception of a European culture among his English readers. It was a

---

[70] His last book in English was, I believe, *A Panorama of Russian Literature*, 1973, when he was eighty-six. This was not, however, the last of his books to be published during his lifetime.

conception, of course, which included the Slav cultures. He had arrived in England at the critical moment, when interest in modernism, including Russian writers, was already in the process of developing, and where there already existed a literary review dedicated to the same goal and supported by distinguished men and women of letters. There were already comparativists in England, but Lavrin was in a unique position to offer an East European perspective. From certain points of view, Lavrin now seems out of date. What he called 'psychocriticism' was based on a naive conviction that an understanding of the writer's psychology—based of course on Freud—is the best route to an evaluation of his work. But it is important to do him justice. He was capable of unexpected and stimulating juxtapositions. His style is always clear and provocative, his insights are often just. He knew how to present the essential in a minimum of space. It would be going too far to say that the major comparativists of our day are disciples of Lavrin, but it can be claimed without exaggeration that his work made a distinguished contribution to the tradition of Comparative Literature among British Slavists and that he helped to make the tradition of Russian literature familiar in England by placing it in its European context. Whatever one's view of Janko Lavrin's scholarship, there is no doubt that in the profusion and range of his writing, in the extent of his reading and personal experience of Slavonic cultures, in his own impact on the literary scene in both Russia and England, he was second to none in his generation. Nor is there any British Slavist whose books have been more widely read and appreciated by generations of students of Russian literature, not only in the English-speaking countries, but also in those other countries into whose languages his books were translated.

Thirdly, one has to make special mention of his contribution to the spread of the knowledge of Slovene literature in England and, indeed, before the First World War, among the Russian literary intelligentsia. This he achieved on a broad scale by the publications of translations, either his own or those of other people whom he encouraged and whose work he facilitated.

Not least important in this connection was his pioneering contribution to the study of Slovene, Serbian and Croatian at Nottingham University. In his own day, such studies were undertaken by a small number of students and the courses offered were occasional, and did not lead to degrees. Subsequently, under the aegis of his former pupil, Monica Partridge, such studies were further developed, a regular supply of lectors and lectrices was recruited in Ljubljana and Zagreb, and degree level courses were eventually introduced, which included the study of literature and Yugoslav history. More students appear to have studied Slovene at Nottingham than at any other British University, at least one to PhD level. Without the foundations laid by Lavrin, this could never have happened as it did. In 2004, the University celebrated thirty years of the Slovene lectorate, but was reminded also of Lavrin's pioneering role dating back nearly ninety years.

Finally, there is his contribution to Slovene literature through his poetry and prose fiction, the latter exemplified above all in his posthumously published book *Med osem in osemdeset*.[71] I am not qualified to pass judgement on his Slovene language publications, though it is evident from the English versions of his short stories that his style is of an old-fashioned variety. Janja Žitknik[72] regards his youthful poetry as second rate but gives an assessment of his prose that is more

---

[71] J. Lavrin (1987).
[72] Žitknik (1996).

sympathetic though not uncritical. David Lavrin believed that his father would really have liked to be a prose writer in the tradition of Gogol and Chekhov but that he was too private a man to realise his ambitions in that sphere. However this may be, his real achievement is in other areas. Above all, he was devoted to the life of the creative intellect in all its manifestations, regarding it as life's highest calling and, together with his wife Nora, bequeathing these values to his sons.

In the twenty-first century, his writings continue to be republished and even published for the first time. Interest in him in his native Slovenia is particularly strong more than 120 years after his birth. Mention has already been made of two recent television programmes,[73] the publication of Nora's sketches of their Slovene honeymoon, and a volume of his correspondence. A second volume of correspondence has also appeared in recent years as well as a Slovene translation of his book on Chekhov.[74] This is all rather impressive for a mere 'journalist with academic pretensions'.

---

[73] The second of these, broadcast in February 2007, contains some rare footage of Lavrin talking about his own life and work, as well as of Monica Partridge lecturing to a class in Slovenia (possibly Piran) in the 1950s.

[74] Dušan Moravec (2002); Dušan Moravec (2004); Nora Lavrin (2004); Janko Lavrin (2005). The last book has the text in both English and Slovene.

The Quiet Don

(1952-1957)

ON Lavrin's retirement in 1952, Dr John Fennell was appointed reader and head of the department. Fennell took up residence in The Park, in a fine red-brick, Victorian house on Duke William Mount, not unlike those houses that grace the streets around the parks at Oxford, to which he was soon to move.

During the Second World War, Fennell had taught himself Russian and had become a member of the Orthodox Church while working for intelligence in the British army in Egypt. He is said to have acted as interpreter for Russian generals in Austria and Italy. A note from 1946[1] refers to a Captain J. Fennell, on loan from the War Office, being one of the instructors on the Cambridge course for military men run by Professor Elizabeth Hill. After the war, he returned to Cambridge, where he had earlier read French and German, as Assistant Lecturer in the Department of Slavonic Studies, working at the same time on his doctoral thesis on the history of the 'Possessors' and 'Non-Possessors'[2] and its reflection in the literature of the end of the fifteenth and the first half of the sixteenth centuries.

He stayed at Nottingham for just four years, and is remembered, as he is also remembered at Oxford, as a shy, self-effacing, highly intelligent, private man. In the words of M. Dimnik, 'Christian values, integrity above all, permeated his academic career.'[3] Though it is said that he could be quite sarcastic, he is also remembered for his kindness and considerateness. He never threw his weight around as head of department and once a year he and his wife Marina gave a party in their house in The Park, usually with one of Marina's Parisian friends, or perhaps a cousin, singing to a guitar.[4]

After his four years at Nottingham, he took up a University lectureship at Oxford, where from 1964 to 1967 he was also Fellow and Praelector at University College; and in 1967 he was appointed to the professorship of Russian in succession to Sergei Konovalov, together with a professorial fellowship at New College. He retired in 1985 and died in 1992, having, largely through his own eminence as a leading scholar on

---

[1] Cambridge University Archive, SLAV 1/B9

[2] Two contending tendencies in the Russian Orthodox Church in the fifteenth and sixteenth centuries, supporting, on the one hand, the right of monastic communities to possess land and serfs and, on the other, the view that freedom of spiritual life was incompatible with the acquisition of lands and the peasants who lived on them. The chief advocate of the former position was St Iosif of Volotsk (1439-1515) and of the latter, St Nil of Sorsk (1433-1508).

[3] M. Dimnik (1994), p. 1.

[4] Many of the details for this chapter have been provided in correspondence with students of the time, principally John Gowling, the late Bernard Johnson, Joan Newiss and Harold Shukman. I have ascribed information to them individually only where I thought it important to indicate a source.

Muscovy, established Oxford as a foremost international centre on research into medieval Russia.

As his stay at Nottingham was a brief one, it is not to be expected that the mark he left there would compare with the mark he was to leave at Oxford, which falls outside our compass here. It is interesting to note, however, that at this time The University of Nottingham was prepared to appoint a young scholar of thirty-four years of age to a readership and headship of department on the strength of a single scholarly article and work in the pipeline, together, no doubt, with some extremely strong references. Nevertheless, they could not be faulted on their choice. It was while at Nottingham in 1955 that Fennell published his first book, an edition of *The Correspondence between Prince A.M. Kurbsky and Tsar Ivan IV of Russia*, annotated and with a translation by himself, and published by Cambridge University Press. While at Nottingham, he must also have been at work on *Ivan the Great of Moscow*, published in 1961.[5]

From the point of view of the development of Russian at Nottingham, however, Fennell's period can be seen in retrospect as a transitional period from the ethos of the gentleman scholar, teaching mostly sub-degree courses, to the modern department developed and consolidated under his successor, Frank Seeley.

The Department of Slavonic Languages, as it was then called, was at this time still in The Orchards, formerly a private house on the University campus. The departmental library and private staff rooms were all upstairs, and a large lecture room downstairs was used for most of the other teaching. Slavonic Languages shared the building with Law. Later, Law was to have the whole building to itself, and later it passed to Politics. Fennell remembers there being only two or three students when he arrived, and University records show two graduates in Russian in 1953, three in 1954, none at all in 1955, six in 1956 and eleven in 1957.[6] The increase was achieved in large measure by recruitment from graduates of the translators' and interpreters' courses in Russian for national servicemen, which were to provide the backbone of undergraduate courses in Russian for several years to come. Military service had been compulsory for young men of 18 years since 1939 and was to cease only in 1960. During the war, Russian courses for servicemen had been run by the School of Slavonic and East European Studies (University of London) and Cambridge University. Between 1951 and 1960, following the establishment of the Joint Services School for Linguists, some 5,000 young men passed through the Russian courses, most achieving an A-level or higher knowledge of Russian, together with specialist training in signals interception; some achieved proficiency in interpreting skills well beyond degree level.[7]

Some of these were to become teachers of Russian themselves and sent their own pupils to study at University in their turn. By the nature of things, these recruits were all men, and would usually teach in single-sex boys' schools[8] in days when co-educational secondary schools were the exception to the rule. Indeed, of Nottingham's

---

[5] For an evaluation of these books and the rest of Fennell's scholarly legacy, see M. Dimnik. *The Penguin Russian Course*, also published in 1961, was apparently written over a mere 6 months in Oxford in 1960.

[6] See 'Graduates of the Department of Slavonic Studies 1916-1991' in Cynthia Marsh and Wendy Rosslyn, eds. (1991), pp. 157-65.

[7] See Geoffrey Elliott and Harold Shukman (2003), which demonstrates how many of the alumni of the Joint Services School for Linguists subsequently rose to positions of eminence in the arts and humanities, and in public life. Apart from published accounts, I am grateful to James Muckle for first-hand accounts of his own experience, and for directing me to key data.

[8] James Muckle points out that some of these young male graduates did in fact go on to teach Russian in girls' schools, and that some of the girls espoused Russian with enthusiasm.

twenty-two graduates in these years, only two were women. One of these, Emmy Voznesenskaya (1956), was later to lecture at The University of Edinburgh and four other graduates, Harold Shukman (1956), Bernard Johnson (1957), Michael Scammell (1958) and A. R. Layton (1957) went on to have academic careers, the first at Oxford; the second at Nottingham and the London School of Economics; the third at Ljubljana, Oxford and Columbia (New York); and the fourth at Salford.

Harold Shukman recalls Fennell approaching a number of *kursanty* on the final year of the National Service Russian Interpreters' Course at Cambridge, who had no plans to go on to university after being demobbed, and suggesting that they consider taking a degree at Nottingham. As Harold Shukman showed interest but had no qualifications, a special entrance examination was arranged for him, which he passed. Similar arrangements were presumably made for others.

Fennell, of course, inherited only Monica Partridge from his predecessor. Dr Partridge, Harold Shukman recalls, taught nineteenth-century literature up to Chekhov and Gorky, Russian Thought (a lot on Herzen) and Serbo-Croat. He also remembers a Miss Heppell lecturing part-time on Byzantium and Kiev during the early part of Fennell's tenure. A serious deficiency of the course at the time was that there was nothing on Russian history after the medieval period. The appointment of Michael Futrell in 1956, beginning in the term after Shukman's graduation, was clearly designed to provide a partial remedy. Futrell, a specialist in Soviet literature, history and politics, was to remain at Nottingham until 1966. Another appointment that dated from Fennell's time was that of V. P. Saulus, an émigré Russian, who served for some years as a lector. In addition, for a while, Professor Kiparsky came over from Birmingham once a fortnight to teach philology.

By the time of Fennell's departure, Nottingham was able to provide students with the traditional range of courses on Russian language and literature from medieval to Soviet times, Russian history and intellectual history, and the history of the Russian language, together with Monica Partridge's growing competence in Serbo-Croat, which justified the department's continued use of the title 'Slavonic' rather than 'Russian' after Lavrin's retirement.

The small department also welcomed distinguished guest lecturers from time to time, and these included Professor B. O. Unbegaun from Oxford, Professor Josip Hamm from Vienna and Arthur Birse, Churchill's wartime interpreter, who had taught on the course at Cambridge.

Interviewed for the centenary edition of *Slavonica*, Fennell remembered it as a happy department: there were some good parties and at least two excellent plays, performed in Russian by the students.[9] Harry Shukman remembers two or three plays put on by the students in Russian. When the new Music School (now the History Department) opened next to Florence Nightingale Hall in 1955-6, it was made available for one week in the year for the Modern Language departments to put on plays. With Emmy Vosnesenskaya directing and acting, they put on several one-act plays by Chekhov in Russian, trying to remember everything they had learnt from the directing of Grech and Pavlov at Cambridge, where Emmy, Eric Dove and Harry had acted in *The Cherry Orchard* and *Three Sisters*.

One graduate of 1958 (John Gowling) recalls that he chose Nottingham because its course seemed more interesting and 'relevant' than those offered at competitor universities at the time. Subsequent discussions with graduates from other

---

[9] John Fennell (1977), p. 15.

universities confirmed this impression. At Nottingham there was good teaching in the language, culture and politics, and a good intellectual training, owing in large measure, he says, to Fennell's scrupulous approach and Futrell's 'dialectics'. Very much later, when he visited Russia, people still said that his verbal skills and vocabulary were very good and his Serbo-Croat was also still serviceable.

Not all the students were ex-servicemen of course, with the advantages of having been force-fed the language before arriving at Nottingham. Joan Newiss (1955-9), one of the few women students in the department, arrived with no previous knowledge of Russian, having A-level qualifications in French, German and Latin. Miss Newiss's course was extended to four years (which later became the norm with beginners) but, in the days before language laboratories existed and intensive language courses had been invented, and the only additional available resource was a Linguaphone course, four weeks in Paris with an émigré Russian family near the end of the first year were not necessarily an adequate substitute. Robert Wood was a contemporary of Joan Newiss and also a beginner, who went into the Royal Artillery after graduation. He remembers that there was only one student in his year with A-level (Alex Boyd), the others being mainly ex-servicemen, and he still regards the experience of studying Russian under John Fennell, Monica Partridge and Michael Futrell as an immense privilege. The period of study in Paris, however, was not particularly helpful for a beginner.

The arrangements for students to spend time with émigré families in Paris had been put in place by Fennell, with the assistance of his wife, Marina, who was herself a Parisian, and knew the Russian families personally. Some Russian families—the Vereshchagins are always mentioned with particular affection—were conscientious and enthusiastic in helping Nottingham students to develop their spoken Russian; others paid them no attention whatsoever; and Nottingham did not appear to monitor the situation very closely. From the point of view of a beginner like Joan Newiss, the course placed too much emphasis on history, literature and philosophy, and by no means enough on the spoken language. This tended to be the case with all language courses at the time, both at school and university, where language was usually seen either as a necessary means to the end of reading the classics in the original, or as a subject for academic study. Proficiency in the written form was given priority over oral competence. For political reasons–the Cold War was at its height and restrictions were placed on ex-servicemen visiting the Soviet bloc–there was, of course, no possibility as yet of sending students to study in the Soviet Union and immerse themselves in the linguistic environment there.

Harold Shukman, however, slipped through the net. He writes:[10]

> I was extraordinarily lucky. In the third term of the first year, we were told that the NUS [National Union of Students] was collecting a representative of each of its affiliated UK universities, of which there were all of twenty (Oxford and Cambridge were not affiliated and so were not included), to form a delegation on Higher Education to go to the USSR for three weeks in April 1954 at the invitation of the Anti-Fascist Committee for Soviet Youth. A lunchtime meeting was held, with the union president in the chair, and I must have stood up and said something, God knows what. Anyway, I soon heard that I would be Nottingham's delegate. I turned out to be the sole Russian speaker on the delegation, an enormous boost for my

---

[10] Private correspondence.

fluency, as I was always surrounded by crowds of Russians—students and ordinary folk in the intervals at concert halls, theatres, in stores or on the street. It was all very memorable. I wrote an absurdly long three-part article on the trip for *The Gongster*, of which they located two parts for me some years ago. The third part is lost. An episode involving Akhmatova, Zoshchenko and our delegation at the Leningrad Union of Writers is described in Michael Ignatieff's book on Isaiah Berlin, and also in Georgy Dalos *The Guest from the Future*.[11]

Ignatieff describes how in May 1954 a party of English university students visited the Leningrad House of Writers. Akhmatova and Zoshchenko, pale and tense, were paraded in front of them. In complete innocence, Harry Shukman asked whether there was a place for satire in Soviet literature. Such questions put the writers in an impossible position; there were party hacks in the room waiting to pounce if they put a foot wrong. Zoshchenko simply replied that it did have a place, a remark that was to cost him dear. Akhmatova said that she agreed, though she did not specify what she agreed with. She imagined that the students had been sent by Isaiah Berlin, with whom she had established a dangerously close relationship when he visited Leningrad in 1945. Of course, not a single one was actually from Oxford.[12]

Harold Shukman was also one of those students—as some years later I was to be myself—selected by Dr Partridge to attend the Seminar za strane slaviste (Seminar for Foreign Slavists) held in the summer vacation at Zadar and Zagreb. Shukman went in 1955. In the genial company of Slavists from all over Europe, and bathed in the Adriatic sun and sea, it was a splendid introduction to the Yugoslav languages and cultures, and an opportunity to gain at least a basic fluency in spoken Serbo-Croat. This year, Monica Partridge turned up herself during the final stages and they went out for dinner with Josip Hamm and other friends. It was evident that they held her in high regard and affection. As we shall see, she introduced another student of these years, Michael Scammell, to Slovene, and Scammell's first academic post was to be at Ljubljana University.

In spite of the fact that groups were small, the style of teaching back at Nottingham was still very formal, and that reflected the relationship between students and staff, and between members of staff themselves. Students did not usually dare to put a question during a lecture, or even afterwards, nor did they dare to offer an opinion unless asked to do so. They were known, addressed and appeared on formal lists as Mr Smith or Miss Brown, and were required to wear black undergraduate gowns for all classes, meetings with academic staff, and examinations. The same requirements were placed on staff, who would not be admitted to formal meetings without them.

Dr Fennell taught mainly in tutorial groups and his style was intimate and restrained. Though not solemn, he rarely joked and was extremely shy. In the first year, he took translation classes (both ways), and students who had learnt their Russian in the armed forces experienced the transition from brutal Soviet-style prose to the more civilised and elegant prose of the Russian classics. He also lectured, fairly formally, on Russian history from pre-Christianisation to Dmitrii Donskoi, and on early and Church Slavonic. His enthusiasm for these subjects was evident and he communicated it to his students. Never talking down, he tried to share his knowledge and enthusiasm with them.

---

[11] Michael Ignatieff (1998); György Dalos (1998).
[12] Ignatieff, pp. 148-169.

Not all students, it is said, felt entirely comfortable with Dr Partridge. However, others testify to her patience and readiness to go off at a tangent if a question demanded it. She taught eighteenth- and nineteenth-century Russian Literature, and Life and Thought. Her courses took the form of lectures. While she lacked Fennell's intimate style, her materials and interpretation were said to be good and she was thought by the students to be as sound as anyone in her field. In the second and third years, she also taught Serbo-Croat, with a heavy bias towards Croat pronunciation, and this too she did well and effectively. One of the students of the time remembers how, in 1953, Fennell interrupted one of her classes to announce that her PhD for her work on Alexander Herzen had just been awarded. They were mightily impressed, and she was justifiably pleased.

On his arrival in 1956, Dr Futrell focussed on Russian nineteenth-century political philosophy (later taken over by Monica Partridge), and on twentieth-century history and literature. He, too, contrasted with Fennell, being much more demonstrative, and occasionally bad-tempered. That apart, he was said to be an excellent teacher, combining lecture-room and tutorial styles. One former student, John Gowling, remembers how he once set an essay on Lenin as a revolutionary. He returned the marked essays at one of his lecture sessions and tore John's essay to shreds because he had described Lenin as the most effective revolutionary of the century. Futrell demanded to know why he had not considered the claims of Kemal Attaturk. At the end of the hour, he stormed out, without giving anyone else's essay so much as a mention. Nervously, the class looked at the marks he had given, and John was amazed to find that he had been given A+, the highest mark that Futrell had ever been known to award. At the next class he was as pleasant as ever. In general, he was more open to questions from students than his colleagues, but only during his Soviet History seminars.

Mr Saulus, like Fennell, is remembered as one of the old school. Everyone got on well with him. He was humorous and a very good raconteur. He told riveting stories about his own adventurous life—he is said to have been a pilot in the Tsar's personal wing—but rarely engaged in actual conversation with his pupils, so that they heard much Russian in his classes but, apart from the lecturettes that they were sometimes asked to deliver, they had little oral practice themselves. Occasionally, he taught some vulgar Russian, but only if he was sure that Dr Fennell would not overhear him.

So far as John Gowling recalls, none of the staff ever asked the ex-servicemen what they had done on their services Russian course, and students assumed that staff already knew, and had been in some way involved themselves. Fennell, he says, made it plain that he had been in the wartime Moscow Military Mission and had worked with the Red Army in the field, but he never gave any details. Futrell never spoke of his involvement, but made it clear that he knew all about their activities. Saulus also seemed to know, but avoided direct reference. There seemed to be tacit agreement never to talk about a distasteful subject.

However, John Gowling recalls a dramatic incident in October-November 1956, when the government was in a tangle over Suez, while the Soviet Union simultaneously invaded Hungary.

> The developing crisis threatened world peace and, the bulk of the undergraduates being on the active reserve, we prepared for immediate mobilisation. Fennell was himself on stand-by. One Friday, at the height of the crisis, some of us had a tutorial with Fennell, before dashing home that evening, firstly, to collect our

uniforms and equipment and, secondly, to say good-bye to our families. As the tutorial ended, Fennell said very gently that he wanted to meet us all again on the following Friday at the same time, but, he was very much afraid it would have to be at Corps headquarters, with us all in uniform. In the following few days the crisis was resolved and we did not meet in uniform, very much to Fennell's and our relief. Had the crisis not been dealt with, the department would have been left with perhaps only half a dozen undergraduates, the Russian lector and Dr Partridge. As Fennell himself commented, the department would have been trying to continue its activities while we were all on active service or in the 'Gulag'.[13]

Harry Shukman (graduated 1956) says that he can recall no Slavonic Society in his day, but John Gowling (graduated 1958) remembers a small Slavonic Society consisting mainly of students from the department, who were sometimes joined by a small group of proto-Trotskyites from the Economics Department. There were some speakers on the then fashionable Mackinder Heartland Theory[14], while others dealt mainly with aspects of Russian culture and politics. The Trotskyites tried to introduce their own speakers, one of whom inveighed against Stalin and state socialism, but they failed to enlist members of the Slavonic Languages Department for their cause.

Students' memories of this period embrace other aspects of campus life too. Since the age of majority was still twenty-one, the University was regarded as acting in loco parentis towards its students and rules and regulations were strictly enforced, not only in Halls of Residence, but also by landladies who provided 'digs'. There was as yet no possibility of living independently in student flats. Local landladies offered bed and breakfast during weekdays and, in addition, Sunday lunch. They also kept a weather eye on student behaviour and morals. There appears to have been no special dispensation for those who, like ex-National Servicemen, might already have attained their majority. In the women's Halls of Residence, Florence Boot and Florence Nightingale (known as F.B. and F.N., and opened in 1928 and 1951 respectively), male guests were allowed after 7.30 only in the presence of a chaperone, and after 10.00 p.m., not at all. Women who wished to be out later, or away at weekends, were required to sign out and sign in, and these regulations were strictly enforced in the case of Florence Nightingale by the fearsome though good-hearted Warden, Miss Audrey Beecham, and in the case of Florence Boot, by Miss Eileen Spellman. Regulations in the men's halls were less stringent in this respect, but Hugh Stewart Hall, under the redoubtable Dr William Neil, was well known for the strictness with which its rules were enforced. Gowns were worn each evening for formal dinners; grace was said in Latin before meals. Wortley Hall, then consisting mainly of rows of free-standing red-brick huts that looked like army barracks, was greatly favoured for its relatively relaxed atmosphere.

Before the Portland Building was opened in 1956, student social life centred on the lower floor of the Trent Building, which contained a refectory in what later became the lower library and is now (2008) occupied by a tearoom, lecture rooms and the Performing Arts Studio. Bridge games were in constant session on the lower corridor. Apart from the high jinks associated with Karnival each autumn, student life was fairly

---

[13] Private correspondence.
[14] The British geographer, Sir Halford Mackinder, who in 1904 proposed a theory according to which 'Who rules Eastern Europe commands the Heartland; who rules the Heartland commands the World Island; who rules the World Island, commands the World.'

restrained. There were fewer than 2,500 students in all during the late 1950s and very little drinking, rowdiness, or litter. Most students were first generation products of the grammar school system, conscious that they had joined a privileged elite, and serious about their studies. Men were constantly aware of the call to military service; women were generally assumed to be there principally to find a husband. In keeping with this ethos, it was assumed that the President of the Union would be a man and that there would be a Lady Vice-president.

This was also the age, before motorways, of hitch-hiking up to university and back home, of trunks delivered to hall or digs by British Road Services, of Christmas jobs delivering mail for the Post Office.

It was in the autumn of 1956 (or possibly 1957, after Fennell's departure) that the department moved from The Orchards to its first home in the 'cowsheds', the temporary buildings behind the new Portland Building. These one-storey, white concrete huts were also reminiscent of military barracks, too much so for the liking of some of the ex-servicemen. The old house had had some intimacy, and the cowsheds were fairly austere by comparison. Moreover, apart from a small residual collection, the departmental library was at this point transferred to the Main Library in the Trent Building, at a time when librarians found it difficult to identify Cyrillic texts. Nevertheless, the cowsheds (later known as Cherry Tree Buildings and demolished in 2004) provided good basic accommodation, with spacious staff rooms along two sides of a corridor, and a seminar room, holding the residue of the departmental library, at the far end. Their exterior aspect was brightened by rows of shrubs running between the rows of huts, and a line of flowering cherry trees bordering the access road that ran from Cut Through Lane to the new Portland Building.

During the period of Fennell's tenure, his colleagues were developing their scholarly reputations. Following the award of her doctorate in 1953, Monica Partridge had been publishing articles on Alexander Herzen and was beginning to work on her Serbo-Croat grammar and reader, while Michael Futrell had in the pipeline several articles on Soviet literature that were to appear in the early part of Seeley's tenure.

It is not clear whether Fennell left at Christmas 1956 to be replaced by Frank Seeley in January 1957 or whether there was a hiatus between his departure in the summer of 1956 and the arrival of Frank Seeley in the summer of 1957. In the latter case, Monica Partridge presumably acted as head of department, but I have never seen any reference to this. If she did, it is perhaps not surprising that she should feel hard done by when, rather than make the arrangement permanent, the University decided to offer the post to a newcomer. At all events, Bernard Johnson noticed that she was not best pleased by this development.[15]

---

[15] Private correspondence with the late Bernard Johnson (graduated BA 1957, PhD 1960; lecturer in the department, 1960-65). According to Nicolas Fennell (John and Marina's son), his mother recalls that Fennell spent one term at both Nottingham and Oxford, commuting between the two, but it is not clear which term this was, so the question remains.

Fruits of Enlightenment

(1957-1967)

The Department in the Late 1950s

FRANK Friedeberg Seeley (1912-2000) succeeded John Fennell as head of the Department of Slavonic Languages in 1957, with the grade of senior lecturer, at the age of 45. He had applied for Fennell's readership, but was told that this would have to wait for a doctorate or a book. Like Fennell's, his publication list at the time of appointment was still rather thin. As with Fennell, a major work was said to be in the pipeline—a book on Dostoevsky. Apart from a translation from the Italian before the war, and a Russian Reader co-edited with Konovalov, Seeley had published just three articles in *The Slavonic and East European Review*, of which one was on the heyday of the Superfluous Man and another on Alexander Herzen.[1]

Not everyone adjusted happily to the change in headship. John Gowling recalls that, by comparison with Fennell, Seeley seemed remote and formal; some had the feeling that he resented being outside Oxbridge and tended to talk down to his students. He taught Russian language and literature and, unlike Fennell, he stressed the psychology of the writer—to the exclusion, it seemed to some, of everything else.

There is some truth in all of this. The word 'cerebral' might have been invented to describe Frank Seeley. Though he had exquisite manners, he often seemed socially ill at ease, and appeared to live in a world in which people were expected to apply the same intellectual rigour to their every casual utterance as they would in the highest reaches of scholarly discourse, and this set standards not only for his students, but also for his colleagues, which few were inclined or equipped to meet. Should students or colleagues fail to meet them, he might seek psychological explanations for the lapse, and this was how he approached the writers he studied, as well as the characters in their works of fiction. A number of students, including Kate Ray (née Jackson), still recall the refined awkwardness of his tutorial coffee evenings in Lenton Hall, where he served undrinkable coffee (made with water straight from the tap, so that the coffee floated around in globules on top of the milk) with the most exquisite cakes, brought back from London, to which he repaired each weekend. Gerry May still remembers the way he folded his paper handkerchiefs.

Bernard Johnson, who graduated in 1957 and experienced the transition as a postgraduate student, called him 'brilliant but stubborn, sensitive but not always sure of his decisions [...] too much of a perfectionist for today's academic world—with the

---

[1] See Malcolm V. Jones (2001). This article includes a bibliography.

result that he never finished his life's work on Dostoevsky. Monica [Partridge] called him a latter-day Oblomov, but perhaps half way between Myshkin and Stavrogin would have been nearer the mark. He was never as flashy as Isaiah Berlin, but having heard them in conversation two or three times [I formed the impression that] he was by no means his intellectual inferior.' [2]

Ruth Morgan (née Fisher) remembers Frank Seeley as 'a reticent and rather shadowy but charming figure in a misty corner of the room'. John Edwards recalls that although the overall content of his degree course did not really inspire him, he found Frank Seeley's option on the nineteenth-century Russian novel quite exhilarating. Kate Hudspith (née Sheaf), whose pupil Patricia Calvert later came to Nottingham to read Russian, remembers him as inspirational, shrewd, humorous and generous.

As an undergraduate myself, I had no doubt of Frank Seeley's superior intellect and learning. He was just what I had hoped to find at university and I counted myself fortunate to have found it by happy accident at Nottingham and to have been able to sit at his feet. He was a perfectionist in all that he did. He describes in the Introduction to one of his books[3] how most of his finely honed articles originated as papers read to various academic societies, how they would then be developed and expanded to become part of lecture courses, before finally emerging in print in various countries and several languages. The process of gestation was that of a more leisurely world in which every semicolon was carefully calculated and where every text was read and reread many times in the process of study, giving the impression of an author with total recall of his material, an encyclopaedic contextual knowledge, and a complete mastery of the nuances of language. It was such papers that he often read to his undergraduate audiences as lectures.

At first educated privately, mostly in France, he had won the Brassey Italian scholarship at Balliol College, Oxford, at the age of seventeen. There he studied classics, philosophy and ancient history, graduating (aged twenty-one) with a first class honours degree, literae humaniores, in 1933, and being awarded the Jenkyns Prize in Classics. It was at Oxford, he later said, that he learned to think, his background in Oxford philosophy and impatience with sloppy and pretentious thinking being everywhere evident in his work. Between 1935 and 1942, he held teaching posts in Italian literature at Oxford and, during 1942, he briefly taught Russian at the Technical Institute in Coventry. In 1943 he was appointed to the post of Lecturer in Russian at the School of Slavonic and East European Studies at The University of London, where he remained until 1957.

Frank Seeley was one of those people who seemed to generate legends. There was the story, for example, about how, in order to help a student in danger of failing her subsidiary Spanish course, he had learnt Spanish grammar over the Easter vacation and announced that it now only remained for him to master the vocabulary. It was also

---

[2] Private correspondence. It will be inferred from Bernard Johnson's comments that Frank Seeley's personality was a complex one. Oblomov is the hero of a novel of that name by Ivan Goncharov, who famously took the first hundred pages to get out of bed, and had grand dreams, which he lacked the energy and motivation to realise. Myshkin is the saintly hero of Dostoevsky's novel *The Idiot* and Stavrogin the intellectual but amoral hero of Dostoevsky's novel *The Devils*. Isaiah Berlin was, of course, widely regarded as one of the most intelligent and accomplished British academics of his time, with a fine record of public service as well as a first rate academic record. His contribution to the study of Russian thought, and his influential position at Oxford and in government circles, contributed much to the strength and even the survival of Russian Studies in Britain during the third quarter of the twentieth century. See Michael Ignatieff (1998).

[3] Frank F. Seeley (1994), p. vii.

said, slightly inaccurately, that he had studied philosophy at Oxford but, having been told at the end of his first year that he was heading for a first, decided to devote his time to Russian studies instead. Surprisingly, this unworldly intellectual owned a low-slung, black sports car (Robert Owen remembers it as a Volvo 66), in which he had driven all the way through Central and Eastern Europe to the first post-war Congress of Slavists in Moscow in 1958, at a time when spare parts for Western cars were unobtainable in the Soviet bloc, petrol stations hidden away out of sight, and fines might be imposed in the Soviet Union for driving a dirty vehicle.

He had had several pieds à terre in Nottingham (a flat in Cripps Hall; another over Fine Fare in Bramcote Lane; another in Lenton Hall when it opened in 1965), but his principal home was in London, at Hatch End, and he commuted every weekend, having persuaded the University that his research materials were all in London libraries. In our final year, he would frequently ask us to leave silently when the phone rang at 1.00 p.m.; he would answer it in Italian, and we later learnt that this fifty-year-old bachelor was talking to his Italian fiancée, whom he married shortly before departing for America in 1967.

Unlike Fennell, Seeley had no wartime record and no experience of the Joint Services Russian Courses. There were probably health reasons for this, possibly connected with the heart problems that beset him in later years. By the time he took over the headship, the Joint Services Russian courses were coming to an end. Compulsory military service for 18-year olds was discontinued in 1960 and was being phased out for some years before that. When I arrived as a student in 1958, at the age of 18, I was expecting to be called up in due course, but the age of conscription had already drifted upwards and by the time I graduated it had been abolished altogether. My first year class consisted of five ex-servicemen, one A-level entrant (from the Latymer School) and two beginners, of which I was one. My fellow-beginner (Joanna Penny) was the only woman on the course and there was rarely to be more than one until the large group that graduated in 1967,[4] Frank Seeley's last year. Arthur Mayer, who had been on the Joint Services Russian Course, and was sent to Cambridge to study the language, recalls that he was expected to continue doing written exercises for the military after completing National Service, and while already an undergraduate at Nottingham.

Most of us, I believe, were first generation university students, and aware of the privilege that this conferred. Few chose their university subjects with a precise career in mind. A general university education, with specialist knowledge to the standard of a good honours degree, was what most sought, in the belief that, combined with personal qualities, this would ensure entry to careers in many fields.

When Seeley arrived in 1957, he inherited Fennell's colleagues; various visiting lecturers continued to fill gaps in the syllabus. Dr Donald Piper came down from Manchester for a year to teach history. So did Dr Veronica du Feu, to teach medieval history. She was succeeded briefly by Dr David Johnson from Birmingham. Then, in 1960, Bernard Johnson, who had by now completed his Nottingham doctorate, was appointed to a permanent post, teaching the History of the Russian Language and Comparative Slavonic Philology. He remained at Nottingham until 1965, when he

---

[4] Most of these will have begun their courses in 1964, though beginners took a four-year course and these will have arrived in 1963. The 1967 group of graduates numbered twenty-one in all, of whom nine were women.

obtained a post at the London School of Economics, where he was to remain until his retirement in 1999.

Nottingham now had its full complement of four full-time permanent lecturers (Seeley, Partridge, Futrell and Johnson) and a lector. Mr Saulus retired as lector in 1960 and was replaced by Arian Kirillov[5] (brother of Irina Kirillova of Newnham College, Cambridge), a talented and highly educated young man with refined English and Russian, who in 1964 was appointed to a lectureship and the headship of Russian at Aberystwyth. Sasha Gillett (née Lubetkin) remembers conversation classes with him and the huge china cat that seemed to mimic his own slightly mysterious smile.

Arian Kirillov was replaced in 1964 by Amelia Cantelli, of Spanish Republican origin, who had been forced to emigrate to Moscow as a consequence of the Civil War. She remained at Nottingham until 1972, when she obtained a post at Oxford. In 1965, she had been joined at Nottingham by Nikolai Naidenov, an émigré Russian, who had fled to the West from a German prisoner-of-war camp at the end of the First World War. Fondly remembered by generations of students, he was to remain until his untimely death in 1980. Meanwhile (1965-67), the department had received its first Soviet teaching assistant in accordance with the recently signed Anglo-Soviet Cultural and Scientific Agreement, under a scheme administered by the British Council. Angelina Kochetkova was an energetic, popular, enthusiastic and highly effective teacher, the first of many who came to Nottingham under the scheme, and was to achieve almost legendary status in the annals of the department.

By the time Frank Seeley left Nottingham in 1967, Bernard Johnson had been replaced by Gerald Stone and Michael Futrell by Gerald Smith, both scholars at the beginning of distinguished academic careers, which they concluded at Oxford as Fellows of the British Academy. As Seeley said in his brief article in the anniversary number of *Slavonica*, the department doubled in size during his tenure. In 1957, it comprised four staff (including one lector) and about thirty-five students; in 1967 it comprised eight staff (including a lector and a lectrice) and about seventy students who, moreover, enjoyed the services of an assistant lecturer in Russian and East European History attached to the Department of History.[6]

Frank Seeley's arrival marked a watershed in several respects, some national and international, some local to Nottingham. On the national stage, the flow of ex-servicemen was drying up, but was to be replaced by an increasing number of applicants from the schools, some of which had sent their modern language teachers on conversion courses (for example, to Holborn College, London) to equip them to teach Russian. It was one of those intermittent periods in the Cold War that saw a burst of public interest in all things Russian and the Soviet Union, and this in its turn attracted a minor upsurge in applications for university places.

Government awareness of the national importance of maintaining a bank of Russian speakers now that the Joint Services courses were coming to an end was reflected in two national reports in the early 1960s, the Annan Report and the Hayter Report[7]. The former was directed mainly at schools and the latter at universities.

---

[5] Arian Kirillov suffered from acute ill health. He was on sick leave for up to 18 months while at Nottingham. During this time the lector's post was filled temporarily by a Russian woman, whose name, regrettably, escapes me. On leaving Aberystwyth, he worked for a while as an interpreter with the United Nations in Geneva, dying in 1987.

[6] F. F. Seeley (1977).

[7] *The Teaching of Russian*, HMSO, 1960, chaired by Sir Noel Annan, and known as the Annan Report; *University Grants Committee: Report of the Sub-Committee on Oriental, Slavonic, East*

Annan mistakenly foresaw the time when Russian would draw level with German as the foreign language of second choice in schools. Hayter set up a number of dedicated university centres in Soviet Studies and, in addition, created some new posts in other universities. Nottingham was to receive three of them, one (Derek Spring) in the Department of History, the second (Brian Falloon) in the then independent Department of Economic and Social History, and the third (Gary Entwhistle) in the Department of Geography. On his appointment, Derek Spring took over the first-year Life element of the Life and Thought course from Frank Seeley and, when Michael Futrell left in 1966, the final year Soviet History and Politics course as well. At about the same time, the three Hayter lecturers established a highly successful Soviet Studies subsidiary course, a two-year course until the Faculty of Arts introduced its one-year unit scheme in the 1970s.

Meanwhile, most of the new universities of the fifties and sixties (Keele, East Anglia, Essex, Lancaster, Sussex, Bath) were to open degree courses in Russian, often within new Schools of European Studies. Some of the older universities and polytechnics were to follow suit.

It was a period of optimism and expansion in Russian studies. The 1950s had seen the foundation of the British Universities' Association of Slavists (mainly for scholars in language, literature and history), the National Association for Soviet and East European Studies (mainly for specialists in the Social Sciences), and the Association of Teachers of Russian (mainly for teachers in the schools, though with significant university participation). 1958 was also to see the first post-war International Congress of Slavists, held in Moscow and attended by a small British delegation including Monica Partridge and Frank Seeley.

Just as importantly, December 1959 saw the signing of the first official Anglo-Soviet intergovernmental agreement on Relations in the Scientific, Educational and Cultural Fields, to be renegotiated biennially until the end of the Soviet period. It was administered by the British Council on behalf of the Foreign and Commonwealth Office and was generally known in the field as 'The Cultural Agreement'. All future exchanges of students, postgraduates and academics were to take place within its framework.[8] The machinery turned out to be creaky and primitive, and vulnerable to inefficiency, delay, suspicion, sabotage and the Kafkaesque workings of the Soviet bureaucracy, not to mention the vagaries of international relations, but it was welcomed as a significant step in the right direction, and enabled many British Slavists to visit the Soviet Union both on courses and individual research visits.

The change of public mood towards the study of Russian was brought about partly through the encouragement of government and its agencies, but more importantly, perhaps, by international events. Following his denunciation of Stalin at the Twentieth Party Congress of the Communist Party of the Soviet Union in March 1956, Khrushchev had proclaimed the principle of peaceful coexistence, notably during a visit to the UK with the Soviet premier, Marshal Bulganin, in April. After the Suez debacle and the Soviet invasion of Hungary later that year, Khrushchev had consolidated his position in the Soviet leadership and, in October 1957, the first

---

European and African Studies, London, 1961, chaired by Sir William Hayter, and known as the Hayter Report.

[8] See 'The British Council in the Soviet Union', in the *House of Commons Second Report from the Foreign Affairs Committee, Session 1985-86, UK-Soviet Relations*, vol. 2, HMSO, London, 1986, pp. 70-4.

sputnik was launched into space, galvanising the attention of the United States and its allies. Then, in November, the Soviets sent a dog into orbit, presaging manned space flight, and engaging public imagination all round the world. Meanwhile, Pasternak had been awarded and had declined the Nobel Prize for Literature.

In spite of continuing ups and downs, there were signs of a thaw both in international relations and on the Soviet domestic scene. In the summer of 1958, Vice-President Nixon visited the American Exhibition in Moscow, where he famously debated with Khrushchev whether all American homes were actually equipped with the modern kitchens on display there. At Khrushchev's invitation, the British Prime Minister, Harold Macmillan, arrived in Moscow in February 1959, wearing a stylish fur hat. In September of that year, Khrushchev visited President Eisenhower in the United States, presenting him triumphantly with a scale model of the first Soviet sputnik. Improving relations between East and West were once again thrown into turmoil, however, when the American pilot Gary Powers was shot down over Soviet territory flying a U-2 spy plane in May 1960. While the public was conscious that the nuclear threat still hung over the world like the sword of Damocles, the promise held out by the policy of détente, with a possible liberalisation of Soviet society in the wake of destalinisation, combined with the glamour of the space race and the fascination of Khrushchev's own mercurial personality, all helped to boost recruitment to Russian courses and interest in the Soviet Union.

The University of Nottingham at the end of its first decade

Nottingham too was undergoing change. 1958 marked the completion of its first ten years as a university, and it is fair to say that the decade from 1958 to 1968 saw its growth to maturity alongside the other great civic universities that traced their origins to the Victorian era. This was true not only of its physical development (the expansion of the Highfields campus, the building of new halls of residence and of Science City) but also of its existing academic departments, their staffing and their syllabuses. It was in fact during Seeley's tenure that a fully-fledged department of Slavonic Studies was consolidated on the foundations laid by Fennell.

At this time, the University was still of modest proportions. In the session 1957-8 there was a total of 252 academic staff and 2,334 students on the two campuses at Highfields and Sutton Bonington[9]. Local residents still referred to the University as 'Highfields College', and it was many years before they registered that they had a university in their midst, or comprehended what a university was[10]. Word got around that the University would no longer accept applicants from local schools. This was of course untrue: it was simply that they were now in competition with applicants from all over the country and even from abroad. A well-known figure on campus in those days was an overzealous Park Ranger, who shooed away members of the public who strayed from the public park onto University land, thus further alienating local residents. The line of demarcation was not everywhere clear. Woodside Road had only

---

[9] J. Wakeford and P. R. Mounfield, eds. (1958), p. 5.

[10] It is arguable whether this is the case even in 2008, when the University has established its place among the top 100 world universities. A recent video, entitled *Nottingham through the Ages*, produced by the *Nottingham Evening Post*, hardly mentions the University.

recently been connected to University Boulevard[11], and red Barton's buses, reputedly driven by retired Second World War fighter pilots, sped along Beeston Lane, still at that time a public highway, joining Derby Road near Lenton Eaves. The Tottle Brook could still be seen passing under a bridge near the west entrance into the paddling pool in the University Park, and an open-air swimming pool, known as the Lido, stood where the Arts Centre now stands. Cut Through Lane (which bore the more sinister name of Cut Throat Lane on some old maps) still designated a footpath that took the pedestrian from Beeston towards the city.

The age of majority was still twenty-one. At the age of eighteen, we noted, you could be hanged for murder and men could be called up for military service, but you could not yet vote. Legally, therefore, the University was in loco parentis in relation to most of its students. Landladies often regarded themselves as being responsible for their students' morals, and were encouraged to be so by Mr Singleton, the University Accommodation Officer, who inspected and approved all student digs personally. My Beeston landlady, a Mrs Collishaw, who claimed that D. H. Lawrence had written a poem for her when she was a girl, took her duties very seriously indeed. She was from Eastwood herself, had once been a primary school teacher, and assumed a special posh accent for talking to her students. No girls were allowed in the house, and a stern lecture awaited any of her students who were spotted with a girl in town. She provided us with breakfast each day and a hot meal ('student pie') on Sundays. She was protected by a large, honey-coloured dog, called Susan, and a son called Peter, who would be invoked from time to time to reinforce her authority. When occasionally he called, we would be bundled out of the way, with the result that he remained a shadowy, faceless, threatening figure, backlit in the doorway of her dark, semi-detached, smoke-encrusted, red-brick Edwardian villa. She had a number of exemplary anecdotes about the retribution that had been visited upon former students who had broken the rules, rules about not leaving football boots around, and having no more than an inch of water in the bath. There was of course no central heating, just hot water bottles and a paraffin heater on cold Sunday afternoons.

In the 1950s, Beeston was still host to the world famous Beeston Boiler Works and, by October, thick fog had usually descended, pollution hung heavily in the frosty air and chilblains began to appear on toes and fingers. In the New Year, the lake in the University Park often iced over, and the Vice-Chancellor might sometimes be seen skating energetically across it. There was a story in circulation about an applicant for a place in the English Department coming up to Nottingham for interview, entering the Park by what he thought was the main entrance to the University by the bust of Jesse Boot, deciding to take a short cut across what looked like a deserted car park, and falling straight through the ice. Having thawed out, the story continues, he was offered a place, but turned it down.

My bank accounts indicate that I received £77 per term in my first year (1958-9), rising to £113 per term in my fourth (1961-2). I paid Ede and Ravenscroft £1. 4s. 6d (£1.22½p) for the hire of a gown for Graduation. A number of students, mostly boys, owned their own cars, and parked them freely on campus; many were pre-war, of the kind that are now treasured by veteran car enthusiasts and lined up in rows in the sunshine once a year in Wollaton Park. It was not unknown in those

---

[11] This must have taken place in or just before 1958, since a town plan purchased in 1958 shows them not yet joined up, as does the aerial photograph on a calendar published by the Students' Union to mark the University's first ten years.

pre-MOT days to find that, owing to brake failure, one of them had run away down the grassy bank in front of the Portland Building and ended up in the lake.

Impressions of an undergraduate

In accordance with the grand design of the first Vice-Chancellor, Bertrand Hallward[12] —whose voice could often be heard booming across the campus—Nottingham had now become an all-day university, and facilities were available in the Portland Building and Trent Library until 10.00 p.m. each weekday. With the opening of the Portland Building (the PB, as it was known) in 1956, the centre of student life quickly shifted there. Hallward insisted that this was not to be thought of as a Union Building, but as a facility that all members of the University might enjoy, the Union Offices occupying only a part of it. As a fresher in 1958, in digs in Beeston, at 50s. (£2.50) a week, I soon got to know the Portland Building well, and spent much time there between lectures and sessions in the Trent Library. In the tunnel that now ran between the Portland Building and the Trent Building, there were rows of tall, khaki lockers, where off-campus students could leave their gowns and books between lectures.

As a fresher, my first acquaintance with the PB was in Week One. There was a programme of events designed to induct the new student. Union societies and sports clubs each had their stalls in the concourse lounges, set out to encourage new students to join and to come to 'freshers' squashes' held in members' rooms in halls of residence.

New students were addressed in the Great Hall of the Trent Building by the Vice-Chancellor, who took the University motto, Sapienta urbs conditur, as his text. There followed an oration from the President of the Union and talks by the Professor of Music (Ivor Keys) and the head of the Department of Fine Art (Alastair Smart), who explained to us that the Music School[13] was situated between Florence Nightingale and Florence Boot Halls because the nightingale symbolised its musical aspirations while the boot symbolised its policy towards its students.

At some stage during the week, we were required to matriculate. This ceremony involved processing across the stage in the Great Hall in our newly acquired undergraduate gowns, and shaking hands with the Dean of the Faculty. We were left with the impression that failure to do this would invalidate everything that we did in the University thereafter, and those who did fail were required to turn up at the Dean's room later, to shake his hand there.

The opening of the PB had freed up space in the Trent Building. The Lower Hall, later to become the Senate Chamber, was still available for social events, but the old cafeteria beneath the Library had become the Lower Library, housing, among other subjects, Modern Languages and Philosophy, on two-tiered metal stacks, the remains of which still provide a balcony for performances in the Performing Arts Studio. There was also sufficient space for the Manuscripts Department, to the east, and a dedicated Periodicals Department, up the steps of the old platform and through a stout, light oak door. I spent many a happy evening in my first year reading and writing in the lower library, which I still associate with sixteenth- and seventeenth-century French literature (Ronsard, du Bellay, Malherbe, Rabelais, Molière, Corneille, Racine). Sometimes, for a change, I would

[12] See Derek Winterbottom (1995).
[13] In the house now occupied (2008) by the History Department.

61

find a seat upstairs, even in the gallery, seeking out relevant books in the history and the geography sections, as well as exploring the holdings more generally. It was a treasure trove, and had all the atmosphere of a real library, full of exciting books, all on open access and available, on completion of a small slip of paper, to be taken home. Library assistants dealt with issues and returns at the desk inside the main door, while Miss Clark, the Deputy Librarian, sat in solitary state at her own desk in the opposite corner by the window overlooking the lake. The Librarian, at that time a senior University Officer, whose name appeared alongside those of the Vice-chancellor and Registrar in the University Calendar, was Dick Smith, and the door to his room was in the corridor just outside.

My first encounter with Frank Seeley had been in February of that year, when I came to Nottingham for an interview, as all applicants were required to do for many years to come. He looked at my application form, asked me if I had any questions for him, and then declared in measured tones, 'Well, Mr Jones, I see no prima facie reason why we should not offer you a place.' Many graduates of the time have similar memories. Terry Sandell remembers that decorating work was being done in the department when he arrived, so he and Frank Seeley ended up sitting on tables. He asked simple but stretching questions, which contrasted starkly with a pretentious interview that Terry had recently had at his first-choice university. Terry came to Nottingham, though he felt slightly cheated on discovering when he arrived that Frank Seeley was no longer there.

In my first year, Mr Seeley took the beginners' language class, using Anna Semeonoff's well-known *New Russian Grammar*, which he corrected as he went. The fruits are to be found in *The Gateway Russian Course*, which, together with Helen Rapp, he later published for the ATR[14]. A quick glance is sufficient to show that for all its many merits as an academic work of reference, its usefulness as an introductory course for schools was limited. As was usual at the time, we were taken through the formal grammar of the language with a bare minimum of practice, either written or spoken, and then left to sink or swim. Mr Seeley would assume that it was helpful to give us parallels in Latin, German and French[15], and this was one of many unspoken assumptions underlying such courses at the time. One graduate remembers his evident disappointment that nobody in the class knew Greek.

It was also assumed that we did not require any motivation to undertake any part of the course (the fact that we were there was thought to be sufficient indication that we were self-motivated), that we had a solid education in the humanities, that we were familiar with English literature and the Classical and Biblical traditions, that we could read secondary material fluently in German and French, as well as in English and Russian, that essays might be set without any reading lists (we were expected to explore the library ourselves), and that we already knew how to write essays without any advice or assistance. Another assumption was that we could somehow make the leap from completing Mr Seeley's introductory grammar course to reading the classics of Russian literature in the original, and to translating E. M. Forster, or some passage on Kemal Attaturk chosen by Michael Futrell, without any further assistance, other

---

[14] Anna H. Semeonoff (1958); F. F. Seeley and H. Rapp (1963, 1964).

[15] Della Thompson has reminded me that 'O' level Latin was still required for entry to Modern Language courses at Nottingham at the time, and that most students of Russian who came straight from secondary school would have studied French and German there. However, this was not always the case with those who had acquired their Russian in the armed forces.

than that provided by grammars and dictionaries, and by the then newly available *Russian Syntax* by Borras and Christian.[16] It was also assumed that we should devote the greater part of our evenings, weekends and vacations to private study. It was understood that some students might have to take vacation jobs to make ends meet; others were reservists whose presence might be required by the armed forces during the summer; but no allowance was made for any of this. Tuition in the spoken language was also minimal. I would sometimes go down to Joanna Penny's room in Florence Nightingale Hall, and there we would listen to the voice of D. S. Mirsky on Linguaphone records together.

The courses that we followed for our Part I examination (normally the first two years, three years for beginners) were laid down in the published syllabus, and we were offered no choice. The same was true in the other departments where we might choose our subsidiary subject. Only in the final year was it possible to select two literature options from among perhaps three or four on offer, alongside a compulsory translation paper, a compulsory English Essay paper,[17] Soviet History and Politics (Futrell) and a compulsory paper in Serbo-Croat (Partridge). The result was a greater spread of performance than one would expect today between those students, who by background or disposition, or both, turned out to be academic high-flyers, and those who floundered about unaided in deep and unfamiliar waters, and were happy to emerge with a third class degree. In its first ten years, the University had awarded only one first class degree in Russian Studies (to Michael Scammell). On the plus side, such courses were genuine voyages of discovery, rather than the guided, package tours that they have since become.

Frank Seeley's lecture notes were written in a small, intricate hand, supplemented by marginal notes in shorthand. I enjoyed his lectures on Russian Life (history) very much, but most memorable were his final year courses on Pushkin and Lermontov and The Nineteenth-Century Russian Novel. Two sequential hours per week were timetabled for each course, over two and a bit terms. The first hour was occupied by a course of lectures, carefully timed to fill the hours available. In the Novel course, we were supposed to cover all the major novels of Pushkin, Lermontov, Gogol, Goncharov, Turgenev, Dostoevsky and Tolstoi. In the second hour, one of us would present a paper for discussion. There was an essay rota covering all the courses for which essays were expected, so that we were not burdened with more than one in the same week. Once the paper had been read, he would offer his own comments, ranging from corrections to our English and queries about the accuracy of our recollections of the text, to a critical analysis of our arguments. Where these were deemed inadequate, as they normally were, he would offer alternatives and speculate aloud on how we could possibly have reached such extraordinary conclusions. Then we were all invited to join in. It cannot be said that discussion usually flowed freely, for we were all aware that the slightest careless remark would become the subject of intense scrutiny, but it was a superb training in disciplined thinking. It was said that, when he embarked on his life-long study of Dostoevsky, Seeley quickly realised that it would be impossible without a thorough and reliable knowledge of modern psychology, with which he immediately began to equip himself. In his knowledge of Piaget, it was said, he

---

[16] F. M. Borras and R. F. Christian (1959).

[17] The questions on this paper were of a general nature, rather like those subsequently set for the Russian Essay paper, only in English. Its object was to test the wider intellectual accomplishments of students.

outstripped any member of the Psychology Department. It should be stressed that his use of developmental psychology was extremely subtle, and its sources eclectic; he was not one of those critics who crudely applied a superficial knowledge of Freudian symbolism to their reading of literary texts.

Dr Partridge lectured to us on eighteenth- and nineteenth-century literature, supplementing D. S. *Mirsky's History of Russian Literature,*[18] which was our Bible. She also lectured on Russian Thought in the second year. Her lectures did not stretch us intellectually as much as Seeley's did, but were reliable, accurate and informative. To liven things up, she would sometimes declaim Russian poetry in a dramatic style that she had learnt from Simon Boyanus in London, inviting us to absorb the sounds and the rhythms, even if the sense generally eluded us. She would set an essay each term, and I remember writing one on Krylov's fables, for which I managed to work my way through a series of fables in Russian, modelling my analysis on my A-level study of La Fontaine. Gerry May remembers how once Dr Partridge made the whole class rewrite an essay on Gogol.

Our essays were hand-written on lined quarto or foolscap paper, and we were not expected to give references or a bibliography. By today's standards they look very amateurish, but technology was still primitive. Few students possessed even typewriters. Essays were returned either individually or collectively during an hour scheduled for a lecture, and usually bore marginal comments and a one-sentence remark at the end, with either a percentage mark or a letter from A to D (or their equivalents in the Greek alphabet), accompanied by subtle combinations of plusses and minuses.

In the second year, Dr Partridge took an unexamined introductory course on Serbo-Croat, shortly thereafter to be published in book form, and continued with the examined Part II course in the final year. The similarities with Russian made it easier than a completely different new language, but it was also easy to confuse them, as she sometimes did herself. She was very keen on our learning passages by heart and parts of some of them still stick in my head. Evidently, I am not the only one. Roger Stubbings caused some amusement many years later on a visit to Yugoslavia when he tried one of Monica's phrases ('Parabrod Jadran ceka na obali') on a Yugoslav guide. He was told with a chuckle that the steamship Jadran was no longer waiting by the shore, as it had long ago gone to the scrapyard.

Dr Partridge's final year option was Selected Nineteenth-Century Russian Thinkers, in which we examined the thinkers we had encountered in the Russian Thought course in more depth and more detail. Herzen was, of course, her favourite. Sometimes she would include a lecture, but mostly we gave papers ourselves, based on our own reading.

Dr Partridge usually seemed genial enough, even kindly, and in my third year she generously offered me extra classes in Russian phonetics to improve my pronunciation. Sasha Lubetkin remembers her with great fondness, respecting her particularly for making her way so successfully in the pre-feminist world. Sometimes, though, she could be unexpectedly fierce. Kate Hudspith (née Sheaf) remembers being sharply reprimanded when discussing whether she should intercalate a year in France as part of her French Studies course (at that time optional). 'She informed me that she did not approve of students swanning off to enjoy themselves abroad and getting out of the way of regular study,' Kate recalls. Ruth Morgan (née Fisher) remembers a row

---

[18] D. S. Mirsky (1949).

about whether or not she should repeat a year, and the unhappy consequences of failing to take Monica's advice. Her 'feminism' too could sometimes take surprising forms. Joanna Hughes (née Penny) remembers being told that it was 'very important for the men to get good degrees but the women should use their time at the university to develop their personalities.'

Dr Veronica du Feu came down from Manchester in my first year to lecture on Old Russian Literature and History. She was a delightful and formidably erudite young woman. I remember her slight, willowy figure, flitting and darting enthusiastically in front of the blackboard, listing the Kievan and Muscovite grand princes and their principalities, and amending them with a flurry of duster and chalk as they died or swapped domains, leaving the blackboard and the class in an amazing state of happy confusion.

There were few handouts in those days, and these were duplicated at the cost of great effort on Xerox stencils which, if they had been used several times, produced texts that were almost illegible. Photocopying machines did exist, but were not yet readily available.

In the following year, 1959, Dr David Johnson visited from Birmingham to teach us the History of the Russian Language. I found it difficult enough mastering the grammar of modern Russian without, at the same time, having to master the complex stages through which it had evolved from the Common Slavonic reconstructed by scholars, through various South-Slav influences, and the interaction of Church Slavonic and vernacular forms of Russian. Bernard Johnson was appointed to a permanent post in 1960. Bernard was still new and slightly nervous when he taught me, but set off on a successful career which was shortly to take him to the London School of Economics.

Dr Futrell's lectures on Soviet Literature in Part I, and Soviet History and Politics in Part II, were quite different from those of his colleagues, and at first I mistakenly thought they were slapdash. They were in fact entertaining, informative, well-structured, and very useful, as later scrutiny of my notes proved. Whereas Seeley would stand gowned at the lectern and deliver his carefully honed lectures formally to his tiny class, exactly as he would have done to a scholarly audience of hundreds, Futrell would seat himself on the desk, throw down a disordered sheaf of notes and talk informally to us in a challenging, even aggressive, way. A journalist in a past life, he was in all ways unlike the Oxbridge model of a lecturer; Joanna Hughes remembers him asking for the 'woman's point of view' on Simone de Beauvoir's *The Second Sex*, which she had recently read. Typically, this had nothing to do with the course. During my period as an undergraduate, he published his *Northern Underground*, in which he controversially argued that Lenin funded his revolutionary activities in 1917 partly from the sale of contraceptives to the troops. Such revelations were a good deal more sensational in the late 1950s than they would be today. On one occasion he told us that he thought today's students were a pathetic lot and that we should do something really daring, such as organising a naked ball. I doubt whether he was impressed when one of our number left a rubber ball on his desk, with a label informing him that this was it.

Futrell's classes on Soviet History did not appeal to Sasha Lubetkin, who graduated in 1964. She was one of those rare students who had been brought up to believe absolutely in the October Revolution, and Futrell's anti-Soviet line was therefore highly uncongenial to her. Her view that the courses in Soviet history and literature were actually courses in anti-Soviet history and literature (neglecting Socialist Realist classics and focussing on those writers whose writing expressed their independence from Soviet ideology) was for many years a standard complaint among visiting Soviet lecturers too. Most students, however, seem to have relished his iconoclastic approach.

Futrell also ran a final year option on the Soviet Novel, which I did not take, reckoning that the amount of Russian to be read in the original exceeded my capacity, especially when taken together with Seeley's course on the nineteenth-century novel.

In researching his book, Futrell had discovered links with Japan that he wanted to follow up, and he could sometimes be found in his private room poring over a Japanese grammar. He also developed an interest in Buddhism, and left Nottingham in 1966 for a chair in Vancouver at The University of British Columbia.

Study visits abroad

Having a French wife, like Fennell, Bernard Johnson took over the organisation of the first year's stay with Russian families in Paris at the end of the summer term. I stayed with the Avierinos in Asnières; others stayed with the Vereshchagins, the Kniazevs, the Kuznetsovs, the Kisselevskys, and others. I do not remember any organised lessons, and my family spoke as much French as Russian; German occasionally too. In fact it was the first time that I had come across a family that seemed to switch fluently into whichever of these languages best suited the subject matter or the person they were speaking to. I learned that there was still a lively Russian émigré community in Paris, visited a Russian pre-revolutionary regimental museum, attended a series of lectures in Russian at the Institut d'études slaves, specially arranged for us, and discovered a marvellous Russian second-hand book shop called Dom knigi in the rue de l'Éperon.

Such things apart, I familiarised myself with the Paris underground and, with the others, visited various tourist spots. Joanna Hughes remembers that her landlord spent all his time at the races at the Bois de Boulogne and recalls meeting a woman who had earned a living shovelling coal on Soviet trains. Almost everyone seems to remember this month in Paris, sometimes for reasons quite unconnected to their course. Peter Ray (1967) remembers seeing the Beatles there in 1965, but hearing none of the music, which was drowned out by thousands of screaming girls. But, when all was said and done, our Russian did not improve as much as we should have liked; we beginners were still too inexperienced in the language to take full advantage of the opportunity; our hosts varied considerably in their commitment to our education; this was in fact the only period of semi-immersion in the language that we had during the degree course and it was therefore only fair that our oral proficiency should not be too severely tested in our finals.

In my first summer vacation, however, I joined an international group of students on a trip to the Soviet Union and the fortnight I spent there was both exhilarating and exhausting. Since we were all English speakers, and carefully shepherded around by English-speaking guides, the opportunity for improving our Russian was limited here too, but it was an important experience from the cultural and political point of view. In spite of Khrushchev's denunciation, Stalin still lay beside Lenin in the mausoleum on Red Square and there were statues, busts and mosaics of him to be seen everywhere, including East Berlin, whose Stalinallee we visited en route. Since the only affordable way to travel for some years to come was by rail, we experienced the transit of West and East Germany, Berlin (divided into zones of occupation, though without its Wall until 1961), Poland, and what is now Belarus, before arriving in Moscow, three days after our departure from London. Most interesting was the occasional encounter with Russians.

Several years later, in the summer of 1967, Sandra Kent (née Suter) was due to go on a trip to Minsk,[19] but, owing to international tensions arising from the Six-Day War, it was deemed unsafe and cancelled. Instead the group was sent on a course in Unterweissenbach in Austria, run by a Dr Dox. Some had board and lodgings with the villagers, others stayed in a hotel that also contained the town slaughterhouse. She remembers sitting in the roof garden and hearing animal screams from down below. Unterweissenbach was occasionally used as a substitute for the Soviet Union by Nottingham students in years to come and contributed to the rich range of experiences available to students on the course.

Social life

There was a Slavonic Society in our day, but I cannot remember it doing anything very Slavonic during my period as a student. Some graduates remember socialising at pubs in town. Yates' Wine Lodge and The Bell are mentioned, as is The Trip to Jerusalem. There was an annual dinner and, on one occasion, Frank Seeley entertained us with an account of his recent visit to the United States, the one that was to lead to his being offered posts in US universities. His speech was characterised by his usual acute observation and subtle verbal wit (what the French would call esprit). It was however rather on the long side, causing Dr Partridge to cancel her own prepared speech, and she was understandably put out.

Gerry May, secretary of the Society at the time, remembers our receiving a visit from the Soviet film star Elina Bystritskaia through the offices of the British-Soviet Friendship Society. So there was at least one Slavonic event. Like a number of other graduates, Gerry went on to teach Russian himself and in the course of time one of his own students, Barbara Honca, came to study at Nottingham. In the 1970s, he regularly brought groups of students to the department's Russian Days.

During the Seeley period, Bertrand Hallward's vision was being expressed not only in the building of Science City and the new Social Sciences Building, but also in a string of new halls of residence that would eventually lead to the closure of Beeston Lane as a public thoroughfare. The first new Hall to be added to the four already existing when Seeley arrived was Cripps Hall (1959), next to Hugh Stewart Hall. There followed in quick succession Lincoln (1962), Derby (1963), Lenton, Sherwood, Rutland (1965), Willoughby, Cavendish and Ancaster (1966), of which the first five were originally for men students and the last three for women.

Most students lived in a hall of residence for a part of their course and some made enduring friendships there. The same was true of the departments in which they took their subsidiary subjects, which occupied a third of their time and effort for the first two years, leading to qualifications at Part I. It was possible to follow any of the subjects taught in the Faculty, including Mathematics, provided that one had the necessary qualifications. French was a particularly popular choice for those who came

---

[19] Since it seems to have pre-dated the first year study visits to the Soviet Union arranged by the department, this may have been one of the courses organised by BUAS, of which mention is made elsewhere.

straight from school. Beginners in Russian normally came with A-level qualifications in French and, if it was their ambition to teach Russian in schools, they were almost certain to have to teach French as well, probably as their main subject. Before the days of Joint Honours Degrees, introduced towards the end of the Seeley period, Part I in French was held to be an appropriate qualification for teaching. The amount of reading to be covered by subsidiary students was prodigious. Although the literature course stopped short of the twentieth century, it covered all the major writers (poets, dramatists, philosophers, novelists) and some of the minor ones, from the sixteenth to the nineteenth centuries. In those two years we read a great deal more French literature than most honours students do today, and there was no sure way of predicting what would come up in the examination.

Examinations

There were departmental examinations at the end of our first year, though they were not taken very seriously. Dr Partridge told us that we ought to be able to pass examinations without any preparatory revision, so we were always on tenterhooks lest she catch us unprepared. However, this never happened. In fact, she once even forgot to turn up at the advertised time for an unofficial examination that she had devised, with the result that after twenty minutes, as was the custom, we all gratefully dispersed. At the end of the second year, we took our Part I examinations in our honours and subsidiary subjects (apart from beginners, who took the subsidiary subject at the end of the second year and the honours subject at the end of the third). We had to pass these examinations, but they were not incorporated in our degree results. There being no compulsory year abroad at the time, even in those languages where this would have been feasible, the final examinations were taken at the end of the third year or, in the case of beginners, the fourth.

Most students of the time will retain a keen memory of their final examinations, not only of those that took place in the Great Hall, where they sat for each three-hour written paper, gowned, at carefully spaced desks, each adorned with a question paper, a piece of blotting paper, a pink-covered answer book, and a short piece of string to tie on supplementary sheets, but also, most particularly, of the viva voce examinations, to which all finalists were subjected.

For the vivas, the entire lecturing staff of the department would assemble in their black gowns behind a table in the seminar room, and each candidate would be summoned from a waiting room, where he or she had been nervously trying to focus his or her mind on a short piece of Russian prose, xeroxed for the purpose, and subsequently to be read aloud to the panel. This exercise completed, there might be a brief exchange in simple Russian, conducted by the External Examiner (in my case John Fennell), and this would be followed by a dissection in English of our hastily written answer papers, from which isolated sentences might be drawn and quoted back for us to justify. All the examiners were expected to participate. Thus were resurrected for public scrutiny words that, several weeks earlier, we had thankfully banished to our subconscious. It may have been Seeley who introduced this system. Although he conducted the vivas with scrupulous fairness and courtesy, that did not greatly diminish the trauma that they induced.

It has to be admitted that not all students appreciated the courses laid on for them. Michael Scammell, in publishing an article entitled 'Examinations are Bunk' in the student magazine *Gong*, left no doubt that he felt the same about the lectures, claiming that most students obtained their degrees on the basis of three months cramming before Part I and a further three months cramming before their finals. With a typical mixture of courtesy and ruthless analysis, Frank Seeley dissected his arguments in a follow-up article in the following number. Typical of students of the time or not, Michael Scammell went on to become a notable Slavist in his own right.

In 1962, I became a postgraduate in the department, supervised by Frank Seeley and, during his visit to the United States, by Michael Futrell. Frank Seeley was just the sort of supervisor that one would expect him to be, superb at textual criticism, though not so well versed in the subject of my work, and blissfully unaware that a postgraduate might need advice on the methodology of scholarly research. All this we were supposed to know intuitively or to find out by ourselves. It was hard work, and lonely work, for there were no other postgraduates, or indeed, staff at Nottingham, who shared my combination of interests. Nor were there teaching opportunities for postgraduates in those days, except for the occasional evening class that might come their way. Among the bright spots were visits to London to work in the famous Reading Room of the British Museum, where Marx and Lenin had themselves once worked and the Russian philosopher Vladimir Solov'ev had seen one of his visions of the Holy Sophia. No such visitation awaited me, though I once encountered the legendary Professor Elizabeth Hill, of Cambridge, leafing through a printed catalogue. The smell of the blue leather upholstery, however, still lingers in my memory and, with it, all the features of a lost world of scholarly endeavour.

While in the United States, Frank Seeley had been offered more than one chair, and although he was undoubtedly happier in the UK, he reasoned that he was unlikely to be promoted at Nottingham without his book on Dostoevsky. He believed that, in any University worthy of the name, merit would be recognised without the necessity of its being proved by publication. Reluctantly, he accepted an offer from The University of Pennsylvania, only to be offered a chair in at least one UK University[20] when it was too late, for one with his moral scruples, to turn down the American offer.

So the Seeley period, the zamechatel'noe desiatiletie (the remarkable decade), as he called it in his article in *Slavonica*, came to an end in 1967 and, to rub salt into the wound, the University publicly advertised the chair that it had denied him. He always remembered these years at Nottingham as the happiest in his career, however, and they were certainly his most successful: he had presided over the transformation of a department that was just finding its feet into one that had become a fully-fledged member of the growing community of Russian and Slavonic Departments that burgeoned in the sixties and early seventies of the last century. And, unlike many of the newcomers, it proved robust enough to endure into the present century. Sometime during this period, the name of the department was changed from Slavonic Languages to Slavonic Studies, reflecting a broader remit than had been implied in its previous title. Throughout the period of Frank Seeley's tenure the department remained in the temporary buildings (the cowsheds) behind the Portland Building, although, to my recollection, it moved within this area once. These unprepossessing, low-slung, brick buildings, painted white inside and out, with their metal-framed windows and central corridors, remain fondly in my mind as the setting of our student years, combining a

---

[20] Rumour has it that the chair in question was at SSEES, though I have also heard it said that it was at Queen's University, Belfast. It is possible, of course, that he received more than one offer.

formality of manners with the intimacy of a small and friendly department. Sasha Lubetkin says that she still thinks of the department there every day, incorporating its buildings and surroundings into the imaginary landscapes of the books she is reading.

The American period of Frank Seeley's career was not a happy one professionally. His lack of sympathy with the ethos of American academic politics and style of teaching was no doubt an aggravating factor. In 1971, he left Pennsylvania and took up a chair at the Binghamton campus of the State University of New York, where he was to remain until his retirement. However, he had married at the time of his move to the United States and this was the beginning of a period of settled, happy and fulfilling family life with his wife Maria and adopted son Mark. The book on Dostoevsky never came, but he continued to publish articles on him, and to give conference papers. In his retirement, he published a fine monograph on Turgenev and two books of collected essays,[21] the last of these in 1999, the year before his death at his home in Texas, at the age of eighty-eight.

---

[21] Frank Friedeberg Seeley (1991); Frank F. Seeley, (1994); Frank Seeley (1999).

From the Other Shore

(1967-1980)

The First Stage, 1967-75

SINCE the retirement of Janko Lavrin, the development of the department had been materially assisted by external events, initially, a flow of undergraduates whose Russian had been acquired in the armed forces, and then, from the late 1950s onwards, the growth of Russian teaching in schools. This last feature reached its peak in the early 1970s and continued to feed into undergraduate recruitment for a number of years to come. Thereafter, in the decade that followed, a combination of worsening public perceptions of the Soviet Union during the Brezhnev era (the so-called period of stagnation from 1964 to 1982) with the closure of many grammar schools and the abandonment of Russian teaching by most of the new comprehensives, caused a serious reduction in the available pool of students with a knowledge of Russian.[1] A few came from families where Russian was spoken, but these were always exceptional at Nottingham. It was widely believed that the Soviet invasion of Czechoslovakia in 1968 also contributed to public disenchantment. Combined with the enthusiastic, and what with hindsight seems the overconfident, expansion of provision for Russian studies in the university sector in the 1960s, this was bound eventually to lead to a crisis of supply and demand. Indeed, Russian studies lived in a constant state of crisis throughout this period and for many years to come. It was destined to be a bumpy ride, whoever Seeley's successor might be.

When Frank Seeley went to America, however, the department, and indeed the subject nationally, were still on an upward trajectory. Admission figures[2] for this period are lacking, but graduation figures give some idea of the general pattern. The department had, as Seeley said, doubled in size over the period 1957-67, and it was now, for the first time in its history, publicly advertising a chair of Russian Language and Literature.[3]

---

[1] See N. S. Sollohub (1967); Daphne West (1983, second edition, 1985); J. Y. Muckle (1989); J. Y. Muckle (1992); J. Y. Muckle (1994).

[2] Application figures from official sources are notoriously unreliable so far as Russian is concerned. This is because an increasing number of applicants wanted to study for Joint Honours degrees with another modern language, and such applications were all entered under the language that appeared first in the alphabet (French and German both coming before Russian). When such figures were circulated and quoted, it frequently appeared that up to 50% of the national pool of applicants to Russian courses actually came to Nottingham, which was clearly not the case.

[3] It should be noted that graduation figures do not necessarily give a true picture of admissions three or four years earlier, for the reason that the proportion of students on three and four years courses varied from year to year. However, graduation figures during Seeley's tenure were as follows: *1958*: 10; *1959*: 3; *1960*: 7; *1961*: 6; *1962*: 8; *1963*: 3; *1964*: 7; *1965*: 7; *1966*: 8; *1967*: 21. If we are thinking of recruitment, then we should add at least the following three years, *1968*: 23; *1969*: 20;

There could hardly have been a greater contrast between the personalities, lecturing and management styles and academic gifts of Frank Seeley and his successor. Having been frustrated ten years earlier, Monica Partridge[4] was finally appointed to the Chair and headship of the department on his departure for Pennsylvania in 1967. She was 52 that year and the first woman professor ever to be appointed by the University. Her combative personality was known to her colleagues, her qualifications were impressive and her vision of the department's future was an ambitious one.

Born in Northampton on 25 May 1915, née Monica Alice McMain, she had attended Northampton School for Girls from 1926 to 1933 and then read French, with Latin as her subsidiary subject, at The University College, Nottingham, graduating with an honours degree in 1936. At the time, Nottingham students read for London degrees. A Cambridge Teaching Diploma followed in 1937, and shortly after this she married Maurice William (Bill) Partridge, who had been a fellow student at Nottingham and who, by the time of her appointment to the Chair, occupied the Jesse Boot Chair of Pharmaceutical Chemistry at the University. He was also a highly accomplished amateur painter and his fine semi-abstract landscapes hung all round the University, and were widely admired and sought after, as they still are today. He had developed his early style on trips to Yugoslavia with Monica, under the influence of the painter Harold Cohen, sometime Fellow in Fine Art at Nottingham.

Soon after the beginning of the Second World War she had taken up the study of Russian with Professor S. C. Boyanus (S. K. Boianus in its Russian form), at that time lecturer in Russian and Phonetics at the School of Slavonic and East European Studies at London University, and formerly professor of English Philology at the Leningrad Institute of Philosophy, History and Linguistics.[5] From 1940 to 1943, she attended classes at the School of Slavonic and East European Studies, and from 1943 to 1947 she taught at Boyanus's School of Russian in London. From 1944 to 1947 she was also a registered postgraduate student at University College, London, holding a Roston scholarship in the Department of Phonetics, where she studied under Daniel Jones. In 1947, she was awarded the Laura Soames Prize for Original Research on the Phonetics of a Language, and served as a part-time assistant lecturer at UCL. She also gave a course of lectures on phonetics at Oxford.

1970: 22. Figures calculated from lists of graduates in Cynthia Marsh and Wendy Rosslyn (1991) , pp. 157-65.
[4] A short biography is to be found in Peter Herrity (1990), pp. xi-xiv. A bibliography of works published between 1946 and 1989 follows (pp. xv-xxi). See also 'Professor Monica Partridge', *The Times*, April 21, 2008, p. 49.
[5] See Monica Partridge (1952-3). The obituary records that Boyanus was initially attracted to drama, which he studied under V. N. Davydov at the St Petersburg State School of Drama. Developing an interest in the relationship between colloquial and dramatic modes of speech, he was later appointed Professor of English Philology at the Leningrad Institute of Philosophy, History and Linguistics. In 1925 he spent eight months in the Phonetics Department of University College, London, where he met and married his principal teacher, Lilias Armstrong. Being obliged to return to the USSR without her, they lived apart for eight years, during which he worked with V. K. Müller on English-Russian and Russian-English dictionaries. In 1934, he obtained permission to live in England and soon afterwards was appointed Lecturer in Russian and Phonetics at SSEES. While there, he published his *Manual of Russian Pronunciation* and, with N. B. Jopson, his *Spoken Russian*. In 1942, he retired and opened his own School of Russian in London. He died in 1952. It was at Boyanus's Russian School, I believe, that Monica Partridge met Kenneth Whibley, later a lecturer at Bangor, who had vivid memories of her at this time.

This period does not seem to have resulted in any formal qualifications in Russian, but her burgeoning interest in this subject, and in phonetics, was beginning to bear fruit and attract recognition; she was also gaining valuable teaching experience, giving lessons to civil servants who were to visit the USSR on scientific and diplomatic missions during the war, and publishing a course on English for Russian speakers in a British Embassy publication in Moscow.[6]

As we have seen, Monica Partridge joined Nottingham University College's Department of Slavonic Languages as a tutorial assistant under Janko Lavrin in 1947. At Lavrin's suggestion, she embarked on her doctoral thesis on Alexander Herzen (*Alexander Herzen: a study of his years in Russia 1812-1847*) and when in 1949 the Scarbrough Report recommended an additional lectureship in Russian at Nottingham, he appointed her Assistant Lecturer to work alongside him.

In 1951, her interest in Yugoslav Studies began to blossom when she first attended the Seminar za strane slaviste at Zagreb, presumably also on Lavrin's recommendation. In the mid to late 1950s, Lavrin encouraged her to become involved in regular English Summer Schools at Piran and Koper in Slovenia,[7] which she undertook at first with some apparent hesitation but later with greater enthusiasm; in the 1970s, these contacts were to bear fruit in departmental links with Zagreb and Ljubljana, and in a steady stream of Yugoslav postgraduates studying in Nottingham's English Department under Professor Vivian de Sola Pinto and Dr Alan Rodway. Among these were the distinguished Croat English literature specialist, Ivo Vidan, and, long before his tragic conversion to the cause of Bosnian Serb nationalism, the noted Shakespeare specialist, Nikola Koljević.[8]

In 1953, as we have also seen, Monica was awarded her PhD on Herzen and, in 1958, along with a handful of other British Slavists, she attended the first post-war International Congress of Slavists in Moscow, where her paper on Herzen was well received by Soviet scholars who had no access to Western archives themselves. In 1962, during Frank Seeley's tenure, she was promoted to the grade of senior lecturer. Meanwhile, she was continuing to work on Herzen and her Serbo-Croatian Grammar, and received support from the Hayter Fund to visit libraries in Moscow, Leningrad and Belgrade. She also visited libraries in the United States, France, Austria and Italy, all the time networking with foreign Slavists and extending her academic links.

Although some who had worked with Monica had doubts about her suitability for the headship, she must have looked a strong candidate when Frank Seeley announced his departure for the United States in 1967. Like her predecessors, she was said to have a major work in the pipeline at the time of her appointment, but, unlike them, she also had publications under her belt. In addition to a number of translations and several early articles on Russian phonetics and stress, she now had eight published articles on Herzen, mostly on his English activities and contacts, and had shown a talent for

---

[6] Monica Partridge (1949).

[7] See Dušan Moravec (2002). The first Summer School was held in 1955 in Bohinj and led by Vivian de Sola Pinto. From 1959 to 1962 they were held in Piran and Koper under Monica Partridge's direction. The eighth and final Summer School was held in 1965 in Ankaran.

[8] Ivo Vidan was later to be one of the department's guests and, according to my engagement diary, a Professor Koljević lectured to the department on March 8 1973. This could have been Nikola Koljević, or his brother, Svetozar Koljević, from Novy Sad, a well-known expert on Serbian and Croatian folk literature. I am no longer certain, but I believe that both brothers lectured to the department on different occasions. Nikola Koljević became Vice-President of the Bosnian Serb Republic under Radovan Karadzić and is believed to have committed suicide in January 1997.

unearthing unpublished letters in West European archives. In 1964, she had the unusual distinction for a Western Slavist of publishing a number of previously unknown letters from Turgenev to Charles Dilke in the prestigious Soviet series *Literaturnoe nasledstvo (Literary Heritage)*. The first edition of her Serbo-Croatian: *Practical Grammar and Reader* appeared in the same year.[9] She now had plans to convert her contacts and activities in Yugoslavia into permanent institutional links of mutual benefit to the department and its Yugoslav partners.

Her East European contacts continued to expand following her appointment to the Chair in 1967. From the early 1970s, she became a member of the British Committee of the Association Internationale des Etudes Sud-Est Européennes, and took an active role in helping to establish the Dubrovnik International Postgraduate Centre, becoming a member of the Executive Committee of its Council. She became an Honorary Vice-President of the Association of Teachers of Russian and, for some years, served as a British member of the International Association for the Study and Dissemination of Slavonic Cultures (MAIRSK[10]).

All this had a bearing on the future shape of the department. Most significantly perhaps, the Serbo-Croat element in the department's work was expanded until Nottingham became, numerically at least, the principal centre for undergraduate studies in this area in the UK. Monica's contacts with the Universities of Zagreb and Ljubljana bore fruit in the appointment of a series of lectors and lectrices in Serbo-Croat from the English Department at The University of Zagreb from 1971, and a lector or lectrice in Slovene from Ljubljana from 1974,[11] the latter fully funded in the early years by the Slovene government. In return, Zagreb made provision for Nottingham students studying Serbo-Croat to spend periods of study there, where they were looked after by past lectors and lectrices. Ljubljana did the same for the smaller number who chose to study Slovene. Monica's efforts to promote Yugoslav studies in the UK became well known in Yugoslavia and in 1980, the year of her retirement (also the year of Tito's death), she was awarded the Order of the Yugoslav Flag with a Gold Star.

From 1971, the first Serbo-Croat lectors and lectrices from the Department of English at The University of Zagreb began to arrive. Their English was fluent and they adapted easily to the British way of life and quickly made friends in Nottingham. Indeed, several brought their teenage children with them, to spend a period in a British school or at the University itself, where they invariably flourished. In this first stage of Monica's tenure, the post was occupied by Stanka Krančević (1971-2), Vjekoslav Karlovčan (1972-3), Steve Maričić (1973-4) and Branko Brusar (1974-5).

Then in 1974, the first Slovene lectrice from Ljubljana joined the department. She was Ljuba Črnivec, who stayed until 1977, and successfully laid the foundations for Slovene studies, a development that was applauded by Janko Lavrin and his previously sceptical associates in Slovenia.

Meanwhile, an annual supply of Soviet language assistants was maintained through the Anglo-Soviet Scientific and Cultural Agreements, their arrival often being delayed by Soviet bureaucracy or reciprocal obstruction by the Home Office, and occasioning a

---

[9] Monica Partridge (1964). A second, revised and improved edition was published by Izdavački zavod in Belgrade in 1972, and a third edition, published by Prosveta, appeared there in 1988.

[10] *Mezhdunarodnaia assotsiatsiia dlia izucheniia i rassprostraneniia slavianskikh kul'tur.*

[11] This had been negotiated on a visit to Ljubljana with the assistance of the young Peter Herrity, newly appointed to the staff of the department.

row with the British Council. Angelina Kochetkova (1965-7) was succeeded by Tamara Amirova (1967-8), Irina Kireyeva (1968-9), Lyudmila Dyachkova (1970-2), Valentina Kleshcheva (1972-3) and Viktoria Surzhina (1973-5). Most of them were women of mature years, with families back home, where they held posts of considerably greater seniority than the one that they occupied in Nottingham. For this reason, Monica insisted on their being called Soviet Lecturers rather than lectrices or language assistants, as was usual in the other modern language departments, though they were actually paid a fraction of the already modest lectrice's salary. They all seemed dedicated to the Soviet system and to the principles of Marxism-Leninism, and most appeared highly resistant to counter-evidence, spending much of their time, it often appeared, trying unsuccessfully to fathom the British way of life and the mysteries of British higher education. Most were provided with accommodation in tutors' flats in Florence Nightingale Hall under its eccentric and colourful warden, Audrey Beecham.

Two Soviet Lecturers stand out as exceptions, however. Lyudmila Dyachkova stayed for two years. She seemed to know hardly any English at all, which must have made life unbearable for her at times. Ina Semyonova, whom I have omitted from the list above, stayed for only one term (Autumn 1969), during which she became convinced that agents of British Intelligence were trying to compromise her and that members of staff in the department were involved in the plot. By chance, I met her in the buffet in the basement of the Lenin Library on a subsequent visit to Moscow. She was not pleased to see me: nothing had happened to change her mind. She was an unfortunate victim of the climate of paranoid suspicion that (not always without justification) prevailed at the time.

There were also occasional Soviet visitors to the department. In recognition of her work on Herzen, Monica had been in attendance when, in February-March 1966, in the presence of a high-powered Soviet delegation, the remains of Herzen's friend Nikolai Ogarev (1813-1877) had been disinterred at Highgate Cemetery for cremation and repatriation to his native Russia. There she met the Soviet writer Vladimir Lidin, representing the Soviet Union of Writers. Photographs of this grisly event were among the first exhibits in the departmental display cabinet, acquired when it moved to the ground floor of the Trent Building in 1968.

Lidin, a brisk and genial elderly writer, who occupied a Moscow flat packed from floor to ceiling with an amazing collection of first editions, visited Nottingham during the 1968-9 session and thereafter was always available at home in Moscow to welcome visitors from the department. Among Monica's other eminent Soviet contacts were Iu. G. Oksman, Iurii Levin, Academician M. P. Alekseev, and the future academician G. M. Fridlender.

Apart from Lidin, the period of her headship saw visits by S. Mashinsky (a Soviet literary scholar), V. G. Kostomarov (principal of the Pushkin Institute for the Russian Language) and A. Parastaev (Cultural Attaché, later First Secretary at the Soviet Embassy), some of whom had close links with the KGB. Monica went out of her way to avoid anything that might compromise her and her colleagues' chances of obtaining entry visas to the Soviet Union; on Russian Days for Schools she was known to suppress questions about Solzhenitsyn, and other matters that might embarrass the Soviet Lecturer.

In 1968, the department decided to send all its first year students to courses in the USSR instead of to Paris at the end of their first year and, with the passage of time, it also became possible for them to spend part or the whole of their third year (the year abroad) in the USSR on programmes of study. During this period, all the three-year modern language courses in the Faculty were transformed into four-year courses, normally with a compulsory year in the target country. Special concessions had to be made for students of Russian, however, since it was often necessary to settle for shorter periods. Degree courses incorporating Serbo-Croat at Honours level were also introduced under various names, and Joint Honours courses with French and German became increasingly popular.

Restrictive admissions quotas for joint honours degrees severely inhibited this last trend, however. This became a serious problem for the department, because a growing number of the best applicants for Russian wanted to study it jointly with French, or sometimes with German, whereas the partner departments claimed that most of their best applicants still wished to study for single honours degrees, and the admission quotas continued to reflect their preferences. When, during the 1970s, the number of schools teaching Russian, which had peaked at about 800 at the beginning of the decade, went into sharp decline, the department introduced annual Russian Days for schools, to support and encourage those that remained.

These were widely appreciated by participating schools, and may even have brought a few more applications to Nottingham, but it was not sufficient to stem the tide. Numbers of graduates in the years of Monica's incumbency tell the tale. From twenty-three in 1968 to a high of twenty-seven in 1973, they dropped to eleven in 1976, and even fell to nine in 1983 and 1984, the last two years falling after her retirement, but recruited while she was still in office.[12] Only after that, for reasons that belong to the next chapter, did numbers begin to pick up again.

The department remained in the cowsheds for the first year of Monica's incumbency, next to the German Department. Though designated 'temporary', they actually survived until the beginning of the twenty-first century, rechristened Cherry Tree Buildings.[13] The access road was indeed lined with flowering cherry trees, which considerably brightened its appearance during the spring months. However, in Monica's second year (1968-9), the department moved into the ground floor of the Trent Building where it was to remain for over 30 years. Here it was situated next to the English Department, in quarters once occupied by Physics[14]—overpainted tiles were still visible on the walls of what had once been laboratories—and most of its staff rooms looked out onto the quadrangle. Others looked out onto the car park between the Trent and the Portland Buildings, which consequently became known to university humorists as 'Red Square'.

In the early years, the Library store was housed in the rooms on the other side of the main corridor, though, on the opening of the new Arts and Social Science Library in 1973, these were converted into classrooms, alongside the dingy but friendly departmental coffee room, whose availability was constantly being called into question by the reluctance of users to wash up their cups. A list of rules for the use of this room

---

[12] The exact figures are *1971*: 25; *1972*: 17; *1973*: 27; *1974*: 18; *1975*: 26; *1976*: 11; *1977*: 13; *1978*: 14; *1979*: 18; *1980*: 14; *1981*: 12; *1982*: 20; *1983*: 9. See Marsh and Rosslyn, pp. 157-65.

[13] Since moving from 'The Orchards' at about the time that John Fennell handed over to Frank Seeley (1957), the Department had occupied two locations in the temporary buildings. I believe that its move from the first to the second location occurred sometime in the early 60s.

[14] I liked to think that Albert Einstein called in there on his visit to the University College in 1930, but nobody has been able to confirm this for me. The Counselling Service now (2008) occupies the quarters that formerly housed Slavonic Studies.

drawn up by Monica in 1968 for the benefit of her colleagues has survived. The corridors were hung with gloomy reproductions of portraits of nineteenth century Russian writers (Tolstoi, Dostoevsky, Turgenev, Nekrasov, Herzen), and pictures of The Hermitage and Lake Baikal, some of which I had myself brought back from one of my early visits to the Soviet Union and donated to the department. Lucyna Perracchi Cavendish (née Makuch) remembers them from the day of her interview in 1978: 'Going down the corridor [...] past the stern portraits of nineteenth-century Russian novelists, I felt I had walked into a pre-revolutionary Russian nobleman's estate. I instinctively knew that this was the place where I wanted to spend the next four years.'

While it was situated here, the department was able to retain a seminar room, to which it brought down from the cowsheds some handsome light-oak bookshelves and cupboards. In the early years, the seminar room, with its large, rubberised, black-top tables set out in a square, was usually available for private study or for staff-student meetings, its tables frequently strewn with tattered copies of Soviet English-Russian dictionaries that, as is the way with unassisted books, had somehow not found their way back to the shelves after use.[15] Later it was also increasingly used for classes.

I particularly recall one meeting in the seminar room in the early years of the Partridge era. Following student protests on university campuses in the United States and on the streets of Paris, student revolt had spread to British campuses by the early 1970s. At the time, students at the new University of Warwick claimed to have uncovered political files on themselves, kept by the university authorities; the mass hysteria reached even Nottingham and, by manipulating the rules governing the calling of Emergency General Meetings of the Students' Union, students 'occupied' the Trent Building, set up a 'Free University of Nottingham' in the Senior Common Room in the Portland Building, and wired up loudspeakers in the Trent quadrangle to give a running commentary on the progress of the revolt. 'Occupation' involved entering and refusing to leave staff-rooms overnight, making revolutionary demands, attempting to break into administrative offices thought to contain secret political files, and engaging in all sorts of activities that secretaries and members of the administration found highly intimidating. It is said that when Gerry Stone, who normally spent long hours working in his room, including evenings and weekends, found it occupied by a group of students from various departments draped across his chairs and floor, he decided to make use of the opportunity to instruct them in Slavonic Philology.

Unfortunately, the then professor of French, Lewis Thorpe, had given a reference for one of his students seeking a placement in a French school during his year abroad, in which he mentioned that he (the student) had been seen parading on campus with a banner calling for his (Professor Thorpe's) execution, and that, as a consequence, he did not feel that he could recommend him as a responsible member of the community. Or so the story went. This reference was channelled through the British Council, where someone leaked it, and the result was furore at Nottingham. His wife, the celebrated translator of Dante and reader in Italian, Dr Barbara Reynolds, was at that time the founding Warden of Willoughby Hall, and she too ran into trouble with her students. Sit-ins continued, over some burning issue or another (often rents), for years to come.

During this particular occupation, when for some reason Monica was away, a meeting took place in the seminar room between the staff and students of the

---

[15] As Della Thompson reminds me, the first *Oxford Russian-English Dictionary* was published in 1972 and its English-Russian one only in 1984.

department, to discuss the situation. I remember saying that I, a lecturer since 1967, was confident that there was no systematic keeping of political files on students because I could not imagine how such information could be collected without involving members of staff like myself; and I had never heard of such a thing. I am not sure whether, in the current atmosphere, I was entirely believed. One of the students of the time was Julian Nundy, who later became a highly successful journalist. When Monica returned, she had wooden blocks installed in all the window frames to prevent entry via the sash windows; they were removed many years later as a fire hazard.

This was a watershed in the life of British universities. After the period of sit-ins, student representation on University committees was increased and various other minor reforms were instituted, but, most importantly of all, the culture of automatic deference to academia and the notion that university statutes and ordinances were immutable began to be questioned. In 1970, moreover, the legal age of majority was lowered from twenty-one to eighteen, and the regulations governing halls of residence were also relaxed. Perhaps change had already been in the air. The wearing of gowns by students had no longer been obligatory for several years. Lecturing staff continued to wear them when teaching, and they were also required for attendance at formal meetings, but most departments, beginning with the scientists and social scientists, gradually abandoned this custom too. Lawrence Weldon, who graduated in 1972, vividly recalls the revolutionary atmosphere of the University at the time, involving the challenging and questioning of authority at all levels. The mood was of course not specific to Nottingham. It was part of an international student movement: among the outward signs of rebellion were men with long hair, girls in miniskirts, flower power, the Beatles, the contraceptive pill, and the beginnings of the drug culture.

Yet Della Thompson (1971-5) recalls that, although students had fun, they were quite sober really – perhaps Nottingham was more staid than some other universities. In the department, most members of staff still addressed students as Mr This or Miss That (occasionally Mrs The Other) for many years to come. This custom occasioned some amusement among students, but at the same time it made them feel more grown-up. In spite of the many new opportunities for kicking over the traces, most students were fairly restrained.

When I returned to Nottingham from The University of Sussex at the beginning of the first year of Monica's tenure, one of Nottingham's attractions was the very strong cast of young scholars already in post, all appointed during Frank Seeley's time. They included Gerald Smith and Gerald Stone, Nicholas Anning and, from 1969 to 1971, Chris Mills, one of Monica's own protégés[16] and a graduate of 1967, with an unusual gift for the South Slav languages and, as one former student, Robert Owen, put it, 'a clever brain and a big heart'. Nicholas Luker, then a postgraduate working on a PhD on Aleksandr Grin, was appointed to a lecturing post in 1970. The two Gerrys, as they were known, were already formidable scholars. Gerry Smith was then working on a London doctorate on Russian poetry; Gerry Stone was a specialist in Sorbian, a Slavonic language spoken on the boundaries of modern Poland and East Germany; Nick Anning was working on his doctorate on Pasternak (never, I believe, completed, but at the time a subject of consuming interest).

---

[16] He is said to have been responsible for correcting the errors in the first edition of Monica Partridge's *Serbo-Croat Practical Grammar and Reader*, but the preface to the second edition makes only general reference to the help of 'several more generations' of students, colleagues and friends.

The pattern of courses—which, as Julian Nundy remarks, was very modern for the time—changed little in Monica's early years. Single Honours students continued to devote two thirds of their first two years to the Honours subject, and the remaining third to the subsidiary subject. The final year was then devoted entirely to the honours subject, though it was possible to take one option from outside. By now there was also a handful of Joint Honours students (their numbers, as we have seen, restricted by miniscule quotas) with French and German, who divided their time equally between the two subjects throughout their course.

All Single Honours students continued to follow two-year Part I courses in Aspects of Russian Literature, Russian Life and Thought, The History of the Russian Language (medieval literature and history had now been dropped, except as they might be touched on in this course), Translation from Russian into English and Translation from English into Russian. There was also the unexamined Serbo-Croat course in year 2, which laid the foundations for a compulsory course in the final year. Students regularly complained about this, on the grounds that they had come to Nottingham to study Russian, not Serbo-Croat, but the department was adamant, claiming that this requirement was known to them when they applied and that most students retrospectively expressed gratitude that they had acquired some knowledge of a second Slavonic language, citing those who had made use of it in employment. There were also weekly Russian conversation classes, taken by Amelia Cantelli and Nikolai Naidenov.

Language classes still consisted principally of prose passages for translation from English into Russian, frequently selected from classic English novels or, occasionally, from history books, and the examination papers were very much the same. Most students still came up with A-levels in Russian, though an increasing number were admitted with lesser qualifications. There was also still a small beginners' class, for which Fennell's Grammar had now been substituted for Semeonoff's.[17]

The non-language courses consisted mainly of weekly lectures and one or two essays per term. These were in due course marked and returned. Occasional seminars for the first and second years were also introduced. A revised notice for the session 1969-1970 that has survived records that in Term 1 there were to be three second year seminars: Lermontov's 'Demon' (Professor Partridge), Turgenev's *Fathers and Children* (Dr Jones), and a topic in Soviet Literature (Mr Anning). In Term 2, the topics were: The lesser nineteenth-century novelists (Dr Jones), Karamzin's *Bednaia Liza* (Mr Smith), Blok's 'Twelve' (Mr Smith). Term 3 was to embrace: Lermontov's 'Demon' (Professor Partridge, again?), Gogol's development as a short story writer (Dr Jones), and an eighteenth-century topic (Mr Smith). How some of these topics could have been covered in a fifty-minute seminar now beggars belief.

In their final year, students chose two from a menu of options, including Comparative Slavonic Philology (Gerry Stone), Pushkin and Lermontov (Gerry Smith and Malcolm Jones), Selected Nineteenth-Century Novelists (Malcolm Jones), Selected Soviet Writers (Nick Anning) and Selected Nineteenth-Century Russian Thinkers (Monica Partridge). There were compulsory papers in Russian Prose Translation, Russian Essay, Serbo-Croat Translation, and Soviet History (taken, after the departure of Michael Futrell in 1966, by Derek Spring, a Hayter lecturer from the History Department.) Two hours per week in the final year were usually devoted to

---

[17] J. L. I. Fennell (1961); Anna H. Semeonoff (1958).

each of the options and to Soviet History, one hour of which was normally taken up by seminars at which students read and discussed essays.

One of Monica's innovations was the introduction of the Part II Russian Essay paper. Teaching for this paper was still rudimentary, and examination performance highly variable. As a consequence, the paper was very difficult to assess fairly, and the process of agreeing marks in examiners' meetings could be a nightmare. Nevertheless, the absence of such a paper had been an anomaly and, with improved opportunities to visit the Soviet Union, less easy to justify. Della Thompson remembers some of the titles that were set as essay topics. Apart from the routine 'Moi vpechatleniia SSSR' ('My impressions of the USSR'), those that she recalls include 'Chelovek i mashina'—khoziain i rab?' ('Man and machine—master and slave?') and 'Chto v zhizni glavnoe?' ('What is the most important thing in life?').

I had no experience of the lecturing style of my colleagues, with the exception of Monica (from my student days) and Gerry Smith, who invited me to join his final year option on Pushkin and Lermontov: he would teach the poetry and I the prose works. I gladly accepted the invitation; I had been convinced by my experience at Sussex of the value of team teaching and of hearing and being heard by one's colleagues. From my own point of view, it was extremely rewarding. Gerry's approach was informal, but also enthusiastic, laced with humour, well-prepared and well-structured, and extremely well-informed. He must have taken his students (and me) through virtually all of Pushkin's and Lermontov's best lyrics during the year-long course, examining them line by line, grouping them and comparing them. Gerry's interest in metrics was fed by an equally strong interest in music – he played in a jazz band – and in underground Russian popular songs. What was timetabled for two hours often stretched into the fourth hour each Friday and nobody became restless or bored; in fact it was the highlight of the week. His was among the most popular of the final year courses on offer. My own main contribution to final year teaching was the Selected Nineteenth-Century Novelists course, which I whittled down to the major novels of Turgenev, Tolstoi and Dostoevsky from the more comprehensive coverage that I had inherited from Frank Seeley.

Although there were departmental examinations at the end of the first year, they still counted for very little. At the end of the second year, students took their Part I examinations. However, it was necessary only to pass them in order to proceed to the final year. The degree class still depended almost entirely on performance in the Part II written examinations at the end of the final year, a combined course work mark for all one's final year courses having the weight of a single paper. The oral mark had no effect at all on the final degree class, though an outstanding performance might get you a star.

However, the civilised tone that had characterised the compulsory final year viva voce examinations under Frank Seeley gave way under his successor to a more inquisitorial one, from which it was not unusual for finalists to flee in tears, to be comforted later by junior members of staff, who would seek them out in their digs or halls of residence to offer reassurance and invite them to the Graduands' Party. Dorothy Strickland, who graduated in 1977, is one graduate who recalls with horror 'a panel encompassing the whole department' that 'discoursed in Russian for what seemed like hours.'

In the early days, study visits to the Soviet Union in the first long vacation were organised through pro-Soviet travel agencies such as Academy Travel and Progressive Tours[18]. Nicholas Luker eventually took over the role of coordinator for the arrangements, and Diuni on the Gulf of Finland and Krasnodar in the Caucasus were favourite spots. Those students who could not, for one reason or another (sometimes because of their health, or the political affiliations of their parents), visit the Soviet Union, might be sent to Unterweissenbach in Austria or to Meudon, near Paris, where there was a Russian Orthodox community that organised language courses. For a while, a handful each year also went to Moscow under the auspices of BUAS, an experience that several, like Ruth Morgan and Roger Stubbings, remember well.

In 1968 the Nottingham group went on a course at the dom otdykha (literally, 'house of rest', in reality a sort of sanatorium) at Abramtsevo, on the road from Moscow to Tula. Abramtsevo was situated fifty kilometres or so outside Moscow in the Russian countryside and had once been the home of the nineteenth-century writer Sergei Aksakov. Later, though still in pre-Soviet times, it was occupied by Savva Mamontov, a rich industrialist who had sought to bridge the gap between the Russian élite and Russian folk cultures.[19]

Sheila Sarkar (née Christopherson), who made the trip by rail, recalls the approach to Moscow lying through woods alternating with marshland, with wooden huts and blocks of flats as they neared the city. The exit from the Belorussky Station was dominated by busts of Marx and Lenin. They had tea at the Hotel Berlin, in a hideously overdecorated room with statuary and fountains; then, after a long delay, they continued by coach to Abramtsevo, following the muddy, potholed track to the dom otdykha, where shortly they were to be inducted into their daily language classes, walks in the woods, films and cultural events, and attempts to mingle with local Russians. One day there was a trip to the monastery at Zagorsk, where the Metropolitan had his office, but most of which had been converted into a museum of 'scientific atheism'; another day took them to Moscow, where 'the streets were full of pedestrians, there were queues around some of the shops and cafés, and melons and ice creams were selling well.' They saw women working on the roads, driving steamrollers, sweeping with twig brooms, shovelling. Then they did all the usual things, visiting the University on the Lenin Hills, the GUM department store and Lenin's Mausoleum on Red Square, the Arbat, Gorkii Street, the Metro, the Exhibition of Economic Achievements, the Kremlin, and much else. Having left home on 17 August, they set off on their homeward journey on 6 September. In 1968, the students were dimly aware that their visit coincided with the Soviet invasion of Czechoslovakia. Gerry Stone, who had stayed on after the Prague Congress of Slavists for a Czech language course, was actually caught up in events there.

My own only first-hand experience of these visits occurred in 1969. This was, I believe, the second such trip, and a member of staff still accompanied the students. The previous year it had been Amelia Cantelli. In 1969, the group was led by Nick Anning.

I took the opportunity to go along in order to visit the Lenin Library and make academic contacts in Moscow. In those days, this was like going to the developing

---

[18] Some graduates of the time recall going on study visits in a group under the auspices of the British Universities' Association of Slavists (BUAS).
[19] See Priscilla Roosevelt (1995), especially pp. 189, 311-12, 316 and 323-24. There are also illustrations of buildings on the estate.

world, with all the added complications of the Iron Curtain and the absurdities of Soviet bureaucracy, designed, it seemed, to keep visitors in a permanent state of disorientation. As well as receiving the usual advice about steering well clear of situations that might lead to being blackmailed by the KGB (e.g. changing money unofficially or selling clothes on the black market), we were advised to take our own toiletries including soap, toothpaste, a plug for the wash basin and, in the case of the women, a good supply of sanitary towels. We travelled by train across Europe, the exhausting journey taking between two and three days, crossing several borders between East and West, and between socialist states, with passport checks, watch towers, guard dogs and armed inspections at night, eventually arriving, hot, smelly and exhausted, by bus.

It was normal for at least one member of any such group to fall ill with dysentery, or something worse. This year Nan Cunningham (now Mrs Taplin) fell ill with meningitis. The adventures that befell her, the misdiagnoses, the lack of suitable transport, the bumpy ride to Moscow over rutted roads in an old coach, the stay in the Botkin Hospital, the arrival of her mother by air, the role of the Embassy doctor, and her eventual recovery, would be worth recounting in detail in another place. A number of students (and I myself on a later visit) were to experience the inside of the Botkin Hospital, where sick foreigners were normally sent. Fortunately Nan was to make a good recovery.

Lawrence Weldon, who was a student on the 1969 trip and served in the Moscow Embassy towards the end of a distinguished diplomatic career, revisited Abramtsevo recently and, although the house (closed in the 1960s) had been spruced up and opened as a Museum, the *dom otdykha* itself was dilapidated, overgrown and abandoned to nature. Only one wing was occupied by a family.

The 1970 trip, as Heather Haslett (née Birch) remembers, was to Sochi, where their 'forays onto the beach gave them unlimited opportunities to try out their Russian' and 'left them aghast at the Russian ladies sunning themselves in their underwear.'

In 1972, Della Thompson was in the group that went to Krasnodar, where she remembers the heat (forty-five degrees) and swimming in a lagoon, and also the stares of the local inhabitants who sometimes barred their way to ask questions.

The beach also plays a role in the memories of Jovan Marcetić, who graduated in 1975. He remembers partying on the beach at Diuni at the height of the White Nights in the summer of 1973, accompanied by hordes of mosquitoes. Recovery from the hundreds of bites took some time, but the appearance of local vodka the following evening went some way to assuaging the embarrassment and discomfort.

One of the undergraduates at the time was Graham Johnston, a mature student who had joined the RAF in 1959 as linguistic interpreter, continued to take every opportunity to develop his Russian and German, and registered on a Joint Honours course at Nottingham in 1968. In 1973 he himself led a group of students on a course in Leningrad and Moscow. One of his abiding memories is the obligatory concert that such groups were required to put on at the end of their course. His group were asked whether they preferred to dance, sing, or 'declaim' a poem. He chose to declaim a poem by Pasternak and froze when he got to the last line, upon which the whole audience of some 1,500 chanted it out. Graham was one of a number of mature students from whose presence the department greatly benefited over the years. He was also one of a number with continuing connections with the Services Language Schools, in their various configurations. In 1997, he became Head of Slavonic Studies at the Defence Special Signals School, where he worked with David Denton, a graduate of 1980, who ran the Serbo-Croat section.

These study visits were of very great value, not only from a linguistic point of view, but also because they introduced students for the first time in their lives to the idea that they might have to submit to cultural norms very different from those they took for granted at home. Boys with long hair and girls in miniskirts were frequently berated in public by Soviet babushki and made to feel that their appearance was a sign of Western decadence. Sometimes they were even spat upon. They were forced to reconsider the then prevalent Western notion that it was their 'right' to dress and behave exactly as they wished. It was a period when, in the West, 'rights', especially 'student rights' were widely regarded as unassailable.

Equally unnerving was the sensation that Soviet shop assistants or waiters (particularly waiters) were doing you a favour by even noticing you, and the suspicion that greeted Western good manners, such as social smiling or holding doors open. Having to make adjustments and blend in with Soviet society often involved a steep learning curve, especially for those who were to spend longer periods there, when the year abroad was made compulsory.

There was not only the question of adjusting to Russian culture and living conditions in the broader sense, but also of taking account of the fact that this was a police state based on fear of the authorities and an alien ideology, which most students had never previously experienced at first hand; and learning to cope with the impasse which occurred whenever conversation ran into a cul-de-sac bounded by an inflexible party line. One of the major hurdles was reconciling the self-evident fact of Russia's backwardness in all but culture, sport, space rocketry and military hardware with its public claims of superiority over all rival systems, claims that most Soviet citizens seemed unquestioningly to accept and were often prepared to argue about vigorously.

As a matter of fact, the language benefits of such short stays in the Soviet Union were less than might have been hoped for. For the most part, our students remained within their own group. This was not just provincialism on their part; the Soviet authorities liked it that way, since it minimised the political contamination to which their own young people might be exposed. Sometimes, special meetings with groups of Soviet youth might be organised, but attempts to follow these up with personal meetings usually proved unsuccessful. Even when such meetings were agreed between individuals, the Soviet side often failed to turn up, having been dissuaded in the meantime by their minders. So, apart from brief exchanges in shops and restaurants and on the beach, conversation in Russian was usually limited to classes with the Russian lecturers on the course. These classes were often larger than the ones at home. Moreover, as soon as the Soviet teachers discovered (on the first day) that there were elementary deficiencies in our students' knowledge of Russian grammar, this would confirm their view that what they needed was a series of lectures and classes on elementary Russian grammar. That was something that could just as well have been provided back in the UK, say on one of the excellent Essex Summer Russian Language Courses. As I have learnt from graduate contributions to this project, students sometimes voted with their feet and went wandering off on their own.

What they did not get, and what they really needed, was total immersion in the linguistic environment, such as many had obtained in France in their teens, by living with a family. That too was ruled out, not only for political reasons, but also because of the very limited accommodation that even well-to-do Soviet families had at their disposal. When the possibility of six or nine months in the USSR at a Soviet University opened up, for example at Moscow or Voronezh, then the linguistic benefits became more palpable, and many of our students came home speaking fluent Russian, some having even acquired potential or actual Russian spouses. If this happened, there followed the lengthy, frustrating, painful business of acquiring an exit visa for the spouse. Sometimes the intervention of the British government was needed to achieve this.

In general, however, though students found the experience of a study visit to the Soviet Union taxing and exhausting, some even falling sick in the process, almost all fell in love with it at some level and could not wait to get back. Perhaps it was in part the enormous satisfaction of having developed new strategies to cope in an alien culture, of having found out how to get around in a country without maps or telephone directories, of having developed an affection for particular places, or of having made friends in spite of official attempts to make this as difficult as possible. Whatever it was, it is a feeling that I share. My memories of the Soviet Union, unlike those of, say, France, are ones of constant frustration, inconvenience, exhaustion, illness and struggle to cope with a system that seemed designed to make life as difficult as possible. But they are also satisfying ones, associated with favourite places, important friendships and some rewarding and unforgettable experiences.

A visit to the Soviet Union in those days usually afforded an opportunity to trawl the second-hand bookshops, and we would pass on to each other information about which ones were currently most worth a visit and how to find them. Soviet books were heavily subsidised, so it was possible to build up quite a good library quite quickly. Otherwise, Soviet books and newspapers were generally obtained from Collet's Bookshop in Museum Street, opposite the British Museum (later removed to Charing Cross Road), which was also heavily subsidised from Soviet sources and the official British agent for all Soviet books and newspapers. Soviet books had a special smell, which soon impregnated any room that contained them.

Some enterprising students found other opportunities to practise and improve their Russian, and sometimes had interesting experiences in the process. Rita Price (née Pildins) remembers how during her second year at Nottingham (1966-67) she responded to a notice on the departmental notice board, placed there by the London-based Educational Interchange Council, which was looking for escort interpreters for a group of visiting Soviet students. These 'students' were all between 30 and 50 years of age, and their itinerary took in London, Stratford-upon-Avon, Nottingham and the Lake District. Rita and a number of other students met them at the George Hotel in town. There were about twenty of them and they came from various republics. All were party members with families at home supposedly guaranteeing their return, and the group included at least one 'minder' and an English speaker who never said anything. One of the younger members, an Estonian, who went back to Cavendish Hall for coffee, buttered toast and Smarties, said he wanted to remain in Britain, then make his way to Canada where he had relatives. But when Rita turned up at the hotel the next morning, the whole party had disappeared. The receptionist gave her a small parcel containing a stump of silver birch with an axe stuck in it, which may have been simply a souvenir, but which she took as a message of defiance. Many years later, in the early 1990s, she found the name of this young man listed as advisor to the Estonian Foreign Minister in a PHARE publication dealing with European aid for the newly-independent Baltic states. Rita was later to work for the Educational Interchange Council herself.

There were several more important innovations in the department in this early period. One, already mentioned, was the institution of Russian Days for schools in the region. The first Russian Day had taken place on Saturday, 10 February 1973. Twenty-five pupils and twenty-one teachers came, mostly from local schools, but a few from as far afield as Scarborough and Scunthorpe. The programme included a 'St Petersburg Miscellany' composed by Monica herself. I gave a lecture on 'The Superfluous Man in Russian Literature' and Nicholas Luker gave one on 'Half a Century of Soviet Literature'. These were followed by an 'Any Questions' panel and a performance by students of the department of Chekhov's *Marriage*, produced by Nikolai Naidenov. John Partington, then responsible for the training of modern language teachers in the School of Education, facilitated the arrangements. This was to provide the model for Russian Days for many years to come.

In 1974, Dr James Muckle was to take up an appointment as specialist in the training of Russian teachers in the School of Education and he was to play a vital part in future Russian Days, drawing on his day-to-day contact with the schools and with active teachers of Russian in the area. James had learnt his Russian during his period of National Service, obtained his first degree at Cambridge and a PhD in Russian literature at Leeds, as well as having behind him a highly successful career as a teacher of Russian in secondary schools, and a record of energetic support for the Association of Teachers of Russian, of which he was in turn Chairman, Vice-President and President. In 1994 he was to be awarded the Pushkin medal by the International Association of Teachers of Russian Language and Literature (MAPRYaL).

I still recall being impressed by the young Cynthia Marsh's rendering of her lines, in impeccable Russian, at that first Russian Day. Cynthia had joined us in 1972. She proved a very fine and innovative teacher and her active interest in theatrical performance was to be a great boon to the department after Nikolai's death in 1980. In fact, a Russian play was often incorporated in the Russian Day programme in later years, first under Nikolai's direction and then under Cynthia's.

During Monica's tenure, encouragement was also given to the student Slavonic Society, though it did not enjoy uniform success. Invitations to outside speakers suggested by the staff were discontinued after Richard Peace, the author of a well-known book on Dostoevsky and professor of Russian at Hull, turned up to give a talk to a group consisting solely of the student President, his fiancée, and three members of staff. Students were happy to meet for visits to the local brewery or parties with no evident Slavonic content, but most were reluctant to turn up for anything bearing on their subject of study. Monica also initiated a series of extra-curricular lectures given by members of staff and the occasional outside speaker, and great pressure was put on students to attend these, but it is difficult to say that they were widely appreciated. An exception to the rule was Susan Coatman (née Bennett) who valued the opportunity they gave to make connections with other disciplines, such as film or fine art.

Much more successful was the inauguration in 1967 or 1968 of *Slavonica*, a magazine edited and published by the students with substantial help from staff, containing articles on Slavonic topics together with the odd translation and some original work (Gill Wightman, later Mrs Gill Chambers, wrote poetry in Russian). The first editor was Jaroslaw Garlinski (graduated 1969), later to teach Russian at Eton. Perhaps the most notable number was the one published in 1977, edited by Mark

Knight (graduated 1979), to mark the sixtieth anniversary of the department, for which he elicited memories from all its heads, past and present. Mark Knight was a friend of Gill's and they were both 'adopted' by the then Soviet assistant Iulia Bulavina; tragically, Mark was killed in a traffic accident in Moscow some years later. In later years, under Cynthia Marsh's direction, *Slavonica* effectively became the vehicle for the programme for Russian Day and the departmental play.[20]

When the Language Centre was opened on the top floor of the Trent Building under Walter Grauberg in the mid-1960s,[21] most established lecturers in the Modern Language departments were reluctant to make use of this newfangled facility, seeing it as more suitable for use in schools; but Gerry Smith created a valuable collection of recordings (now, sadly, lost). Charlotte Sing, who was to become Russian specialist librarian at the John Rylands Library at The University of Manchester, vividly recalls the engrossing and rewarding sessions with Gerry listening to magnitizdat recordings of Bulat Okudzhava. Chris Mills and Amelia Cantelli also made increasing use of it, as Cynthia Marsh and I did too in future years. We tended to see it as an ancillary tool, however, not as the principal means of inculcating the forms of the Russian language. Nevertheless, with time it became clear that it would be particularly valuable for teaching our increasing numbers of beginners.

Meanwhile, in 1973, the Trent Library was abandoned to the Law Library,[22] and a new state-of-the-art Arts and Social Sciences Library was opened on what had previously been the bowling green of the University Staff Club. In the 1990s it was to be named the Hallward Library, after the University's first Vice-Chancellor. This grand new building, which won architectural prizes, had many advantages— individual carrels for library users, for example, and a great deal more space—but in the view of some it lacked the atmosphere associated with traditional scholarship. It also let in water through its flat roof, more than once seriously damaging irreplaceable items in the Slavonic collection.

The civilised habits of Library use soon gave way to barely suppressed chatter, the smuggling in of food and drink, and the more frequent abuse and theft of books. It even became the preferred location for student sit-ins. Mobile phones and computers were still to come, but the atmosphere of the Victorian library soon gave way to that of the airport concourse. Slavonic books and other Arts subjects were located on the top floor quite close to the top of the staircase, and Slavonic periodicals were on open access on the opposite side of the building.

However, Nottingham was very fortunate at the time in having its own qualified Slavonic Librarian in the person of Garth Terry, a graduate of the department of 1968, who had completed an MPhil on the Macedonian Revolutionary movement in 1974. All too soon, Garth was to take early retirement for health reasons, but continued to work as a dedicated bibliographer and even to set up his own private press (the Astra Press), in order to publish bibliographies and scholarly works by other British Slavists in a variety of fields. Down the years, he also collaborated with colleagues in Nottingham's Department of Slavonic Studies in publishing, editing and contributing

---

[20] We presume that the present-day academic journal published from Manchester University adopted the name in ignorance of ours.

[21] A language laboratory was first opened in the Trent Building in 1963 when a technician was appointed and its operation supervised by Walter Grauberg (Education), Brian Tate (Spanish) and Monica Partridge (Slavonic Studies). In 1965 Walter Grauberg was appointed the first Director of the newly created Language Centre on a half-time basis (the other half of his time retained by Education).

[22] Now, having passed through various hands, it is occupied by the Graduate School (2008).

to scholarly publications. He remains a firm and invaluable friend of the department at the beginning of the twenty-first century.[23]

Few of our graduates in those days made direct use of their Russian in future employment, though there were still posts available for those who wanted to teach, provided that they could offer French (or occasionally another subject) as well; some of these took the PGCE course in the School of Education with James Muckle. One of these was Jovan Marcetić, who gratefully describes James's 'caring support and constant encouragement'. Others found employment with the monitoring service at GCHQ in Cheltenham, and these, together with those who sought posts in other security-sensitive areas, would be the subject of personal and highly secretive visits to their tutors by rather sinister members of the security services, who described themselves as members of the Ministry of Defence. They would ask a series of questions about the personal habits of the applicants, especially any that might make them vulnerable to blackmail by foreign agents. Since I never had this sort of knowledge, I doubt whether I was of any use as an informant, and I used to joke (though it may well have been true) that the visits resulted in more additions to our own files than to those of the students under investigation. One of those who briefly worked at GCHQ was Heather Haslett (née Birch), who later went to become a freelance translator and interpreter, and is currently teaching Russian as part of the International Baccalaureate.

Mention must also be made of departmental secretaries. Some would have put them first, for they were in many respects the pivot round which the administration of the department revolved, and the ultimate insurance against academic inefficiency. With their own room in the department, they were normally the first port of call for any student, colleague or visitor seeking information, reassurance or personal advice. During this early period there were three Slavonic secretaries, Sheila (surname unfortunately lost to the record, to 1969), Jane Dewick (1969-71), and Pat Morris (1971-74). Of these, Jane was to play a particularly notable role in the history of the department, for she returned to resume her post from 1990 to 2003. During the remainder of Monica's tenure, Irene Dale (1974-75) and Ann Collins (née Hall; 1975-1981) were to occupy the position.

The secretary's principal piece of equipment in those days was her typewriter, together with stationery, carbon paper, correcting fluid, Tipp-Ex and stencils (which we called Xeroxes after Rank Xerox, the firm that manufactured them). Our own secretary also had a typewriter with Cyrillic keys. In those days, her (largely unspecified) duties included answering the phone, collecting the post, taking down dictation from the head of department, typing letters, documents and teaching materials, and, if time permitted during the vacations, articles being prepared by academic staff for publication. Failing that, it would be back to the knitting. If materials had to be duplicated, as was the case with passages for translation into Russian or Serbo-Croat, she would type these on stencils, correcting any errors with correcting fluid and typing them over. She would then take the stencils to the duplicating office, situated on the corridor leading to the tunnel between the Trent Building and the Portland Building, and collect them for the relevant member of staff when they were ready. Photocopiers were not introduced to the Faculty much before

---

[23] Mention should also be made of his highly efficient and approachable successor, Deborah Bragan-Turner, whose ready assistance on Level 4 was for many years highly appreciated by staff and students alike.

the end of the 1970s, at about the same time that golfball and daisy-wheel typewriters made their appearance.

In reality, though, the secretary's most important function was to act as a point of contact, and sometimes as a buffer, between members of staff, the staff and students, the department and the rest of the world (which extended from other departments in the University to embassies, the British Council, parents, staff working abroad, and many other types of enquirer). It could be both an essential and uncomfortable position to occupy. But the secretary's door was always open; she would know where everyone was, or how to contact them, and also served, when necessary, as a friend and confidante to both staff and students, with the result that she was the person most likely to be able to answer your question or enquiry. Indeed, she was the one you were most likely to be able to find.

If, as Lucyna Peracchi Cavendish remembers, it was 'a department that combined egalitarianism, personal warmth, academic excellence and intimacy' this was in no small measure due to the moderating role of the departmental secretary.

Unfortunately, all was not well behind the scenes. Most students may have been unaware of it, but others sensed that something was wrong; a few knew the whole sad story.

A former student remembers that Monica's relationships with her colleagues had deteriorated badly by the early 1970s and recalls how Nick Anning and Chris Mills, who had become his personal friends, were thoroughly disenchanted with her management style. The clouds were gathering and it seemed that little could be done about it.

One by one her colleagues sought and found posts elsewhere. Nick Anning was the first to go, when he was appointed to a lectureship at SSEES in 1970, subsequently to abandon academic life for a successful career in journalism, where, with his buccaneering spirit, he probably felt more at home. In 1971, Gerald Stone went to a fixed-term appointment at Cambridge, designed to modernise Russian language teaching there, and within a year was appointed to a Fellowship at Hertford College, Oxford, where he remained until his retirement. Gerald Smith found a permanent post in Birmingham's Russian Department. He was subsequently to spend some years in the United States before his appointment to the professorship of Russian at Oxford in 1986 in succession to John Fennell. Chris Mills failed to find an alternative academic post and, in desperation, joined the BBC Monitoring Service at Caversham (1971).[24] Finally, Amelia Cantelli found a position teaching the Russian language at Oxford (1972). With the contraction of the subject and the freezing of posts from the mid-1970s, such movement was to become increasingly difficult.

With these departures in the early 1970s, the vacant posts were filled by Peter Herrity from The University of Ulster at Coleraine (a Serbian specialist in place of Gerry Stone's Sorbian, and the last member of staff to have learnt his Russian in the armed forces); Wendy Rosslyn (from SSEES, working on the twentieth-century Russian poet Bagritsky, but notionally responsible for eighteenth-century Russian in

---

[24] Tragically young, Chris died a few years after leaving Nottingham. My last surviving correspondence with him is dated 1974.

place of Gerry Smith); and Cynthia Marsh (latterly from the Central London Polytechnic, but originally a Nottingham graduate herself and working on a PhD on the twentieth-century Russian poet, Voloshin). Nicholas Luker (an Oxford graduate who had been awarded a Nottingham doctorate on the Soviet novelist Aleksandr Grin in 1971) completed the team, replacing Nick Anning's expertise in Soviet literature.

Of the team that Monica had inherited, only Nikolai Naidenov and I remained by the mid-1970s. In 1973, I had been promoted to the grade of senior lecturer, and senior members of the Faculty hoped that with colleagues whom she had picked or recommended for promotion herself, and a better gender balance in the department, Monica would now feel happier, and that the department would prosper. Having decided to stay at Nottingham when an opportunity to move had presented itself, it was a hope that I fervently shared, and indeed there were promising beginnings.

But tragedy was to strike in the summer of 1973, when Bill Partridge, now Deputy Vice-Chancellor, and engaged in the demanding business of negotiating on behalf of the University with its technicians, suddenly died of a heart attack at home at the age of 60. He had been at work on a canvas in a new experimental style. Monica tried to carry on as normal, but the loss inevitably took its toll and was to some degree irreparable. Everyone tried to be supportive. She was given study leave for the whole of the academic year 1974-75, during which I was acting head of department. Some hoped that she might decide to take early retirement now (she would have been 60 in 1975), but those who knew her best thought this unlikely.

Before concluding this section, I cannot resist passing a comment on the lifestyle of members of academic staff in those far-off days. It was very widely believed by members of the public, and even by some students, that since there were only thirty weeks of term in the calendar year, academics had twenty-two weeks of holiday. This misconception seemed impossible to eradicate, even among close friends, who would congratulate one cheerily on the beginning of 'the holidays' at the end of June each year, thereby unwittingly, if only fleetingly, putting the friendship at serious risk.

In fact, our terms of appointment allowed us six weeks holiday each year, to be taken during vacations. I myself never took more than three to four weeks, plus the occasional public holiday (though the University actually remained open on bank holidays that fell within term time) and although some colleagues, being human, no doubt abused the system, I believe that my own practice reflected the norm. Nor did the fact that there were no prescribed hours of work each day, apart from attendance at designated classes and meetings, mean that we worked fewer hours than other professionals. In fact, many of us would work at home each evening and at weekends, up to sixty hours in a normal week, and much more if we had an article or book to finish, or examination papers to mark. The additional pressure on female staff with children, or single parents of either sex, does not need to be spelled out.

As with all professionals at the time, it was assumed that you would work as many hours and as many weeks in the year as the job in hand, your head of department, and your sense of professional duty required. Professor Partridge even arranged examiners' meetings for Sunday evenings, and no enquiry was ever made as to whether this encroached on private life, family time, or even on religious commitments, at a time when Church attendance was still quite common, and most commercial enterprises were closed on Sundays.

On the positive side, however, there was still enough flexibility in the daily round to take morning coffee in the Senior Common Room or lunch in the University Club with colleagues from a range of other disciplines and there to share one's academic interests as well as to exchange views on institutional developments or examination procedures. Had there not been, I should have felt sorely disappointed after my Sussex experience, but at Nottingham too, at this time, there were rich opportunities for interdisciplinary cross-pollination, often feeding into one's own research and teaching.

As a rough and ready guide, academics were (and probably still are) expected to devote a third of their time to teaching, a third to research and publication, and a third to administration. But, as we were soon to discover, a credibility gap was opening up between academia and government, which the public was all too ready to credit in those anti-establishment times. As the era of Wilson and Heath in British politics drew to a close, the image of the Oxbridge don dining sumptuously, living in an ivory tower, sipping sherry in the Senior Common Room and enjoying endless vacations while the country was sliding into economic chaos, was all too plausible.

The Second Stage, 1975 to 1980

On the surface, the department's work carried on as usual. Numbers of *Slavonica* continued to appear; Russian Days, accompanied by a play, adapted, or sometimes even written, by Nikolai Naidenov, were held annually; graduands' parties were held each year after the final examinations, usually at the home of a member of staff; visits to the Soviet Union, courses and examinations, with accompanying successes, failures, triumphs and disappointments, all went on as before, as did the various personal dramas of staff and students.

Jovan Marcetić remembers the staff of the department with great fondness: 'heroic, knowledgeable and totally caring and friendly', 'open-minded, brilliant lecturers and motivators'. All members of staff, he recalls, were 'dynamic, on-the-ball, at the cutting edge, and ensured that all students took an active part in tutorials and contributed positively'. Nikolai Naidenov was 'much loved by all who came into contact with his caring and encouraging nature'. Another graduate (Dorothy Strickland) remembers Nikolai playing Russian folk music. And on the subject of music, Della Thompson recalls the importance of Russian songs in studying the language and learning about Russian life and culture. They were regularly included as part of the curriculum on courses in the Soviet Union and in her year the students' singing was led by Mick Stevens, a talented guitarist and singer-songwriter, whose recordings of his own compositions are only now, posthumously, being re-issued and receiving recognition.

Soviet lecturers too came, made their mark, and went. Iulia Bulavina was the Soviet lecturer (1975-76), followed by Natasha Fiodorova (1976-7), Nelli Shevelyova (1977-8), Svetlana Navalnaya (1978-9) and Tamara Kapitonova (1979-80).

On the Serbo-Croat side, Branko Brusar was followed by Mira Vlatković (1975-6), Maja Dubravčić (1976-7), Vera Andrassy (1977-8), Ivan Pletikosa (1978-9) and Maša Marušić (1979-80). Meanwhile, Ljuba Črnivec was succeeded as Slovene lectrice by Srečko Fišer (1977-9) and Božena Činkole (1979-84).

In the mid 1970s, the destination for the first-year study visits to the Soviet Union was Kalinin, (formerly, and again since the end of the Soviet Union, Tver'), situated on the railway line between Moscow and Leningrad. Dorothy Strickland remembers the organised visits to collective farms and schools. The group was supposed to be accompanied by local students wherever they went, but they took it in turns to distract them so that they could wander around unchaperoned, eat the fantastic ice cream, drink

HEADS OF DEPARTMENT IN THE TWENTIETH CENTURY

Janko Lavrin (1918-52)

John Fennell (1952-1957)

Frank Seeley (1957-67)

Monica Partridge (1967-80)

Malcolm Jones (1980-97)

Peter Herrity (1997-2001)

Monica Partridge (1963-64), Malcolm Jones (1974-75) and Peter Herrity (1989-92, 95-97) were also Acting Heads of Department during their predecessor's period of tenure.

Staff and graduands 1968

Back two rows: Nikolai Naidenov, Michael Brownbill, Jo Howard-Smith, Garth Terry, John Murray, Gerald Smith, Michael Phippard, Andrew Thatcher, Michael Barnard, Nicholas Anning, Robert Owen, Simon Barton, Janet Boyd, Christopher Mills, Gerald Stone, Andrew Taylor
Middle row: Linda Proffitt, Tamara Akhvlediani, Monica Partridge, Malcolm Jones, Amelia Cantelli, Roger Stubbings
Front row: Rita Pildins, Sarah Vickers, Frances Howard-Gordon, Janet Elston, Valerie Griffiths

Absent but member of this group. Brian Davis !

Staff 1997

Back row: Adriana Krstič, Wendy Rosslyn, Lisa Lacy, Svetlana Clark, Nicholas Luker, Rachel Farmer, Irina Shlumukova, Monika Savage, David Norris, Vladislava Ribnikar. Front row: Lesley Milne, Peter Herrity, Jane Dewick, Malcolm Jones, Stephanie Brunger, Cynthia Marsh.

Cynthia Marsh, Lesley Milne and Wendy Rosslyn have served as Head of Department in the twenty-first century.

morale, and Russian was now widely perceived as a lame-duck subject, whatever Atkinson's recommendation for a particular department might be. Nottingham was not mentioned in the recommendations at all, which meant that Atkinson was, for the time being, content to let things continue there as they were. All the same, had the University wished to phase Russian out, a golden opportunity was about to present itself with Monica Partridge's impending retirement.

In retrospect, it may be difficult for an outsider to understand why the report created such widespread dismay. As Atkinson said, there undoubtedly was overprovision, to an extent that was unlikely to be fully compensated by the introduction of beginners' courses. What needs to be realised, however, is how much extraordinary personal commitment had been involved in getting Russian off the ground in UK universities, and in sustaining it, especially in the new universities of the 1960s, and how much genuine and largely selfless enthusiasm had been devoted to trying to achieve a major objective of the Scarbrough Report (1947), which had stressed the importance of building up 'an academic tradition comparable in quality with those of the major humanities and sciences'.

Apart from quoting these words, Atkinson made no mention of this effort, of the quality of the scholars who would be displaced, or of how such a tradition might be built up and sustained if many of the best young scholars were to be unceremoniously removed from the scene whenever student recruitment flagged. It was this omission that caused the sense of outrage. Though Atkinson stressed that it was not recommending redundancies, salt was rubbed into the wound by the suggestion that those academics who were surplus to requirements might be moved into Russian Studies without language, into the teaching of English as a foreign language, into extramural studies and the provision of short courses tailored to the needs of industry and commerce, or into University administration.

While accepting the Report in general, the UGC, to its credit, set up a scheme under Professor Martin Harris to facilitate the movement of such scholars to the survivor departments. Dr Lesley Milne was to come to Nottingham under this scheme in 1989, when the department at Hull was closed.

Once the dust had settled, however, it became clear that the other professors of Modern Languages at Nottingham saw the survival of Nottingham's Department of Slavonic Studies as an endorsement of its relative strength, and the presence of Serbo-Croat and Slovene in its curriculum (duly noted by Atkinson in one of its annexes) as a particular asset. This local expression of support must have influenced the University in its decision to advertise the chair on Monica's retirement in 1980, and to revise its title from professor of Russian Language and Literature to professor of Slavonic Studies. Whereas the conjunction of dates could have been fatal, it was in fact turned to our advantage.

Monica's departmental colleagues were by now beginning to establish solid academic reputations themselves. They had all developed their own distinctive styles of teaching and were beginning to lay the foundations for successful careers as scholars. PhDs had been awarded to Nicholas Luker (1971), Peter Herrity (1974), and Cynthia Marsh (1979), while Wendy Rosslyn had acquired an MPhil from London. All had been busy publishing articles in academic journals. My own first book on Dostoevsky (*Dostoyevsky, the Novel of Discord*) had appeared in London and New York, followed by a collection of articles on Tolstoi of which I was the editor (*New Essays on Tolstoy*. Nicholas Luker had published monographs on *A. I. Kuprin* and

The Forgotten Visionary: Alexander Grin, and had also written a book on Grin for the Bradda series. Other work was in the pipeline, including important scholarly monographs by Peter Herrity (who was promoted to the grade of senior lecturer in 1977), Cynthia Marsh and Wendy Rosslyn. These were to be published in the first half of the next decade (see the next chapter).

Many students remember Monica with fondness; she could go to great lengths to help lame dogs over stiles and could be generous in her support for those who showed promise in her own field, especially in Serbo-Croatian Studies. Some went on to do postgraduate work under her auspices, including several young Canadian Slavists. Similar warm memories are expressed by the series of lectors and lectrices from the English Department at The University of Zagreb who taught at Nottingham from 1971. While aware that Monica could be a problematic head of department, they frequently add that she was always kind and supportive to them personally. Harry Shukman, who served as external examiner for an extended period, said that she was always quite sweet to him.[29] At some point she gave support to all her colleagues and many of her students. She enjoyed the friendship and esteem of a number of eminent European Slavists and British scholars from various fields and she was a force to be reckoned with in the field of Slavonic Studies for many years. However, there is no denying that she could be an extremely difficult colleague. Whenever Monica encountered opposition, or felt that her authority was being slighted, or that she was receiving less than wholehearted support, a storm was likely to blow up, and the collateral damage would not necessarily be limited to the department, or even to the University. She tended to attribute the obstacles that she encountered to the personal ill will of people intent on obstructing her. Paradoxically, I cannot think of a single instance in which this was true. While her fierceness could be an effective weapon in her struggle to promote the subject, not all her colleagues and associates found it easy to deal with on a regular, day-to-day basis. With a few notable exceptions, her relationships with UK Slavists were less warm than those with her European colleagues, and she never achieved representative office among them.

Yet Monica's overall vision was a broad one and her legacy substantial: it was a vision that saw the department playing a leading role on the international as well as the national stage, at a time when some heads were content to run their department as though it were a higher-level school, and leave the rest of the world to look after itself. By her energetic contributions to International Congresses and other scholarly events abroad, as well as by a series of invitations to influential Soviet figures, she raised and maintained the department's profile on the international stage, managing to create in some quarters a highly flattering impression of her own and the department's achievements. She took up her post at a time when the post-war fortunes of Russian studies were just reaching a peak and when, making use of her East European contacts, she might reasonably have expected to build an even more impressive edifice on the foundations laid by her predecessors.

In fact, within a few years, the process was to go into reverse. This was one objective source of her frustrations, which any head of department, ambitious for her subject, would have had to face. The institution of Russian Days was a creditable response.

---

[29] Private correspondence.

In the end, however, the department survived, many students benefited from its courses, most of her colleagues went on to have distinguished careers, and the positive features of her legacy are still intact. The period saw real achievements with which any head of department might justifiably feel satisfied. To use the jargon of the time, it 'tunnelled through' the steep drop in recruitment of the 1970s and emerged unscathed by the Atkinson Report, when other well-established departments did not. Moreover the department's foundations, though severely tested from within and without, remained firm.

Most notably, Monica could take the credit for carrying the torch of Yugoslav Studies through the Fennell and Seeley periods, and for subsequent successful institutional developments during her own. The Serbo-Croat and Slovene dimensions of its work continued to flourish after her departure, under Peter Herrity's oversight, with major contributions from David Norris, and with the indispensable assistance of native lectors and lectrices.

Secondly and crucially, the importance that she attached to her colleagues' continuing research and publication was to play a vital role in the department's fortunes when the UGC began its Research Assessment Exercises in the mid-1980s. Not all Russian departments placed such emphasis on staff research and publications, and some were subsequently to pay the price for this omission.

During the thirteen years of her tenure, Monica continued to publish an average of two academic articles a year and to accumulate material for the long-planned book on Herzen. In 1980, she retired at the statutory age of sixty-five and, in her retirement, with funding from MAIRSK, she organised an International Herzen Conference at Nottingham in September 1982, whose proceedings were subsequently published as a book.[30] Then, in 1983, her contribution to the field of Slavonic Studies was publicly recognised by the award of an honorary doctorate by The University of Kiev. To the best of my knowledge, she was the only British Slavist ever to be honoured in this way by a Soviet University.

A short biography of Alexander Herzen appeared in 1984 and a collection of her essays in 1988,[31] while in 1990 a group of colleagues and professional associates, including the future Academician G. M. Fridlender from Leningrad and Professor Rudolf Filipović of the Yugoslav Academy of Arts and Sciences, presented her with a Festschrift on the occasion of her seventy-fifth birthday.[32] It was published by Garth Terry's Astra Press. At about this time, she was elected an Honorary Fellow of Fitzwilliam College, Cambridge, to which she made a gift of a selection of her late husband's paintings. Later, she was made a member of Pembroke College, Cambridge, where she endowed an academic travel scholarship, and to which she eventually bequeathed the fine collection of water colours that she and Bill had assembled during his lifetime. The major book on Herzen, which was to have overturned prevailing views on his life and work, never appeared, and it is possible only to guess at the revelations that it was due to contain—her published work leaves few clues—but she left a series of articles on him, some of which are still important points of reference for scholars working on his biography. Monica continued to live in the Nottingham area until her recent death, aged ninety-two, on 19 March 2008.

---

[30] Monica Partridge (1985).
[31] Monica Partridge (1984); Monica Partridge (1988, second, revised edition, 1993).
[32] Peter Herrity (1990).

In 1980, the challenge for her successor would be to seek to raise the department's levels of undergraduate recruitment, while ensuring that its national and international profile (in research and service to the profession, as well as in undergraduate teaching) continued to move in the direction signalled by Scarbrough. The department awaited the outcome anxiously.

The Weather Clears

(1980-1997)

Overview

IF Lavrin's was a pioneering period, Fennell laid the foundations for a modern department, which Seeley turned into a reality, and Partridge's tenure was notable for the vigorous development of the Serbo-Croat and Slovene dimensions of the department's work, I had the good fortune to preside over its affairs as it evolved into one of the leading Slavonic Departments in the UK, with healthy undergraduate recruitment, high quality teaching, and an acknowledged reputation for research of international significance.

But it was a hard struggle to begin with, and the omens did not seem particularly good. As Wendy Rosslyn reminded me in conversation recently,[1] survival was top of our agenda for many years to come—or so it seemed—and, though this would obviously depend to some extent on our own individual and collective efforts in the fields of teaching and research, it was affected no less, perhaps more, by events that came at us out of the blue, and over which we had no control. Equally important would be to have sympathetic friends (preferably one of ourselves) in high places. If much of Monica Partridge's energy had been invested in developing the South Slav aspect of the curriculum, a good deal of mine was to go into supporting the subject locally and nationally. In the end, fortune would smile on us, but this was not always obvious to everybody at the time, and our nerves were often fraught.

When I retired in 1997, the range and content of the Russian courses offered by the department was very much as it had been in Seeley's day. An exception was medieval history and literature, which we were now no longer able to cover fully. Peter Herrity still taught the History of the Russian Language and Comparative Slavonic Philology; History and Politics as such had gone, but a course in Russian History taught by Derek Spring was available in the History Department. Serbo-Croat and Slovene continued to thrive and to develop under Peter Herrity and David Norris. Life and Thought was taught by Cynthia Marsh and by me. A wide range of Russian literature courses, taught by Wendy Rosslyn, Nicholas Luker, Lesley Milne, Cynthia and me, was also available.

However, the early 1990s were to prove another watershed in the history of UK universities, even more radical in its effects than that of the early 1970s. The

---

[1] Conversation with Professor Wendy Rosslyn, 20 December, 2006.

model previously underlying most British universities, including Nottingham, had been that of the scholarly community, a community of which undergraduates were for a few short years privileged to be part. In the 1990s this model was progressively to give way to that of the corporate business, or perhaps to an uneasy compromise between the two. One of its manifestations at Nottingham was the introduction to the University of semesters and the modular system. This gave students a freer choice of courses (now called modules) in each of their three years at Nottingham, including more from outside the department, and enabled us to introduce strategically designed courses that would not have been thought worthy of a whole year's work. It also gave staff longer periods of study leave, and this was by no means a trivial consideration, as we shall see.

The downside was that students were no longer required to cover the whole range of courses of the traditional degree established under Fennell and Seeley. In fact, we were sometimes heard to complain that it was now possible to get a first class degree in Russian at Nottingham 'without ever having read of word of Pushkin'. I am not sure whether this was literally true, but it was too close to the truth for comfort. Seen as a comprehensive academic grounding in the subject, there were therefore drawbacks to the new system, but from the point of view of undergraduates, few of whom wished to become academics themselves, the new flexibility was to be welcomed. Those who did could now enhance their range and qualifications at MA level before proceeding to a PhD. Although our new degree courses were patchy by comparison with the traditional European courses in Slavonic Philology,[2] they came to resemble North American courses more closely and, we believed, were in some respects more demanding than these. Anyway, as we were constantly reminded, students were now to be regarded as customers purchasing a product, not as pupils owing respect and deference to the eminent scholars at whose feet, for a few short years, they would be privileged to sit. Such attitudes were reinforced by the introduction of student loans in the 1990s, together with new mechanisms for quality assessment and control, and procedures for students to assess the quality and effectiveness of the teaching that they received.

Russian and Slavonic Departments were of course affected no less by the great historic changes in the Soviet Union and Eastern Europe, changes that not only strengthened their position but also demanded a response.

Apart from all this, technology was marching on too. It can safely be said that the student experience at the end of this period differed in many significant ways from that of the graduate of 1980.

The First Stage 1980-6

Following the pattern of previous chapters, I should begin with some biographical details of the new head of department. It was now twenty-two years since I had matriculated as an undergraduate. Born in the Somerset village of Stoke-sub-Hamdon in January 1940, I had been educated at Cotham Grammar School, Bristol, before taking up Russian as a beginner at Nottingham in 1958, convinced that there was a serious imbalance in the foreign languages prioritised by the British

---

[2] 'Philology' in Europe covering the whole range of language and literature courses, not just the academic study of language, as is usual in English.

educational system, and that change was in the air.[3] In other words, I was a product of the post-war grammar school meritocracy, and just too young for military call-up. From 1965 to 1967, I was Assistant Lecturer in Russian in the School of European Studies at the new University of Sussex. Then, in 1967, I was encouraged to return to Nottingham, where in 1973 I had become a senior lecturer. What could the department expect?

My own pedigree was at first sight more conventional than that of my four predecessors. Lavrin had had no formal degree qualifications at all; Fennell's first degree had been in French and German, followed by a doctorate in medieval Russian history; Seeley's first degree was in Classics, Philosophy and Ancient History; Partridge's was in French, with a doctorate in Russian Thought. All had acquired their Russian privately.

By contrast, like most of my colleagues, I belonged to a new generation of British Slavists,[4] with a first degree and PhD in Russian Studies, both gained at Nottingham. By the time of my appointment to the chair at the age of forty, I had published my first book[5] and a number of articles on Dostoevsky, had edited a book on Tolstoi,[6] had working contacts with the Dostoevsky Group in the Institute of Russian Literature of the Soviet Academy of Sciences in Leningrad (Pushkinskii dom) and was a founding member of the International Dostoevsky Society. A co-edited book on Dostoevsky was in the pipeline. I had also been Vice-Dean of the Faculty of Arts and Secretary of BUAS. As in 1967, the chair had been publicly advertised and external candidates interviewed but, like all chair appointments in Slavonic Studies at Nottingham in the twentieth century, there was to be an internal appointment.[7] As with my predecessors, the University no doubt made its choice as much on perceived potential as on past achievement.

The two major influences on my academic values and my approach to my subject had been Frank Seeley and my experience at Sussex. They merged in the importance I attached to interdisciplinary study.

From Frank Seeley, apart from a shared interest in the Russian novel, I learned that a university is about thinking, problem-solving and asking questions in a rigorous and disciplined way; and that, whatever the discipline, it is the job of the university lecturer to encourage the student to do the same. Scrupulously acquiring, marshalling and passing on information and skills, though crucial to the operation, is but a preparatory stage. To use an expression that came into fashion during this period, we were teaching 'transferable skills'.

It is gratifying to hear from graduates who have moved into other spheres that we achieved some measure of success in this. In the words of Marcus Richardson, who graduated in 1996, 'each and every member of staff [...] taught us how to think critically, how to construct arguments, and how to present our ideas to people. And

---

[3] This was of course an illusion.

[4] There was an intermediate stage consisting of those professors of Russian who had first studied Russian in the armed forces and who were a few years older than me. Peter Herrity, who took over the reins of the department while I was a Pro-VC and for a few years thereafter, became head of department in his own right in from 1997 to 2001, and was promoted to a chair in 1999, belonged to this category, so Nottingham did not miss out on this generation.

[5] Malcolm V. Jones (1976).

[6] Malcolm V. Jones (1978).

[7] A more detailed biography is to be found in Sarah Young and Lesley Milne (2006), pp. 255-8. There is also a bibliography (pp. 259-68).

even at that time, I knew that whatever direction my life would later take, even if I went into a career that had no obvious connection with my degree studies, I was getting first-class training in essential skills.'

I had always been deeply uncomfortable with the restraints imposed by the study of national cultures in isolation, especially when institutionalised within single-discipline departments. It was at Sussex in the 1960s, with its abolition of departments, its student-centred learning, and its fostering of interdisciplinary study, that I found my spiritual home, teaching on The Modern European Mind course, which was based on a selection of the great books of American, English and European Literature, Philosophy, Religion, Sociology and Psychology: hence my support throughout my years at Nottingham for developments that transcended disciplinary and departmental boundaries. Locally, this was to be expressed in support for IRSCEES and Critical Theory; on the national stage, for BASEES,[8] Area Studies, the Humanities Research Board of the British Academy and other interdisciplinary bodies; and, on the international stage, for the International Dostoevsky Society: I was a founder member of all of these bodies. I hope that some of this fed through to my students, if only indirectly.

It was also at Sussex that I first encountered the philosophy of Karl Popper, which continued to influence my thinking and working methods throughout my career, even when the waves of structuralism and post-structuralism in their wilder forms threatened to drown us in the 80s and 90s. Popper tells young scientists (i.e., scholars of all kinds) that they are badly advised if they are told to 'go round and observe,' and that they are well advised if their teacher tells them to 'try to learn what people are discussing nowadays [...]. Find out where the difficulties arise [...]. In other words, you should study the problem situation of the day.'[9] That was always my guiding thought too: don't ask 'what are authors trying to say,' but 'what problems are they trying to solve?' These were often problems that they shared with writers in quite different fields.

On my appointment in early 1980, I lost no time in making contact with Janko Lavrin and visited him in London. I did not know John Fennell well, but he had turned up unexpectedly, like Evgraf in Doctor Zhivago, at key moments in my professional life, as external examiner for my first degree, at my first International Congress of Slavists at Warsaw, and as one of the external assessors when I was appointed to the chair. Since my graduation, I had come to know Frank Seeley well and became one of the few Europeans who knew him by his first name (Americans, to his chagrin, simply assumed that they should use it without being asked). We kept up a regular correspondence for over thirty years—from the time of his departure to the USA until his death in Texas in the year 2000;[10] I would see him from time to time at International Dostoevsky Symposia, and I visited him and Mara once at their home at Binghamton in the State of New York. Monica Partridge was of course still around the University in her retirement and retained a room in the History Department until it was required for other purposes.

The first event of the summer of 1980 was a tragic one. We had all assumed that the much-loved Nikolai Naidenov would continue to serve as Russian

---

[8] The Institute for Russian, Soviet and Central and East European Studies and The British Association for Slavonic and East European Studies, of which more below.

[9] Karl Popper (1963), p. 129.

[10] I have about seventy-five letters from Frank Seeley together with copies of a number of my replies.

language assistant alongside the continuing stream of Soviet lecturers. Sadly, this was not to be. Nikolai had been brought up in Tambov during the period of politically induced famine before the war, reaching adulthood just as Hitler invaded the Soviet Union. Drafted into the Red Army, he was taken prisoner by the Nazis, where he remained in a prisoner-of-war camp until the end of the war. Hearing rumours (which turned out to be true) that Stalin was sending ex-prisoners of war straight to the camps, he decided to set off westwards, ending up in England, where he pretended to be Ukrainian to avoid deportation back home. Paul Szyszczak recalls him telling his class that he temporarily assumed the name of Makarenko at this time. Having settled, and obtained British citizenship, he worked for a while in a factory in the north of England, eventually being appointed lector in our department in 1965, under Frank Seeley. Monica Partridge persuaded the then Registrar (Alfred Plumb) to give him the ill-paid, but pensionable, post of language assistant. Nikolai had congratulated me with particular warmth when I was appointed to succeed Monica in 1980. But he died on holiday in Rumania in the summer of that same year, having had a last glimpse of his native Russia. Technically he was still a deserter from the Red Army and, reluctantly but wisely, he decided that he could never risk going back to the Soviet Union itself. We held a memorial service in the University Chapel, and for many years his photograph hung in the corridor of the department. Warm memories of Nikolai have been a constant refrain in graduate contributions to this project, together with a sense of privilege in having known someone with his experience of life.

Following Nikolai's death, we appointed Liza Lacy, a Russian from Leningrad who had married an English businessman and now lived in Nottingham, as full-time Russian lectrice. She occupied this post until 1984, when financial stringency obliged us to appoint Russian lectrices on a part-time basis. For the next few years Marina Firth (1984-86) and Natasha Romaine (1986-87) served as Russian lectrices, while Liza returned in this capacity in 1987. She continues to teach in the department, now a familiar, well-regarded and experienced teacher of Russian.

I was entirely comfortable with the main lines of Monica's vision for the department. Student recruitment was still worryingly low, and the cloud of Atkinson still hung over the whole profession, but the University agreed to a replacement for her expertise in Serbo-Croat, and we determined to maintain our links with the schools, to promote and nurture the department's research activity, and to develop its profile on the national and international stage, hoping that the tide of public opinion would turn and that recruitment would pick up again.

We also made some minor changes in our domestic arrangements. For example, we abolished Sunday evening examiners' meetings and compulsory viva voce examinations for finalists; we also introduced the custom of minute-taking at staff meetings and the systematic filing of examination results. Later we would be one of the first departments to institute an annual review meeting.

Colleagues would now teach the field of literature that best reflected their research interests, rather than being allocated to different centuries: Wendy Rosslyn would teach poetry; Cynthia Marsh would teach drama; Nicholas Luker would teach Soviet prose fiction; Peter Herrity would have overall responsibility for language work and continue to teach the History of the Russian Language and

Comparative Slavonic Philosophy; I should teach nineteenth century prose fiction and intellectual history. When David Norris, fresh from his degree in Serbo-Croat at SSEES, was appointed in 1981, this enabled us to continue teaching Serbo-Croat to degree level and to welcome lectors and lectrices from Zagreb each year as usual. The links with Ljubljana were also reaffirmed, Peter Herrity's expertise in this area remaining a key factor.

Paul Szyszczak, who was a student during the period of transition (1978-82), remembers the happy atmosphere in the department at the time. He writes:

> The memory of my time in the Slavonic Studies Department is one of fun. To any casual visitor who might have strayed into our small corner of the Trent Building and passed through the austere and characterless corridor of the department [the same corridor that had so impressed the young Lucyna Makuch], that might seem impossible. However, being a small department, there was a great bonding among the students and staff, noticeable more, I think, with the arrival of Professor Jones at the helm. His open, approachable style brought a new spirit and signs that a certain glasnost would arrive somewhat earlier in our small corner of the Slavonic world than in those countries we were to study and visit.

Every change in the headship in the days before it rotated among senior members inevitably affected the atmosphere in the department. Lucyna remembers thinking that 'if an earthquake had hit the department or the Russians had invaded, [Professor Jones] would have been neither shaken nor stirred.' It is nice to know that this is how it appeared: I can remember occasions when my calm was severely tested.

One of my early memories is of the then Dean, Professor Robin Storey, calling to announce conspiratorially that, according to the most recent staffing formula, Slavonic Studies was due to 'lose' two of its six full-time members of staff. This would have undone the work of more than a decade in a single stroke, not to mention the effect on the unidentified colleagues concerned. Following the principle of glasnost, I felt that this unwelcome news had to be shared with colleagues, but under such circumstances it was difficult to preserve the atmosphere of relaxed collegiality to which we all attached such importance.

The filling of the chair in 1980 and the appointment of David Norris in the following year had been important gestures of support by the University in the wake of Atkinson, but evidently we were not yet out of the wood. The whole University system was put under siege by the new Thatcher government, and placed in a position of 'severe financial stringency'. It was expected that there would be thousands of academic job losses across the country, with the closure of small departments and the further rationalisation of 'minority subjects'. In pursuit of these aims, the government was to abolish legal tenure for academic staff, thus changing their terms of appointment so that they could be more easily made redundant. In such a situation, a department like ours—still suffering from undergraduate recruitment problems and grossly overstaffed by current norms— was in the firing line. Fortunately the University managed to avoid redundancies, which would in any case have been legally dubious under the Statutes of the time, by introducing from 1981 a voluntary early retirement scheme for members of the University over 55 years of age.

The first five years did not therefore feel much like a honeymoon. Every single year, it seemed, we had to fight anew for funds to send our first-year students on study trips to the USSR and Yugoslavia, and anxiously re-argue the case for the appointment of lectors, the easiest posts for the University to cut. Every year, we were made to wait until the last moment for authorisation to re-appoint. Each summer consequently saw a last-minute rush to obtain visas and work permits for our overseas lectors and lectrices, time that could have been spent more advantageously on scholarship and research. Our colleagues in the other Modern Language departments were spared this additional anxiety, since their lectors and lectrices came from the European Union, but some senior members of the University were heard to argue that all linguists in the Faculty should be able to teach any and all of the languages it offered, ours (they presumably thought) being such an undemanding discipline.

In the event, the flow of lectors and lectrices from Yugoslavia continued unabated. The Zagreb lectors and lectrices usually stayed with us for a year. Over this period we enjoyed the services of Branko Brusar again (1980-1), Ivan Matković (1981-2), Dora Maček (1982-3), Damir Kalogjera (1983-4), Maja Bratanić (1984-5) and Mladen Engelsfeld (1985-6). Our Slovene lectors and lectrices tended to stay with us longer and were paid by an agency of the Slovene government in accordance with an arrangement negotiated in the early 1970s by Monica Partridge and Peter Herrity. In 1980, the Slovene lectrice was Božena Činkole (1979-84). She was followed by Tone Perčič (1984-5) and Jože Iskra (1985-8).

With very few exceptions, where personal or other problems arose, all our former Yugoslav colleagues fitted into the department happily and well. Like our Soviet lecturers, almost all lived in tutors' flats in Nightingale Hall. Some continued to bring their children and to have them educated at the nearby Margaret Glen Bott Comprehensive School or to take courses at the University itself. In general, they were a joy to have in the department and contributed massively to the popularity of our courses in Serbo-Croat and Slovene. It was in fact during this period that one of our graduates, David Denton, obtained the first Nottingham PhD in Slovene Studies for his thesis on *The Life and Works of Ciril Kosmač* (1984), an outcome that must have delighted the 97-year-old Janko Lavrin.

Until 1992, when arrangements under the Cultural Agreement began to break down following the dissolution of the Soviet Union, and the British Council evinced a desire to treat the countries of the former Soviet bloc as 'normal', we also continued to receive Soviet Lecturers. In this way, we enjoyed the services of Olga Shcherbakova (1980-1) and Marina Akhvlediani (1981-2). For reasons that now escape me, but were probably financial, there was a break in the supply from 1982 to 1986, when it resumed with the arrival of Zoia Markova (1986-7).

If public support for Russian was flagging in the early 1980s, there were encouraging signs with regard to student and teacher exchanges. In 1981, The Russian Language Undergraduate Study Committee (RLUSC as it became known) was established as successor to a smaller committee known as the V/2/d Committee, after the relevant paragraph in the Anglo-Soviet Cultural Agreement. Nicholas Luker was to be a loyal and effective representative on RLUSC for many years. The ten unpaid members were all full-time lecturers in British universities and polytechnics, and administered schemes whereby students of Russian were placed on ten-month courses at the Maurice Thorez Institute in Moscow or Voronezh State University (thirty-eight places), five-month courses at the Pushkin Institute in Moscow (fifty places) and three-month courses at the Leningrad, Minsk and Voronezh State Universities (114 places).

As RLUSC itself reported, students' living conditions varied and in some centres were poor. 'There is, however,' it went on reassuringly, 'no correlation between material conditions and the benefit students derive from their stay.' There was also a V/2/c agreement operated by the British Council for postgraduates, about which the same could be said. As President of BUAS from 1986 to 1988, I was briefly to sit on the postgraduate selection committee. As the eighties unfolded, many of our students were to obtain places on these schemes, as well as to benefit (or otherwise) from arrangements that Nottingham negotiated privately.

When in 1982 I was pressed to stand for the Deanship of the Arts Faculty, I was disinclined to turn down an opportunity to get closer to the places where our fate would be decided. My responsibilities as Dean would extend to the whole Faculty, but the fact that I should be present and involved in discussions which might bear on our fate would, I hoped, in itself be sufficient to give us that extra degree of security that was needed to stabilise the situation. As a former Vice-dean, I also knew that the ability to influence events depends on the acquisition of reliable and up-to-date information, and that the best way to acquire such information (and indeed to contribute to it) is to be present where it is being generated.

To what extent the survival of the department, and indeed that of other small Arts departments, owed anything to my efforts as Dean during these crucial years, I cannot now honestly say. Vice-chancellor Basil Weedon, though he was always alluding threateningly to 'the problem of small departments',[11] closing 'the Department of Tibetan Studies' (code for Slavonic Studies) and pressing the Deans to identify the weakest links in their Faculties, never did in fact close any departments at all.[12] Although it was difficult to discern in him any special sympathy or understanding for the Arts, he tried at all times to be even-handed, and clearly did not want to rupture the institution.

Decanal duties did not absorb all my time. Thanks to the advent of the BBC Micro computer in the mid-1980s, I was able to maintain research and publication at a reduced level, and my colleagues did even better. This was the beginning of the computer age as it affected the non-specialist. It was to be many years before personal computers appeared as of right on the desks of Arts academics, and the era of the Internet and email was still well in the future. However, apart from making use of word processors, some people were beginning to advocate a number of more sophisticated uses for computers in the Arts, including the field of poetics. Wendy Rosslyn made an early contribution with her article on 'COCOA as a tool for the analysis of poetry'[13].

---

[11] 'The problem of small departments' was greatly exercising the UGC at the time.

[12] Geology was the only department at Nottingham to close at this time. But this happened only after its academic staff had jumped ship in anticipation of its closure. Professor Weedon was not pleased. To my knowledge no Dean ever offered a view on the 'weakest links' in his Faculty.

[13] Wendy Rosslyn (1975).

Student recruitment was at its lowest ebb in the decade from 1972-82. This was a national problem related to the decline of Russian in schools, which Atkinson had noted but had done nothing effective to alleviate. At the beginning of the eighties, strenuous efforts were made at Nottingham to boost recruitment generally and to publicise our own courses.

A key role in the campaign was played by Cynthia Marsh, who organised Open Days and regularly coordinated the annual Russian Days for fifth- and sixth- formers. Not a few graduates have commented on the combination of friendliness and authority with which she welcomed them and the decisive role that this played in their choice of Nottingham to study Russian.

Russian Days went from strength to strength in these years and frequently included a Russian play, which Cynthia produced and sometimes scripted herself. In 1981, a Russian Christmas Play (*Petrushka, a Christmas drama of the Astrakhan Seminary*) was performed in St Mary's Church, Nottingham, and succeeding years saw performances in Russian of Gogol's *Marriage* (1982), Chekhov's *Uncle Vania* (1983), Maiakovsky's *Bedbug* (1984) and Gogol's *Government Inspector* (1985). Cynthia was also to become a driving force in the Lace Market Theatre in town, where over the years she was to promote, and produce, a number of Russian plays in English translation.

Links with schools were maintained and developed through collaboration with the School of Education, where James Muckle continued to be responsible for the training of prospective teachers of Russian on Nottingham's Postgraduate Certificate of Education course. At the same time, Nicholas Luker maintained effective personal links with schools in the Midlands where Russian was still taught, through both lecturing and examining. For some years, he also assisted recruitment through his enthusiastic and dedicated adult education work.

These efforts were beginning to make a discernible impact by the mid-eighties, but the department was aware that unforeseen circumstances could just as easily reverse the trend. The more recruitment depended on attracting beginners, the more it depended on the public perception of Russian as an interesting and useful subject, and the more it depended on able language students being willing, often in defiance of the best advice of their teachers and parents, to take the risk of reading a 'difficult' language of which they had no previous knowledge, and for which the use in future employment was highly uncertain.

As Paul Szyszczak remarks, the department attracted some really strong and interesting personalities among its students at this time, and was itself a melting pot of cultures: 'a mixture of those with 'O' or 'A' level qualifications, those who might have learnt at home with parents of Slav descent, and those who just wanted to learn Russian and/or Serbo-Croat from scratch.' He reflects: 'I dare say the unorthodox choice of studying Russian at university at that time did attract the unusual in people.'

It was at this point that history offered a helping hand. Following the short reigns of Andropov and Chernenko, Mikhail Gorbachev was elected General Secretary of the Communist Party of the Soviet Union in March 1985 and, perhaps for the first time in almost seventy years, the Soviet Union began to assume a humanly engaging aspect. The Iron Curtain itself unexpectedly began to show signs of rust, and was to crumble away or be torn down completely by the end of the decade.

This is not the place to revisit the heady years of glasnost and perestroika; of the personal rapprochement between Gorbachev and Reagan; of the facilitating role played by Margaret Thatcher; of the end of the Cold War; of the impact of these events on the East European satellite states and the eventual collapse of the Soviet system and the disintegration of the Soviet Union itself. Let it simply be said that international events on this scale favoured a welcome resurgence of interest in and support for Russian and East European Studies in our universities, of which Nottingham was glad to take advantage. Support from government and the University was matched by improving levels of student recruitment.

In 1981, there had been twelve graduates, followed by twenty, nine, nine and thirteen in the following years. In 1986 there were also thirteen, but in 1987 only nine again. Then numbers began to pick up, with twenty-one graduates in 1988, and seventeen, eighteen and twenty-one in the following years. Bearing in mind that by this time all Modern Language students were on four-year courses, it is evident that the resurgence pre-dates the advent of Gorbachev, but there is no doubt that the new atmosphere greatly assisted and helped to sustain it.

Apart from David Norris's appointment, the only changes in academic staff during the first five years had been among lectors and lectrices. But there were also changes in the secretary's office. Ann Collins (née Hall) left us in 1981 after five years' loyal service, subsequently to reappear as one of the secretaries in the adjacent English Department. She was replaced from 1981 to 1983 by Jolanta Murjas, herself of Polish descent, and the only one of our secretaries with a degree in Russian. Her knowledge of the subject and her wry sense of humour made her a welcome addition to the department. She was succeeded from 1983 to 1986 by Heather Phoenix, whose happy personality and lively efficiency contributed not a little to raising everybody's spirits. She left all too soon to read for a degree in Drama at The University of Manchester.

1986

1986 deserves a section to itself. In that year the department celebrated the seventieth anniversary of Basil Slepchenko's arrival to teach Russian at The University College, with a gathering of more than a hundred graduates, including one of Lavrin's own students (the Revd C. H. Stephens), who had studied in the class described by Nancy Binyon in a previous chapter. Also present was a representative of the Chamber of Commerce through whose interest and support the study of Russian at Nottingham had originally taken wing. 1986 turned out to be a memorable year in other ways as well, some planned, but some quite unexpected.

Glasnost and satellite technology now made it possible for us to receive Soviet television for the first time. It is difficult to convey just how sensational this development was. For most of the Soviet period there had been an effective communications barrier between the USSR and the rest of the world, which sometimes seemed as remote from each other as two parallel universes. The news that did come out via Radio Moscow or the Soviet News Agency TASS was heavily censored and politically slanted, and our own broadcasts to the Soviet Union frequently jammed. We knew from Western intelligence sources that rockets could explode, riots take place and planes crash on Soviet soil without the news ever leaking out at the time, even within the Soviet Union itself, where such rumours were subsequently dismissed as bourgeois falsifications.

Now, suddenly, we were able to see Soviet TV programmes (officially beamed at the Soviet Navy) directly, on a set rigged up for us by a sales representative in the car park of the Trent Building. The experience was surreal. Before long, the University had been persuaded to allocate funds for the purchase of a satellite dish, which was erected on the roof of the Trent Building during the Spring Term of 1986. Receivers were installed in the Language Centre and at the back of our departmental coffee room behind the partition that Monica Partridge had put there to house a Soviet radio and stereo player that I had once purchased in Beeston for family use, under the mistaken impression that it would be more sensitive to Soviet radio broadcasts. It cannot, unfortunately, be said that the facility was much used by staff or students at the time. Soviet TV was itself not very gripping, the quality of sound and vision was highly variable, and it was difficult to incorporate broadcasts within the teaching programme, but at the time we believed that the possession of a Soviet TV might make all the difference to our undergraduate recruitment. Much later, it became possible to watch both Russian and Yugoslav TV in the Language Centre and to make much more systematic and imaginative use of it.

On the international scene, events were also continuing to unfold. On 26 April 1986, there was an explosion at the Chernobyl nuclear reactor. Like other universities, we had students in the vicinity in their year abroad. Effective emergency action was taken by RLUSC, the Committee set up by British universities to organise undergraduate study visits to the Soviet Union, chaired at the time by Dr Derek Offord of Bristol. We immediately took steps to change the destination of our first year students, who had been due to go to Minsk for their summer course. The Registrar agreed to make extra funds available, if necessary, to enable them to go somewhere safer. Stephanie Briggs (née Batty) remembers that Chernobyl occurred nine months after their first visit to Minsk, when she was halfway through her second year. Her third-year trip to Minsk occurred a year after the accident. She was there from March to June 1987. 'We all fretted and dithered about returning to the Soviet Union after Chernobyl,' she recalls, 'regardless of where we were due to go, but I was assured that Minsk was unaffected by the radiation drift. It had drifted north and east from Chernobyl towards the other side of Belarus. In fact people had been evacuated to Minsk from Chernobyl because it was considered so safe. So I took a deep breath and went.'

There were still concerns about Chernobyl four years later. The British Council reported in 1990 that Kiev now seemed to be clear of radiation, but the situation in Minsk was less certain. Food from the contaminated area had been distributed far and wide, and it had been necessary to devise ways of testing it for safety. Alex Harrington remembers how they went to Obninsk at the end of the first year (1992), a provincial town dominated by its own nuclear reactor. 'One of the girls had been given a portable Geiger counter by her mother and I remember it crackling insistently in the background whenever it was switched on.'

From the department's point of view, the most important development of 1986 was the announcement of the results of the first national Research Assessment Exercise (or Research Selectivity Exercise, as the first round was known). This exercise, run by the University Grants Committee (UGC), was designed to inform research funding to universities, subject by subject, on a new selective basis. When the results were published in June 1986, research in Slavonic Studies at Nottingham was awarded the highest possible grade. Suddenly, from being a Cinderella subject in danger of extinction, we were perceived as one of the jewels in the University's crown, and our credibility soared. In the RAEs that followed, Slavonic Studies at Nottingham scored 4 out of 5 in 1989[14] and 1992.

The research achievement of the last fifteen years had indeed been notable. PhDs had been awarded to Nicholas Luker (1971), Peter Herrity (1974), and Cynthia Marsh (1979) and Wendy Rosslyn had acquired her MPhil from London. By 1988, both she and David Norris had submitted for Nottingham PhDs, which were to be awarded in 1989. But it was scholarly publications that really counted.

Nicholas Luker was by far the most prolific author of books at the time. He had published a string of six, of which his monographs already mentioned on Kuprin and Grin were the most substantial, but also included a book on Grin in the Bradda series and an anthology (edited and translated) on the work of the 'Znanie' School. In 1987, he was to publish another anthology on Alexander Grin and to edit a series of essays entitled *Fifty years on: Gorky and his time*, for the Astra Press.

In addition, Garth Terry and I edited *New Essays on Dostoyevsky*, which we dedicated to Janko Lavrin; Peter Herrity published his *Jezik Emanuila Jankovica*; and Cynthia Marsh brought out her *M. A. Voloshin: artist-poet. A study of the synaesthetic aspects of his poetry*. In 1984 Wendy Rosslyn's *The Prince, the fool and the nunnery: the religious theme in the early poetry of Anna Akhmatova*, appeared. In 1982, David Norris published his translation of Edvard Kardelj's *Reminiscences: the struggle for recognition and independence, the New Yugoslavia, 1944-1957*, and in 1988 he was to edit and publish *Miloš Crnjanjski and Modern Serbian Literature*.

There were, of course, many articles published in academic journals during these years as well, some arguably as important as the books, but too numerous to list here. Monica Partridge's own publications continued to augment the department's research profile: in 1984, after her retirement, her *Alexander Herzen, 1812-1870* appeared and her flow of scholarly articles also continued for a number of years.

The number of these books published then and later by the Astra Press is not coincidental. Garth Terry, a former student of the department who had subsequently taken a Master's degree in Macedonian History, had for some years supervised the expanding Slavonic collection in the University Library to the great advantage of the department. Obliged to retire early owing to ill health, he had set up the Astra Press from his home at Cotgrave (later Keyworth). Its first publication was the second volume of his own multi-volume bibliography of academic articles on the languages and literatures of Eastern Europe.[15] Thereafter, he continued to publish bibliographies, monographs, Festschrifts and collections of essays in the Slavonic field, not only for colleagues at Nottingham but throughout the country, and even abroad.

Nottingham's contribution to national and international research was, however, not limited to its publications. From 1984, Peter Herrity had been British representative on the International Commission for the Slavonic Literary Languages, and in 1985 I became General Editor of Cambridge Studies in Russian Literature, a

---

[14] To be exact, Russian scored 4 and other Slavonic languages 3 in 1989, but in retrospect this 3 can be seen as an aberration.
[15] Terry (1982). Further volumes in the series appeared in 1985, 1988, 1991, 1994 and 1997.

Literature in Leningrad. More happily, in the summer, an honorary doctorate was conferred on Professor G. M. Fridlender of the Institute for Russian Literature, and chief editor of the Academy Edition of the Complete Works of F. M. Dostoevsky, the only Soviet participant in the Dostoevsky Symposium of 1986.

Behind the scenes in the 80s and 90s

At the end of 1988, I handed over the headship of the department to Peter Herrity for four years. In 1986, the then Vice-Chancellor, Professor Basil Weedon, had invited me to serve from 1987 to 1991 as a Pro-Vice-Chancellor of the University, on the understanding that this would be followed by a year's research leave. I had been canvassed for this position once before, at the close of my period as Dean, and had then declined. Professor Weedon, however, was now about to retire and we had no idea who his successor might be, or what attitude he or she might take to Slavonic Studies. At such a critical time, it would have been irresponsible, I thought, to reject the invitation.

The new Vice-Chancellor was Professor Colin Campbell from Queen's University, Belfast. In his first year as Vice-Chancellor, it became clear that major changes were in the air and that Pro-Vice-Chancellors' duties would in future take up at least 80% of their time. He readily agreed to the appointment of Peter as acting head of department, while I retained overall responsibility for the department's research. This was the first time that the University had authorised a non-professorial head in a department containing a professor, and it was a significant tribute to Peter's competence and the esteem in which he was held.

Fortunately, despite the difference in our personalities (noted, incidentally, by a number of graduates), Peter and I always worked together very harmoniously. He was able to give the department the sort of constant daily attention and direction that I no longer found possible, while I was able to contribute relevant intelligence from the world outside. His brisk efficiency and attention to detail made him a popular choice and he soon impressed not only his departmental colleagues but also outsiders who had to deal with him. It was not an easy period, and he recalls having to fight many battles on committees and on Senate.

Slavonic Studies was one of the first departments that Colin Campbell visited following his appointment in 1988. He was particularly impressed by the growing student numbers and by the potential for interdisciplinary work created by the foundation of IRSEES in the new situation developing in the Soviet Union and Eastern Europe, and saw my appointment to the Wooding Enquiry (see below) as a vote of confidence in the department, and as an indication that it was now safe from outside threats. In the University Plan for his third year in office, he was to include support for a post in Soviet Economics and also for a series of IRSCEES visiting research fellows from Central and Eastern Europe, who would collaborate with Nottingham colleagues in research projects. The first of these were to arrive in the second semester of 1992-93. Most were by the nature of things to go to History and the Social Sciences, but the department also benefited from the scheme.

Into my work as Pro-Vice-Chancellor had to be woven departmental teaching and also an increasing number of outside commitments, seen as helpful both to the University and to the subject area. I did not realise at the time to what extent my involvement in the process of forming the British Association for Slavonic and East European Studies was going propel me into discussions with government ministers, high-ranking civil servants and national lobbying on behalf of the profession over the next ten to fifteen years, activities involving the heads of funding councils, senior businessmen and prominent members of the two houses of parliament. It would also lead to my membership of two official national enquiries into Soviet, Russian and East European Studies, which sought to strengthen the subject nationally and to provide additional funding[25]. Following a term as Vice-President of BASEES from 1988 to 1990, I also became Chairman of the Coordinating Council for Area Studies Associations from 1991 to 1993, and a member of the Area Studies Monitoring Group from 1991 to 1995. Experience gained on these bodies led to invitations to sit on further committees (including three Research Assessment Exercise panels for Russian and other Slavonic Studies), and to serve almost uninterruptedly on chair appointments committees at other universities for more than a decade. From 1994 to 1997, I was also the only Slavist on the newly established Humanities Research Board of the British Academy (now the Arts and Humanities Research Council).

My diary for this period shows frequent visits to London: for meetings with the Minister responsible for Higher Education, George Walden M.P. (a Slavist himself) or his successor Robert Jackson M.P.; to give evidence to the House of Commons Foreign Affairs Committee; to engage in consultations on the new Cultural Agreement; and to liaise with the British Council and the Director of SSEES (Professor Michael Branch). The writing of articles and letters to the press, to Vice-Chancellors thinking of abandoning Russian, and sundry other activities supportive of the profession nationally, including meetings at Highgrove House and St James's Palace,[26] also took up much time. As President of BUAS, I had also become involved in facilitating the relocation of Slavists whose departments were closing following the Atkinson Report, through discussions with Professor Martin Harris,[27] who had been deputed by the UGC to oversee the process.

In such ways we were able to contribute to the strengthening of the subject nationally over the last fifteen years of the twentieth century, and it was the background against which our own local strategy had to be planned.

By the end of the 1980s and the beginning of the 1990s, our own position was therefore considerably strengthened. We were even approached informally to discover whether we should be prepared to receive another Russian Department in its entirety, a proposal that was ruled out because of the improbability of our recruiting sufficient undergraduates to justify the additional staffing.

In the academic year 1988-9 negotiations for Lesley Milne's transfer from The University of Hull reached completion and, as we have seen, she joined us in the following year. It was also the year in which the first ever conference of the newly formed British Association for Slavonic, Soviet and East European Studies came to

---

[25] These were the 'Wooding Committee' (*Enquiry into Soviet and East European Studies*, set up by the Department for Education and Science to report to the Universities Funding Council), of which I was a member from 1988 to 1989, and the Higher Education Funding Council for England's *Review into Former Soviet and East European Studies* from 1995 to 1996.

[26] These were meetings of the Area Studies Monitoring group, chaired by the Prince of Wales.

[27] Sir Martin Harris was then Professor of Linguistics at the University of Salford and a member of the UGC; he later became Vice-Chancellor at Essex (1983-7), then Manchester (1992-2004). I was to meet him in each of these capacities in later years and also as Chairman of the HEFCE/CVCP/SCOP Review of Postgraduate Education, of which I was a member in 1995-6. He is currently Director of Fair Access at OFFA and Chancellor of the University of Salford.

Nottingham;[28] and in which the department published the Festschrift for Monica Partridge, to which reference was made in a previous chapter. In this year too, Wendy Rosslyn and David Norris were awarded their PhDs; Russian at Nottingham scored a four in the second Research Assessment Exercise; and Wendy Rosslyn organised an international conference on Anna Akhmatova in Florence Boot Hall.

The Anna Akhmatova Centenary Conference, which resulted in the two volumes of articles mentioned above, was in all respects a highly successful event. It took place from 10 to 14 July 1989. Relations with the Soviet Union had improved to such an extent since the Dostoevsky Symposium in 1986 that it proved possible for a strong contingent of Soviet scholars to participate, including T. V. Tsiv'ian-Mikhailova, N. V. Koroleva, S. A. Kovalenko, V. G. Admoni, V. V. Ivanov and Z. B. Tomashevskaia. Half the papers were in English and half in Russian, and a substantial article on the conference subsequently appeared in the Russian-language newspaper *Russkaia mysl'* in Paris.[29] Perhaps even more memorable was the fact that Josip Brodsky, the émigré Russian poet, sent a new poem to the conference with permission for its publication.

As summer ended and the year drew to its close, the historic events in Eastern Europe were reaching their climax.

On 11 September 1989, Hungary opened its borders to East Germans seeking to go to the West, and television cameras showed them leaving in their droves. By the end of the month, tens of thousands were fleeing via Hungary, Poland and Czechoslovakia. Following a visit to East Germany by Gorbachev in October, German cities were rocked by pro-reform marches and on 18 October the veteran East German leader Erich Honecker was briefly replaced by Egon Krenz. In November, finally, the borders between East and West Berlin were opened and the Berlin Wall came down.

Back at Nottingham, Sir Bryan Cartledge, a former British Ambassador in Moscow with whom I had worked on the Wooding Committee, gave the first IRSCEES public lecture on 21 November, which drew a massive audience in the Great Hall, while Derek Spring was making progress with a book to be published under the aegis of IRSCEES on *The Impact of Gorbachev*.[30] In the same month the Arts Faculty gave permission for him to advertise an honours degree course in Soviet and East European Studies, by way of expanding the subsidiary course that he had successfully run for so many years in association with Gary Entwhistle and Stuart Thompstone,[31] and which a number of our students had followed. The new course, which was to run alongside the separate Joint Honours course in Russian and History, incorporated modules and drew in other staff from the Faculty of Law and Social Sciences (including Bill Lomax, Anthony Kemp-Welch and Richard Popplewell). Although it had only a tiny admissions quota and some students felt rather isolated, it was a fitting response to the events of the time and a small-scale success. The first intake was in 1991-2.

---

[28] It was soon to make Fitzwilliam College, Cambridge, the permanent venue for its Easter Conference, as had previously been the case with NASEES.

[29] 'My rabotali v dukhe sotrudnichestva', interview with Wendy Rosslyn by Sergei Dediulin, *Russkaia mysl'*, No. 3786, 28 July 1989, p. 10; see also p. 11.

[30] Derek Spring (1991).

[31] Stuart Thompstone (History) was Brian Falloon's successor in the post established by Hayter and became an active and valued member of IRSCEES, later serving as its Secretary.

The historic events of 1989, culminating in the resignation of Todor Zhivkov in Bulgaria, the Velvet Revolution in Czechoslovakia, the death of the dissident physicist Andrei Sakharov in the Soviet Union, and civil war followed by the execution of the Ceaucescus in Rumania, did of course prompt further responses by the British government, whose Prime Minister, Margaret Thatcher, justifiably prided herself on having acted as a catalyst for these events. Among those public bodies with which we had the closest contact, the British Council was allocated an extra £2m for Eastern Europe on top of £1.5m in the previous year.

We hoped that we might benefit in some way from these developments, in conjunction with the recommendations of the Wooding Report. However, it soon became clear that, in spite of our long association, the British Council's extra funding was not to come the way of Slavonic Studies Departments. It was granted in recognition of the new opportunities opening up for the discharge of the Council's central mission, the dissemination of British culture abroad. And the response to the Wooding Report was also disappointing.

While the Report was warmly welcomed by the Committee of BASSEES, there was much buck-passing between the Department for Education and Science and the newly established Universities' Funding Council under its chief executive Sir Peter Swinnerton-Dyer. The UFC protested that the Enquiry had been imposed on it by the DES without special funding, and the DES stonewalled. More to the point, perhaps, Wooding was swiftly being overtaken by events, for the Soviet Union and Eastern Europe that it had taken as a given a year or so before was now crumbling before our eyes, and the new configuration that emerged would require a more complex response.

However, by the summer it had been announced that The Foreign and Commonwealth Office had allocated a sum from its own resources sufficient to part-fund ten new lectureships in Soviet and East European Studies for a period of three years. The scheme was to be administered by the British Council,[32] and a competition was held in December, from which Nottingham emerged with a new post in Geography and Management, to be filled in April 1991 by the young Soviet economist Igor Filatotchev, one of the first of the new breed of post-Soviet specialists to be appointed to a post in a UK university. He was to work with Professor Mike Wright in the East European Privatisation Research Group.

In addition, the government claimed that it had allocated extra funding to the Economic and Social Research Council for East European Studies and that, apart from this, it was up to the UFC and individual universities to respond as they saw fit. In other words, having set up the Wooding Committee in the first place, government now washed its hands of the whole matter. It was more interested in channelling resources into the Know-How Funds that were being set up to assist East European countries in the transition to market economies and parliamentary democracy. In November 1990, moreover, Margaret Thatcher resigned and her position as Prime Minister was taken over by John Major.

During these years of change, at the turn of the new decade, the department too tried to take advantage of the new opportunities. It set up exchange arrangements with The University of Moscow (MGU) and with an institution of Higher Education in Kiev.

---

[32] For this reason, it was widely, but mistakenly, known as the British Council Lectureships Scheme.

At the beginning of December, however, the British Council reported that its Moscow office could not cope with the changed situation. With increased staffing levels, it was going to have to revert to the normal type of British Council operation, and cease to support Russian and Slavonic Studies as it had done in the past. It was now no longer necessary for it to get involved in exchanges in order to get a foot behind the Iron Curtain. The Soviet Union was moving to a money economy (khozraschet) and previous arrangements negotiated under the Cultural Agreement were breaking down, sometimes in mid-operation. Felicity Cave, on behalf of RLUSC, tried heroically to sort out problems on the ground as they arose. Available accommodation was miserable. Some students had been thrown out onto the street from the Hotel Universitetskaia when more important guests arrived. No guarantees had been given to students at the Pushkin Institute after 1 January 1991; the Maurice Thorez Institute had given a written undertaking, but its value was not clear. The Moscow University exchange involving SSEES, the Polytechnic of Central London, Birmingham and ourselves was encountering real difficulties: students had been placed in private flats, where hosts received no payment but where the students were expected to give English lessons; but food shortages were placing an extra burden on the hosts and money was going astray. We were advised that the Cultural Exchange programmes would probably collapse during the current academic year, and that the postgraduate exchange would not work at all. Costs were soaring.

So while the British Council was talking about new opportunities for itself, it was leaving us in the lurch in a situation of growing chaos. The following year, 1991, saw a visit to Nottingham by Professor Svetlana Terminasova of Moscow State University to try to sort out the problems with our exchange programme. Unfortunately they were foredoomed. Students' parents were increasingly inclined to hold us legally responsible for the shortcomings of our Soviet partners and this was a risk that, whatever our personal sympathy for our Soviet colleagues, the University was not willing to assume.

On the other hand, public interest had resulted in increased student numbers studying Russian, and we experienced an upward surge in admissions that peaked in the late 1990s. In fact in 1988-89 we seriously overshot our intake quota for the first time, and there were 30 first year honours students, the largest group since the heyday of the early 1970s. Colleagues naturally worried about teaching loads, but increased teaching loads were shortly to become official university policy as the new Universities Funding Council[33] allowed student numbers to expand, and this was the only effective way, apart from public appeals, for the University to generate the extra income it needed to invest in the future.

One positive effect of the extra income was the ability to make extra promotions. There had been a promotion drought in Basil Weedon's last years. In some years, there had been no more than one promotion to a senior grade in the whole of the Arts Faculty. Under Colin Campbell, increasing the number of promotions for the many deserving candidates who had been held back for financial reasons became a priority, and Nicholas Luker was the first in our department to benefit from the new policy. He was deservedly promoted to the grade of senior lecturer in the academic year 1988-9. There were, of course, other

---

[33] Set up by the government to succeed the University Grants Committee in 1989, it adopted a policy of allowing subject provision to be determined by market forces.

deserving cases queuing up behind him. Cynthia Marsh was promoted to Senior Lecturer in 1991, and Lesley Milne and Wendy Rosslyn were promoted to readerships in 1992 and 1993 respectively. All these promotions recognised significant all-round performance in teaching, administration and research, while the readerships laid special emphasis on research performance. Lesley Milne, who had become an internationally recognised pioneer in Bulgakov studies, had by this time followed up her earlier work with a critical biography of Bulgakov, published by CUP in 1990.[34] Wendy Rosslyn, who had made her mark in the field of Russian women's poetry, had now supplemented and complemented her book on Akhmatova's religious poetry (1984) with two volumes of articles by leading international scholars on Akhmatova and, with Cynthia Marsh, had co-edited a volume to celebrate the department's 75th anniversary[35].

I resumed the headship of the department from 1992 to 1995 and then again passed it over to Peter for the last two years before my retirement (1995-97) in recognition of further outside commitments. I also had the assistance of two part-time personal secretaries at this time, Melanie Cumpston (1995-96) and Stephanie Brunger (1996-97), who were a great help to Jane as well. Both were highly professional and adaptable, and an enormous help to me personally. Melanie went to a post at Oxford when she left, and Stephanie became Secretary in the Philosophy Department.

1992-97

The old world order was evidently collapsing: by the beginning of 1991 the USSR had effectively ceased to exist. During the year, Boris Yeltsin became the first freely elected President in the history of Russia. In August, there was the coup against Gorbachev, still the titular head of a fast disintegrating Soviet Union. Although he returned following a demonstration of popular support for Boris Yeltsin, he was forced to resign in December when his post was abolished and a new, loose federation to be known as the Commonwealth of Independent States was established. Peter Hoare, the University Librarian and a member of IRSCEES, had been among the crowds in Moscow when the coup collapsed.

At least one former student of the department had an even more privileged view of history as it was unfolding in the early 1990s. Terry Sandell, who had graduated in 1970, and had a distinguished career with the British Council, was extensively involved with the Soviet Union, including a period as Cultural Attaché at the Moscow Embassy in the late 1970s and early 1980s. He returned to Moscow in early 1989 as the first Director, British Council, Soviet Union[36]. He recalls,

Of numerous memories of that historic period, one was of meetings with Anatolii Sobchak, whom I had known as an academic and who had become Mayor of St Petersburg (and was being groomed as Gorbachev's successor). We used to meet in his office and one day he said that he had become so busy that in order to follow up anything from our meetings he was going to ask one

---

[34] Lesley Milne (1977), (1983), (1990).

[35] Wendy Rosslyn (1984), (1990), (1991).

[36] When the USSR ceased to exist, Terry became Director, FSU/Russian Federation and was awarded the OBE for his contribution to Anglo-Soviet/Russian relations in 1991.

of his staff to take notes and do the necessary. The person concerned sat in a corner and was Sobchak's Head of Foreign Relations, one Vladimir Putin!

Meanwhile, Slovenia had voted for independence from Yugoslavia in December 1990, to be recognised twelve months later with relatively little resistance, but Croatia and Bosnia-Herzegovina had also declared their independence and most of the former Yugoslavia was edging towards a bloody and lengthy civil war. 1991 saw the destruction of Vukovar and the shelling of Osijek, Vinkovci, Karlovac, Split and Dubrovnik. The whole of our target area was in a state of flux, or worse, with little certainty as to how things would work out. The subsequent problems still haunt the former Yugoslavia and will do for many years to come. In the last decade of the twentieth century they seemed to have no end.

Several of our graduates found themselves involved in these events, both in the former Yugoslavia itself and also at the International Tribunal at The Hague. One of these was Marcus Richardson, who took advantage of the opportunity to study Serbo-Croat at Nottingham, conscious that war was raging in the former Yugoslavia and that he knew almost nothing about the language, culture and history of that part of Europe. When Marcus graduated in 1996, David Norris encouraged him to apply for the post of English lector at The University of Belgrade. He soon found that Belgrade was not the hostile, violent, depressing place that he had feared and he was overwhelmed by the friendliness of the people. Before long, he found himself caught up in protests against the Milošević régime. At the time it felt as though he was witnessing and participating in a genuine revolution. On returning home, he went to Oxford for a taught Master's degree in Slavonic Studies, after which David Norris drew his attention to the fact that the United Nations International Criminal Tribunal for the former Yugoslavia was looking for translators from Bosnian/Croatian/Serbian into English. Ten years later he is still working for the Tribunal, one of the longest serving members of his department, and has meanwhile also kept up his Russian. He remembers with gratitude being taught by Višnja Josipović (1992-93), Dave Norris and Peter Herrity, as well as the support that he received from his tutor, Cynthia Marsh. In his judgement, Nottingham is unbeatable for the expertise offered by the staff and the overall student experience.

Unfortunately, Višnja and Damir Kalogjera (1993-94) brought the traditional flow of lectors and lectrices from Zagreb to a close. In 1994, we had regretfully to discontinue the Zagreb link. For historical reasons combined with our own current funding arrangements, we found ourselves with a full-time Serbo-Croat lectorship for a handful of students, combined with the equivalent sum to distribute among three part-time Russian lectrices for a much larger number. This position could no longer be sustained as student recruitment on Russian courses began to rise. Fortunately, Vladislava Ribnikar was available to take over their role and she has remained to give sterling service to the department ever since, adding her expertise in Critical Theory to the attributes usually expected of a lectrice. But we were deeply sorry to have to sever the Zagreb link at a time when our Croatian colleagues felt beleaguered as a result of the developing political situation in the former Yugoslavia. Such straws in the wind are a sufficient reminder that although our overall position was increasingly secure, our financial position was always extremely tight.

Other students of the time have memories of events in Russia. In 1993, Alex Harrington went to Moscow and attended classes at the Moscow State University (MGU), lodging with a family on the Lomonovskii Prospekt, not far from the statue of Gagarin. It coincided with the power struggle between Khasbulatov and Yeltsin. She vividly remembers visiting a friend who lived not far from the White House and being confronted by rows of riot police as she emerged from the Metro station. In the same year, James Tyrrell spent three months in Minsk. They arrived in Moscow on 17 September when there was no sign of the events about to unfold, and left for Minsk two days later. They heard about the siege of the White House but it was taken very calmly in Minsk, where life remained unchanged as the events in Moscow unfolded, and the same apparatchiki remained in charge.

During this period Elena Anderson (1991-5), Janna Kazarian (1992-4), Irina Shlumukova (1994-2005), Svetlana Clark (1995–present) and Natasha McGrath (1997-9) succeeded one another as our Russian lectrices. Irina was to leave us for Birmingham in 2005 while Svetlana, under a new type of contract, continues to work happily and effectively in the department to the present day.

In the first half of the decade, we also benefited from the presence in the department of two guest lecturers from Russia, Viktoria Tikhomirova (1993-94), who was head of the Department of Slavonic Languages at Moscow University and had made our acquaintance while on an exchange course in the School of Education, and the distinguished specialist in Russian Literature and Music, Marietta Tourian, who came to us on a three months' IRCEES research fellowship from St Petersburg in 1994.

Adriana Krstič continued the tradition of lectrices from Ljubljana from 1993 to 1997. Happily, the arrangement had survived the tricky period of transition from a Communist order to a parliamentary democracy and a market economy that marked the break-up of the old Yugoslavia.

The historic changes in the former Soviet sphere coincided with reforms in higher education at home. As previously indicated, the turn of the decade was in many ways a watershed in the evolution of UK universities. This is not the place to analyse or even to describe the nature of these changes in any detail, but some account must be given, because they fundamentally reshaped our courses and the student experience.

The whole university world was undergoing radical changes and Nottingham, under its new Vice-Chancellor, was usually ahead of the field. In 1991-92, the old degree structure that had existed at Nottingham since Lavrin's day was finally abandoned, and modularisation came into force. So did semesters, though terms somehow survived uneasily alongside them. The academic year was divided into two semesters for academic purposes, with the first semester starting in late September and second at the beginning of February, while the usual breaks continued to be taken at Christmas and Easter, fracturing the first and second semesters at those points. Each module would last one semester and would count for a prescribed number of credits, at the end of which it would be examined. Students had to accumulate a given number of credits in order to graduate. A wide variety of new forms of assessment now also began to be introduced, with a growing preference for various forms of course work assessment. All this had to be set out clearly in the Module Handbook for each module, with its aims and objectives, dates for submission of work, penalties to be exacted for late submission, and a rigid timetable of lectures, seminars and assignments. Similar things were going on at other universities at the same time. The idea was to create greater flexibility for students to design their own courses and for transfer from one institution to another. It would also, it was thought, make it easier for students to spend time abroad at universities that operated a semester system, and for international students to spend short periods at Nottingham.

It was a response to the changing environment in which universities operated and led to far-reaching changes in universities themselves. The old assumptions about the background, motivation and education of first year undergraduates had to be completely revised, as students now often came up to read Arts degrees with little knowledge of history, philosophy, the Biblical or classical traditions, literature or grammar (of their own language or any other). Moreover, the range widened to include more mature students, and a greater ability range, while the University as a whole recruited a growing number of students from overseas with very different assumptions about the nature of education itself. It was not only students' background that had changed. So did their expectations. Increasingly they demanded, and we provided, carefully defined tasks, with clear aims and objectives, from which we dared not diverge for fear of appeals. We could not, as in the old days, go off at a tangent in our lectures to indulge a particular interest that we shared with the class; nor could we revise the course half way through to acknowledge that some subjects were proving more productive with this particular group than others. Nor for that matter could we afford to be ill in term-time, because the timetable was so tight that it would be virtually impossible to reschedule the missed hours.

Another factor that had to be taken into account was the worsening financial position of our students. As grants were phased out and replaced by student loans from 1990-91, students increasingly found paid employment in the evenings, at weekends and during vacations, times that we had traditionally assumed were available for reading, study and writing, as well as for learning those non-academic social skills that should have been transferable to the world of employment.

These pressures not only crowded out the time available for academic work, but also the time traditionally devoted to extra-curricular activities. It was as students that our generation had learnt how to speak in public, chair meetings, organise national conferences and practise other leadership skills that were to stand us in good stead in our subsequent careers. Such skills could be acquired in the activities of the Students' Union and its many clubs and societies. Now there would be all too little time for students to gain these experiences.

We had always noticed that under the old system students' motivation, and regular attendance at classes, seemed to flag in the second year, when they were no longer fresh and enthusiastic and not yet confronted by final examinations. Under the modular system, every module was to be examined at its close and every second year module would count in one way or another towards the final degree classification, so a consistent effort would have to be made throughout the course. Now, success would depend upon constant attention to work throughout the three years at Nottingham and not on performance in a month's diet of written examinations at the very end, as they had been in earlier times.

At first sight, the new system would work to the disadvantage of our beginners. Our so-called intensive language courses had always involved far fewer contact hours than those in the polytechnics. Now the hours permissible for the teaching of individual modules were to be further curtailed. Something had to be done about this, for if there was a common complaint about our courses, it came from students whose interest was in the language itself and who professed no particular interest in literature or history. The new system did in fact make it possible for students to choose a combination of modules that all but eliminated literature, though we continued to try to persuade them that an essential part of their education in Slavonic studies, and of understanding Russians and Yugoslavs, was familiarity with the great works of literature from the target countries, especially those that had achieved international status. We usually succeeded in this, but in addition we incorporated an oral element in virtually all our language courses for the first time.

The variety of degree courses offered by the department in various combinations was also to increase. In addition to Single Honours Russian for post-A-level students and for beginners, there were Joint Honours post-A-level courses in Russian and French, German, Hispanic Studies, Portuguese, or History; while beginners could take the same combinations apart from the one with Portuguese. The department itself offered Joint Honours with Serbo-Croat. Other possibilities included the study of Russian and East European Studies, drawing on the expertise available through members of IRSCEES, and the recently established degree courses in Modern European Studies and Modern Language Studies. Meanwhile, Russian, Serbo-Croat and Slovene were offered as minor subjects within other degree courses, including modules that could be studied by non-linguists using translated texts.

There were of course disadvantages to the new system. Among the casualties was the post-examination period in the summer, which Cynthia Marsh had used to rehearse and produce the departmental play. For a while at least it proved possible to incorporate it in one of the new modules. Gorkii's *Vassa Zheleznova* (a project with the Lace Market Theatre) was produced in 1994, with Chekhov's *Seagull* (also in 1994) and Andreev's *Love Your Neighbour* (1995). The Russian play, along with the first year study visit to the Soviet Union, and (of course) the coffee room, had done more than anything else to create the sense of camaraderie that had long prevailed in the department.

The next few years saw the new system bedding in. Among the new modules were Wendy Rosslyn's first year Learning Strategies course, and final year courses on Intertextuality: Pushkin and Akhmatova, and Russian for Business Situations, Cynthia Marsh's new course on Transferable Skills, and David Norris's on Theories of Literature. Cynthia's innovative language teaching was later to win her a Dearing Award.

One noticeable feature of the new system was that more good students achieved an upper second honours degree class, with the result that the threshold of disappointment moved up too. In the past, the distribution between upper and lower second class degrees had been much more even and both were regarded as 'good honours degrees' for teaching purposes. Some have inevitably ascribed this to a process of 'dumbing down'. Most university lecturers would probably disagree with this. I have no doubt that the quality of the best students under the new system was as high as it had ever been, and some of my best memories of intelligent, well-motivated undergraduates relate to the end of my career. Certainly, the focus was narrowed and much more attention was now paid to teaching and acquiring relevant skills, skills which in the past students had been expected somehow to acquire unaided. The Teaching Quality Assessment process saw to this. The result was that a growing number of graduates really did acquire the transferable skills that were so much talked about. No longer were essays presented in semi-legible handwriting on sheets of paper of varying size: they now had to be word-processed, spellchecked, and have proper footnotes, references and lists of works consulted, all in accordance with the departmental style sheet—a document that also included detailed advice on avoiding plagiarism. And, when returned, essays were accompanied by comments from the tutor under a number of different headings on a standard sheet. A degree of professionalism had entered both student work and staff feedback that had previously been lacking.

This was in some measure due to the spread of computer technology and the increasing availability of word processors. Students of the time will remember the room full of word processors on our corridor almost opposite my office. It is still there in 2008, though the department has moved. But it was, in fact, only just before my retirement in 1997 that each member of staff eventually had a word processor on his or her own desk. The University was slow to accept that the Arts Faculty needed the new technology as much as the scientists, who usually had other funds to call on. Even lecture rooms equipped with slide projectors were the exception in 1997, and PowerPoint was still a thing of the future. Still, there was no doubt about the direction things were taking. Before long our old-fashioned world of books and libraries would be incorporated into a brave new world of Information Services.

If the new system imposed extra burdens on students, the same was true for staff. Russian Days for schools went by the board: flexibility on one front had led to inflexibility on others. It is perhaps symptomatic that the last major international conference in the twentieth century organised wholly by members of the department took place from 16 to 19 April, 1991. This was the Bulgakov Centenary Conference, organised by Lesley Milne and her Cambridge colleague Julie Curtis. About 50 distinguished Bulgakov specialists from Canada, Czechoslovakia, France, Germany, Hungary, India, Poland, Russia, the UK and the USA took part and the proceedings were, for the most part, published in *Bulgakov, the Novelist-Playwright* (1995). In spite of the excellent cooking provided by Florence Boot Hall, the vegetable lasagne served for lunch on Wednesday, 17 July was identified as the source of an outbreak of food poisoning that laid low a number of eminent participants. Fortunately, all survived and none sued.

However, IRSCEES was active on the conference front, and other opportunities for interdisciplinary conferences presented themselves.

In 1994, a conference on Fantastic Realism and Russian Literature was attended by colleagues from Nottingham, Sheffield, Bristol, Derby, St Petersburg and Belgrade. In 1995, a conference on D. H. Lawrence and Russia, organised by the D.H. Lawrence Centre, involved members of the department and drew invited Slavists from Britain and the USA. In 1996, IRSCEES celebrated its tenth anniversary with a conference organised by the department, attended by distinguished outside speakers including Professor Michael Kaser and Sir Norman Wooding. In the same year, the Russian writer Vladimir Voinovich, on whom Rachel Farmer had written her PhD thesis (1997), lectured in the department, as did visiting Slavists from other countries. All the staff participated actively in conferences abroad and maintained research links with specialists in the target countries and around the world.

The number of students on the MA by Research course established in 1994 was increasing and some of them proceeded to PhDs, gaining teaching experience in the process. The RAE submission for 1996 counted eleven. A regular staff and postgraduate research seminar was established, all under the eye of a newly established departmental Research Committee.

And research publications were also continuing to appear. Between 1990 and 1996, members of staff had a total of nineteen volumes published, of which seven were original monographs and the remainder edited collections of articles or translations. Among these were Nicholas Luker's *In Defence of a Reputation: essays on the early prose of Mikhail Artsybashev* (1990); *The Short Story in Russia 1900-1917* (1991); *From Furmanov to Sholokhov, an anthology of the classics of socialist realism* (1992); *Yury Miloslavsky. Urban Romances, edited and translated by Nicholas Luker and others* (1994); *After the Watershed: Russian Prose 1917-1927* (1996). There also appeared Cynthia Marsh's *File on Gorky* (1993); David Norris's *The Novels of Miloš Crnjanjski: an approach through time* (1990) and *Teach Yourself Serbo-Croat* (1993). My own *Dostoyevsky after Bakhtin* was published in 1990 and *Dostoevsky and the Twentieth Century: The Ljubljana Papers* in 1993.

In 1991, Peter Herrity had been promoted to a readership and he became a member of the editorial board of Studia Slavica Savariensia in 1992, the same year in which Wendy Rosslyn was awarded the Heldt Prize for the best translation by a woman in Slavic Studies by the American Association for the Advancement of Slavic Studies, and became joint editor of *The Central and East European Gender Studies (UK) Newsletter*. By 1996 she had completed her book on Anna Bunina (1997).

Meanwhile Lesley Milne had become a member of the International Academic Council of the State Russian University for the Humanities in Moscow, Cynthia Marsh was diversifying into drama as performance and, from 1995 to 1998, I served as President of the International Dostoevsky Society.

Apart from reading for publishers, refereeing for journals, external examining for other universities and the reading of papers at conferences in this country and abroad, members of the department gave guest lectures between 1990 and 1996 at the universities of Ljubljana, Szombathely, Moscow and Klagenfurt (Peter Herrity); Amsterdam, Otago, Wellington and Auckland (Nicholas Luker); Leningrad and Kiev (Lesley Milne); Belgrade and Monash (David Norris); Marburg (Wendy Rosslyn); and Oxford (the 1991 Ilchester Lecture), Oslo, Moscow, Bergen, Lille and Queensland (myself). Nicholas Luker, Wendy Rosslyn and I also spent periods lecturing at universities overseas.

In 1994 the Vice-Chancellor appointed me founding Associate Dean of the Graduate School and I was also Acting Dean of Arts again for a spell. As indicated previously, substantial outside commitments, in which the University wished to support me, led to my asking Peter to take over the headship of the department again from 1995.

One of these outside commitments was membership of a new Review of Russian and East European Studies, this time undertaken by the Higher Education Funding Council (HEFCE)[37] itself, and therefore more likely to be properly funded. In the event, HEFCE, recognising the need to re-equip the field to deal with the reconfiguration of the old Soviet bloc, was to allocate £2,475,000 to fund thirty-three new posts for an initial three years. Nottingham was to secure three of these. Katy Pickvance was to join the Department of Geography and the School of Social Studies, Vanessa Pupovac (a graduate of our own department) was appointed to the Department of Politics and the School of Social Studies, and Adam Swain joined the Department of Geography and the School of Management and Finance. Each of these posts carried a commitment to admit students studying for degrees in social sciences with a Slavonic language component taught by our department, and an additional allocation of student places was made to enable this. It was a fitting development to greet the tenth anniversary of IRSCEES in 1996 and marked its most substantial success to date. The experiment proved less successful than had been hoped but a number of students took advantage of the new opportunities.

Meanwhile, 1995 had seen a visitation from a panel set up by the Teaching Quality Assurance Agency. At the time, we were pleased with the result, doing as well or better than other Modern Language Departments at Nottingham under a new system of assessment, which nobody as yet quite understood. We scored nineteen out of a possible twenty-four points. This subsequently turned out to be disappointing by comparison with the dazzling results of similar Russian and Slavonic departments in other universities. It may have been partly because we were overwhelmed by the phenomenal amount of paperwork required (TQA officers in some departments were reported to be on the verge of nervous breakdowns and whole shelves were lined with bulky files of material required—though hardly read exhaustively—by the visiting teams); but it may not be irrelevant that only one member of our visiting panel came from a department remotely like our own.

Our own students, past and present, were glowing in their support and it soon became clear that even our competitors thought that we had been hard done by. However, the outcome of the TQA exercise was by no means a disaster, and it did no damage to our credibility or to our ability to attract excellent students. Numbers remained buoyant. As James Tyrrell, who had retired from the Law in 1990 to become one of a number of mature students in the department, wrote some years later, 'I am grateful to all who taught me for their devotion and never-failing helpfulness. I think the courses I did were excellent, and I cannot think how they might be improved.'

1996 brought even better news, with the results of the latest Research Assessment Exercise. Of all the departments of Russian and Slavonic Studies in the United Kingdom, Nottingham's was the only one to score a 5*A. The 5* meant that its research was deemed to have reached international excellence in a

---

[37] So far as England was concerned, HEFCE had taken over from the UFC in 1992. Wales, Scotland and Northern Ireland had their own arrangements.

majority of its areas of activity and national excellence in all the others. The A meant that its entire full-time academic staff had been included in the submission.

I remember Peter Herrity telling me how he had attended the meeting of heads of department in the Great Hall where the Nottingham results were flashed up onto the screen, beginning with the 5*s and proceeding downwards. For some reason, he did not notice Slavonic Studies on the first slide and he sat there growing more and more nervous as the lower results were announced and Slavonic Studies failed to appear among them. It was only when colleagues started to congratulate him after the meeting that the penny dropped. How pleased Janko Lavrin and his successors would have been, especially with the fact that the department's work in Serbo-Croat and Slovene had played a full part. Colin Campbell was also delighted with our success. As a member of the panel myself[38] I had of course known this gratifying result for some time but was bound by confidentiality.

With IRSCEES ten years old and attracting fresh funding, with the department doing creditably in the TQA and outstandingly well in the RAE, with undergraduate recruitment buoyant and the new modular system bedded in, with other activities reaching fruition, with several colleagues poised for professorships, it seemed a good time to hand over to a successor. I therefore opted to take early retirement in February 1997 in order to devote myself full-time to research for the next decade. Although there was to be a brief hiatus before a new professor would be appointed, I knew that the department would be in safe hands.

In retirement, I continued to research and publish, and supervised Sarah Young's doctoral thesis on Dostoevsky; Sarah was subsequently appointed to an assistant professorship at The University of Toronto, from which she moved in 2007 to the School of Slavonic and East European Studies (SSEES) at University College, London. I also had the pleasure of assisting Wendy Rosslyn in the supervision of Alex Harrington's PhD thesis on Akhmatova. Subsequently, Alex was appointed to a lectureship in Russian at Durham.

1998 saw the publication of *The Cambridge Companion to the Classic Russian Novel*, which I had co-edited with Robin Feuer Miller of Brandeis University, and of a Russian translation of *Dostoevsky after Bakhtin*. 2004 saw the appearance of a Chinese edition of the same work, while in 2005 *Dostoevsky and the Dynamics of Religious Experience* appeared. By this time, various of my articles were appearing in publications of the Russian Academy and other overseas presses.

I was more than delighted when in the same year over twenty colleagues from ten different countries presented me with a Festschrift edited by Sarah Young and Lesley Milne and published by James Muckle, the owner of Bramcote Press.[39] In the following year I was asked to collaborate in the television programme on Janko Lavrin to be broadcast by Slovene TV in February 2007, an enterprise that brought me together once again with the Lavrin family and became the starting point for this book.

---

[38] For those unfamiliar with the procedures of the RAE panels, I should make it clear that members are barred from discussions of their own departments and required to leave the room while they are taking place.
[39] Sarah Young and Lesley Milne (2006).

For the first decade of my retirement, during which I was styled professor emeritus in residence, I continued to be heavily involved in professional activities. In 2002, I became a member of the International Commission for the History of Slavic Studies and in 2005 I was elected an Honorary Life Member of British Association of Slavonic and East European Studies which, together with Martin McCauley, I had brought into being in 1988. At that point health factors obliged me to pause and, on reviewing the situation later, I realised that I had fallen too far behind in my specialist subjects to resume research and publication in these areas: the present project resulted.

It was now eighty years since Basil Slepchenko had taken up his lectureship in Russian at The University College. Up to and including the point of my retirement, the department had, like most Arts Departments, had only one professor at any given time, and had been exceptional in allowing a rotation of the headship.

Now all this was to change, together with continual progress on the curricular and technological fronts that would require the input of another author better acquainted with the current scene than I am. Russia's position on the international map was also to see radical changes, as was the situation of the new states carved out of the old Yugoslavia. Inevitably, student experience was to mirror all these developments and the courses offered would be supplemented and modified to keep pace with changing academic interests, new technological developments, fresh opportunities for travel, and the march of history.

During my tenure, Peter had acted as head of department from January 1989 to summer 1992 and again from summer 1994 to February 1997. Following my retirement that month, he became head of department in his own right until his own retirement in 2001, having meanwhile been promoted to a professorship in 1999, following completion of his *Slovene: a Comprehensive Grammar*, to be published by Routledge in 2000. To him and his colleagues belong the last three years of the twentieth century.

Peter I

(1997–2001)

IN February 1997, Peter Herrity became head of department in his own right and was promoted to the chair of Slavonic Languages in 1999, retiring in 2001. Looked at another way, he had already served as head of department for six years and was now to give independent leadership for the last three years of the century, during which a collection of his articles (*Jezička razmatranija, Zavod za udžbenike i nastavna sredstva*, 1991) appeared in Serbian translation, as well as his *Slovene, a Comprehensive Grammar* (2001).

Peter had been educated at Hastings Grammar School and had done his National Service in the Intelligence Branch of the Royal Air Force, where he learnt his Russian. From 1957 to 1961 he worked at the Foreign Office, following which he obtained a first class Honours degree in Russian Language and Literature at King's College, London, with French as his subsidiary subject. In 1965, he had registered for a PhD at SSEES on the Serbian literary language of the eighteenth century, and had spent the year 1966-7 at The University of Novy Sad, followed by five months in 1968 at The University of Moscow (MGU). The degree was awarded in 1974. In the meantime (1968-71), he had been employed as lecturer in Russian at the New University of Ulster, to be appointed lecturer in Russian and Serbo-Croat at Nottingham in 1971, following Gerald Stone's departure for Cambridge.

As we have seen, he had been promoted to the grade of senior lecturer in 1977 and to a readership in 1991. Unlike previous heads of department, his chosen field was that of Historical Linguistics and Comparative Slavonic Philology, though some of the theses he had supervised related to the contemporary language. In 2004, as the department celebrated thirty years of the Slovene lectorate in the presence of the Slovene Ambassador, Peter was presented with an award from The University of Ljubljana in recognition of his contribution to Slovene studies. He continues in retirement to pursue his academic interests and to publish in the field of Slovene language. Between fifteen and twenty students continue to study Slovene in the department each year, most, but not all of them, reading for degrees in Modern Languages.

Although there were no changes in the permanent lecturing staff during these three years, an important innovation was the establishment of a lector's post for the teaching of the Polish language. Monika Savage, herself a graduate of the department, was appointed in 1998. In fact, Polish had occasionally been taught at Nottingham before. Janko Lavrin had offered Polish classes. Leszek Kukulski had taken an extra-curricular class in 1963-4. Peter himself had supervised Zofia Weaver's PhD thesis on *A Semantic Analysis of Comparative Structures in the Modern Polish Language* (1980), but this was the first time that Polish had been offered as part of the undergraduate degree programme.

Natasha McGrath joined the group of Russian lectrices from 1997 to 1999 and Sabina Grahek was Slovene lectrice from 1997 to 2000. Sabina knew the area of Slovenia where Janko Lavrin had been born and where relatives still lived, and contributed some fascinating contemporary photographs to the departmental archive.

One of the last public events in the old department on A floor of the Trent Building was the Exhibition associated with the University's Jubilee Day Celebration in 1999, when a programme of events was laid on in the department for graduates of Slavonic Studies. Monica Partridge was in attendance, as well as current staff and a host of graduates of many different generations.

The same year saw David Norris's promotion to senior lecturer and the advertisement of the chair that I had vacated two years previously. To my delight, the successful candidate was Lesley Milne, who became head of department herself on Peter's retirement in 2001. Lesley had graduated with First Class Honours in Modern Languages at Cambridge in 1969 and had stayed to study for her PhD at Girton College from 1969 to 1972, followed by 10 months at Moscow University (MGU) in 1970-71, and a further five months in 1972-73. Following the award of her doctorate in 1975, she was a lecturer in the Department of Russian at The University of Hull from 1975 to 1989 when, as we have seen, she transferred to Nottingham, being promoted to a readership in 1993. By this time, she had established an international reputation for her work on modern Russian literature, in particular the life and work of Mikhail Bulgakov. In 2000, assisted by Evgeny Dobrenko, Rachel Farmer and other colleagues, she was to organise and preside over a highly successful international conference at Nottingham on Russian Humour and Satire, attended by leading Russian scholars. In Lesley, the department had acquired a new professor with the energy and imagination to lead it into the new century. Once again the University had advertised internationally for a professor of Russian and discovered that the best candidate was already in its midst.

It was to be the department's last three years on the ground floor of the Trent Building, marking the disappearance of the famed coffee room, the display cabinet, the gloomy pictures of nineteenth-century writers (some of them now replaced by reproductions of paintings by Kandinsky) and the departmental seminar room, where generations of undergraduates had written their essays or thumbed through tattered dictionaries attempting their prose translations. For some time now, the Seminar Room had been timetabled for occasional classes, and used increasingly by other departments besides our own.

There was also soon to be an end to the arrangement by which each department would have its own secretary with her separate room, where she could be consulted at any time. Jane Dewick reduced her commitment in 1998 and was joined on a part-time basis by Sue Drury until 2001, before retiring herself in 2003. Alex Harrington recalls that it would be impossible to imagine a more efficient or warmer departmental secretary than Jane and her farewell party at the home of Wendy Rosslyn and her husband Roger Bartlett (himself a professor of Russian History at SSEES) was a suitably warm occasion.

Alex was not the only one to regret the move to Floor B when it took place in May 2000. She had been a member of the department in various capacities from 1991 to 2001, collecting a BA, MA and PhD en route, as well as teaching undergraduates. Throughout that period, she recalls, the department's location on the ground floor of the Trent Building had given it a definite identity. Students would lounge around in the coffee room between classes, leave belongings behind to pick up later, and chat to members of staff and students who came in. In particular she laments the department's loss of autonomous space and the University's increasingly corporate feel. Fortunately, she reflects, many things remained constant, especially the commitment and talent of the teaching staff.

Other graduates confirm this impression. Corinne Redwood, who went on to work in the Registrar's Office, recalls that one of the best things about the department at this time was the continuing sense of community, partly due to its size, but also to the people and the staff.

Kate Curran, who graduated in 2000, also remembers how friendly and helpful the staff were. She remembers how Dr Luker made them jump with fright with his vivid storytelling in literature lectures; the pleasurable challenge of Svetlana Clark's lessons; and her first year trip to Russia and the year abroad in St Petersburg where she taught English. After working for a while for a charity she took the PGCE course under Dr Philip Hood at Nottingham, and worked in Nottingham schools for three years teaching Modern Languages (mostly French and German). She managed to introduce Russian as a lunchtime club and as an optional subject for beginners at the Bluecoat School between 2005 and 2007. She is one of many who have spent part or the whole of their careers teaching Russian in schools.

With minor adjustments, the same words might have been written by students almost half a century earlier. Now, however, they were living in a much more complex and structured world, in which paperwork proliferated and communications with staff were conducted as often by email, or during prescribed office hours, as by knocking at one's tutor's door as one passed.

During these last few years of the century, much time and attention had to be given to arrangements for new appointments as well as to the physical move, but everything else went on very much as usual.

To be continued...

I shall make no attempt to chronicle the next decade in any detail, a period during which the department, now transferred to C Floor in the Trent Building, and renamed The Department of Russian and Slavonic Studies, continues to make strides in both research and teaching within the context of the newly established School of Modern Languages, of which Lesley Milne is the current Head.

As we have seen, the summer of 2000 saw a major conference on Two Centuries of Russian Humour and Satire, organised by Lesley and attended by almost sixty participants, including the Russian writers Liudmila Petrushevskaia and Vladimir Voinovich. In 2001, the University awarded an honorary doctorate to Voinovich and the Research Assessment Exercise brought a grade 5. Wendy

Rosslyn (2002) and Cynthia Marsh (2006) have both been promoted to Chairs and have both had turns at heading the department. At the time of writing, this role falls to Cynthia.

New staff have arrived and two have come and gone again. Evgeny Dobrenko was appointed to a readership in 2000, and promoted to a professorship in 2003, but left for Sheffield in 2007. Dejan Djokić also worked in the department from 2003 to 2007. They both brought considerable strengths to the department, which it was sorry to lose.

Meanwhile, 2007 saw the appointment of Polly McMichael, Siggy Frank[1] and Vladimir Zorić to lectureships, and Rolf Hellebust to a senior lectureship or, as it is now called, an associate professorship. Just before this book went to press, Monica White, a medieval historian from Stanford, was appointed to the vacancy left on the retirement of Wendy Rosslyn. She is expected to take up her post in September 2008. Alenka Jensterle-Doležal was Slovene lectrice from 2000 to 2001; Andreja Ponikvar from 2001 to 2005, and Ivana Petric Lasnik from 2005 to the present.[2] Ivana has been particularly active in association with the celebration of Slovene Culture at Nottingham and has given generous help with the Slovene references in this book.

Following a highly successful conference, a collection of articles on the former Soviet bloc countries entitled *After the Fall*, edited by Roy Bradshaw, Nick Manning and Stuart Thompstone, and published by Olearius, St Petersburg and Nottingham, was published in 2003 under the auspices of IRSCEES. The Institute, now renamed NIREES (The Nottingham Institute for Russian and East European Studies) in 2006, continues to be active under the chairmanship of Adam Swain.

By way of summary, and at the risk of some repetition, I shall give the final word to a recent graduate. Michael Snook, who graduated in Russian and Serbo-Croat as recently as 2007, writes in response to our enquiry for graduates' impressions of their period of study:

> My fondest memories of my time at Nottingham are of the staff, the friendly atmosphere of the department and of the luck I had in being based mainly in the Trent Building. In terms of staff, I feel glad to have encountered and learned from such an enthusiastic and knowledgeable group of teachers. In particular I remember that staff made students feel welcome; they always said hello in the corridor and would open their door to you whenever you needed their help [...] I guess we were and are the product of a generation focused more on marks, results, exams and ticking boxes rather than being led by our instincts, learning for fun and out of an interest in the subject. I know that several members of staff expressed their regrets that this was the case. Nonetheless I feel the great thing about my time studying Russian/Serbian at Nottingham was a sense of unity. Everyone knew everyone in the Slavonic Department and we all got on well.

He goes on to mention his special gratitude to Nick Luker, David Norris and Vladislava Ribnikar, Svetlana Clark and Wendy Rosslyn, Nick for his unfailing

---

[1] Siggy is due to take up her post in 2009, when her Leverhulme Fellowship expires.
[2] By arrangement between the two departments, Andreja and Ivana have both visited SSEES at UCL to teach a class on Mondays.

support, encouragement and good humour, David and Vladislava who pushed him to reach degree standard in three years, Svetlana for her no-nonsense approach to oral lessons and Wendy for the delights of poetry. He felt privileged to have studied Slovene in his final year. The teacher, Ivana Petric Lasnik, was simply superb—enthusiastic, friendly, knowledgeable. Other students, needless to say, have particularly warm memories of other members of staff. Like other students, Michael, who is now studying Law in London, had the good fortune to witness the reaction to historical events while he was abroad. He was in Belgrade when Slobodan Milosević died and Montenegro became independent.

He concludes:

> I have no regrets whatsoever about my decision to study there [at Nottingham]. My most vivid memories are of the friendly atmosphere, the excellent teaching, the great fun I had on my year abroad, and the skills I learned which I hope to put to good use in the future.

And, allowing for differences in circumstance, that is very much what the majority of students of Slavonic Studies at Nottingham University in the twentieth century have told us. It augurs well that they are still saying it in the twenty-first.

As we have seen, the experience of reading Slavonic Studies at Nottingham, as in other universities, has radically changed over the years. Some changes have to do with the subject itself. The languages and the cultures have themselves evolved and been affected by revolutionary political changes in the countries involved. Though they have left deep traces on these countries, the Soviet Union and its post-1945 sphere of influence in Eastern Europe have come and gone.

Other changes have to do with the evolution of UK universities and the structure of their degrees, the intellectual demands they make and the perceived purpose of a university education and the relationship between teacher and taught. It would have been interesting to trace the reasons students have given for taking up Slavonic Studies over the years, but this lay outside our remit.

Yet other changes have to do with the technological means at the disposal of staff and students in the course of study, and the relative ease of communication between the UK and the target countries in the present-day world. All these and other factors have led to changes in the content of courses in Slavonic Studies and the research interests of academic staff. Some courses, thought essential in the past, have now been abandoned and others, that might have been thought peripheral—such as art and architecture, critical theory, film, popular culture and émigré literature—have achieved new prominence. Some, like medieval literature, have disappeared for a while, only to be restored. It goes without saying that the range of Soviet literature studied today differs greatly from that studied under Lavrin or Michael Futrell.

With the retirement of the generation of academic staff whose careers began in the 1960s and 1970s, a living sense of continuity with the department's roots will finally be broken. But what we can be sure of, as this story shows, is that the future will bring new and unexpected developments, and no doubt fresh crises, and that the department will enthusiastically adjust to meet them. *Forsan et haec olim meminisse iuvabit.*

APPENDIX

THIS list of staff of the department from 1915 to the present is as complete and accurate as it has been possible to make it. We apologise for errors and omissions and should welcome corrections. Deaths have been indicated in the footnotes only where we have definite knowledge. A decision was taken to omit those who have lectured in the department from time to time on a part-time or short-term basis, as it proved impossible to compile a complete and reliable list. The following abbreviations have been used: P professor; R reader; SL senior lecturer; FT full-time; PT part-time; H of D head of department

Permanent lecturing staff

Basil Slepchenko[1]	1915-18
Janko Lavrin[2]	1918-42, 1944-52
(P 1921)	
Monica Partridge[3]	1947-80
(SL 1962, P and H of D 1967-80)	
John Fennell[4]	1952-7
(R, H of D)	
Michael Futrell	1956-66
Frank Seeley[5]	1957-67
(SL, H of D)	
Bernard Johnson[6]	1960-5
Gerald Smith	1964-71
Gerald Stone	1965-71
Nicholas Anning [7]	1966-70
Malcolm Jones	1967-97
(SL 1973; P 1980; H of D 1980-8, 1992-5)	
Christopher Mills[8]	1969-71
Nicholas Luker	1970-present
(SL 1988)	

---

[1] Died probably in early 1950s.
[2] Died 13 August 1986.
[3] Died 19 March 2008.
[4] Died 9 August 1992.
[5] Died 12 June 2000.
[6] Died 8 June 2003.
[7] Died 2003. In fact, I think he left Nottingham in December 1969.
[8] Died mid-1970s.

Wendy Rosslyn	1971-2008
(R 1993; P 2002; H of D 2004-5, 2006-7)	
Peter Herrity	1971-2001
(SL 1977; P 1999; H of D[9] 1989-92,	
* 1995-97 1997-2001)*	
Cynthia Marsh	1972-present
(SL 1991; P 2006; H of D 2005-6,	
* 2007-present)*	
David Norris	1981-present
(SL 1999)	
Lesley Milne	1989-present
(R 1992; P 1999; H of D 2001-4)	
Evgeny Dobrenko	2000-7
(R; P 2003)	
Dejan Djokić	2003-7
Polly McMichael	2007-present
Rolf Hellebust	2007-present
(SL)	
Vladimir Zorić	2007-present
Monica White	from 2008
Siggy Frank	from 2009

Departmental secretaries[10]

FT Sheila ?	19??-69
FT Jane Dewick	1969-71
FT Pat Morris	1971-4
FT Irene Dale	1974-5
FT Ann Collins (née Hall)	1975-81
FT Jolanta Murjas	1981-3
FT Heather Phoenix	1983-6
FT Carole Eyre	1986-90
FT Jane Dewick	1990-8, PT 1998-2003
PT Melanie Cumpston*	1995-6
PT Stephanie Brunger*	1996-7
PT Sue Drury	1998-2001
PT Lisa Murphy	2001-07
PT Mary Browne	2003-4
PT Ann Howe	2004-present
PT Leilani April	2006-present

Lectors and lectrices, language assistants, 'Soviet lecturers', etc.

Russian

FT V. P. Saulus	1955-60
FT Arian Kirillov	1960-4

---

[9] Peter Herrity served as head of department while MVJ was engaged in other activities on behalf of the University.

[10] From late 1960s. Records are lacking for the earlier period.

I am delighted now to be able to send you a copy of *Slavianskii mir* and thank you for your cheque. I shall be interested to read any comments you may have.

I look forward to meeting you at the reunion if you are able to come.

Malcolm Jones

If your copy is in any way damaged in the post, please do not return it, but keep it for the moment and inform James Muckle at Bramcote Press, 81 Rayneham Road, Ilkeston DE7 8RJ (or jymuckle@ilk81rr.orangehome.co.uk). It will be replaced.

FT Amelia Cantelli	1964-72
FT Nikolai Naidenov	1965-80
FT Angelina Kochetkova†	1965-7
FT Tamara Amirova†	1967-8
FT Irina Kireyeva†	1968-9
FT Ina Semyonova†	1969 (autumn term only)
FT Lyudmila Dyachkova†	1970-2
FT Valentina Kleshcheva†	1972-3
FT Viktoria Surzhina†	1973-5
FT Iulia Bulavina†	1975-6
FT Natasha Fyodorova†	1976-7
FT Nelli Shevelyeva†	1977-8
FT Svetlana Navalnaya†	1978-9
FT Tamara Kapitonova†	1979-80
FT Olga Shcherbakova†	1980-1
FT Liza Lacy	1980-4, and PT 1987-present
FT Marina Akhvlediani†	1981-82
PT Marina Firth	1984-86
PT Natasha Romaine	1986-7
FT Zoia Markova†	1986-7
FT Elena Stolyarova†	1987-8
FT Natasha Papkovich†	1988-9
PT Olga Smirnova	1989-91
FT Evelina Zolotovskaia†	1989-91
FT Galina Babina†	1991-2
PT Janna Kazarian	1992-4
PT Elena Anderson	1991-5
PT Irina Shlumukova	1994-2005
PT Svetlana Clark	1995-present
PT Natasha McGrath	1997-99

Croatian and Serbian**

FT Stanka Krančević	1971-2
FT Vjekoslav Karlovčan	1972-3
FT Steve Maričić	1973-4
FT Branko Brusar	1974-5
FT Mira Vlatković	1975-6
FT Maja Dubravcić	1976-7
FT Vera Andrassy	1977-8
FT Ivan Pletikosa	1978-9
FT Marija Marusić	1979-80
FT Branko Brusar	1980-1
FT Ivan Matković	1981-2
FT Dora Maček	1982-3
FT Damir Kalogjera	1983-4
FT Maja Bratanić	1984-5
FT Mladen Engelsfeld	1985-6
FT Marka Filipović	1986-7

FT Višnja Šepčić	1987-8
FT Vera Andrassy	1988-9
FT Jasna Bilinić-Zubak	1989-90
FT Vjekoslav Karlovčan	1990-1
FT Marija Marušić	1991-2
FT Višnja Josipović	1992-3
FT Damir Kalogjera	1993-4
PT Vladislava Ribnikar	1994-present

Slovene ¶

FT Ljuba Črnivec	1974-7
FT Srečko Fišer	1977-9
FT Božena Činkole	1979-84
FT Tone Perčič	1984-5
FT Jože Iskra	1985-8
FT Ksenija Slabe	1988-90
FT Metka Čuk	1990-3
FT Adriana Krstič	1993-7
FT Sabina Grahek	1997-2000
FT Alenka Jensterle-Doležal	2000-1
FT Andreja Ponikvar	2001-5
FT Ivana Petric Lasnik	2005-present

Polish

| FT Leszek Kukulski | 1963-4 |
| PT Monika Savage | 1998-present |

IRSCEES Visiting lecturers

| Marietta Tourian | 1994 |
| Ivan Esaulov | 2001 |

* Malcolm Jones's personal secretaries
** All those named in this list apart from Vladislava Ribnikar were members of the English Department at The University of Zagreb, who came to Nottingham under an arrangement made by Monica Partridge and R. Filipović in the early 1970s.
† Supplied through the British Council Soviet language assistants scheme under the Anglo-Soviet Cultural Agreements
¶ The Slovene lectors and lectrices were originally supplied under an agreement negotiated by Monica Partridge and Peter Herrity in the early 1970s and fully financed by Ljubljana until the independence of Slovenia.

BIBLIOGRAPHY

THE Bibliography contains publications by members of the Department of (Russian and) Slavonic Languages/Studies only when they have been mentioned in the text of the book. Correspondence with alumni and former members of staff is acknowledged in the introductory chapter.

Unpublished materials

Lavrin, Janko, The Lavrin papers, Department of Manuscripts and Special Collections, University of Nottingham.

Minutes of the Leicester Chamber of Commerce, 1915-20, held at Record Office for Leicestershire, Leicester and Rutland.

Minutes of the Nottingham Chamber of Commerce Council Meeting, 13 April 1915, pp. 19-21. Two bound volumes of printed minutes dated 1915-18 are held in the Hallward Library, University of Nottingham, uncatalogued.

Note on John Fennell, Cambridge University Archive, SLAV 1/B9.

Slepchenko, Basil: curriculum vitae of 1931 (typescript, 1 p.).

Slepchenko, Basil, Testimonial by A Bruce Boswell, Professor of Russian, dated 28 Nov. 31 (typescript, 1 p.).

Slepchenko, Basil, Grant of British nationality by naturalisation, 28 June 1930. National Archives, Kew, certificate 18419, HO 144/11688, disclosed by request under Freedom of Information Act.

Smith, Gerald, 'Interview with Emeritus Professor Janko Lavrin at 28 Addison Gardens, on 30 January 1974', Leeds Russian Archive (Ms 400/3).

Published materials

Annual Report of the University College Council, University College, Nottingham, 1921.

Barnes, Frank, *Priory Demesne to University Campus, a Topographic History of Nottingham University*, The University of Nottingham, 1993.

Beerbohm, Max, 'On Speaking French', in *And Even Now*, Heinemann, London, 1920, pp. 289-99.

'The British Council in the Soviet Union', in the *House of Commons Second Report from the Foreign Affairs Committee*, Session 1985-86, UK-Soviet Relations, vol. 2, HMSO, London, 1986, pp. 70-74.

Borras, F. M., and Christian, R. F., *Russian Syntax, Aspects of Russian Syntax and Vocabulary*, The Clarendon Press, Oxford, 1959.

Butler, John, *Wonders of Spiritual Unfoldment*, Shepheard-Walwyn, London, 2008.

Dalos, György, The *Guest from the Future: Anna Akhmatova and Isaiah Berlin*, John Murray, London, 1998.

Dediulin, Sergei, 'My rabotali v dukhe sotrudnichestva', interview with Wendy Rosslyn, *Russkaia mysl'*, No. 3786, 28 July 1989, p. 10.

Dimnik, M., 'John Fennell's Contribution to Slavonic Studies', *Oxford Slavonic Papers*, new series, XXVII, 1994, pp. 1-22.

Elliott, Geoffrey, and Shukman, Harold, *Secret Classrooms, an Untold Story of the Cold War*, St Ermin's, London, 2003.

Edgerton, W. B., 'The history of Slavistic scholarship in the United States', J. Hamm and G. Wytrzens, eds., *Beiträge zur Geschichte der Slawistik in nichtslawischen Ländern*, Verlag der Österreichischen Akademie der Wissenschaften, Vienna, 1985, pp. 491-528.

Fawcett, A. Peter, and Jackson, Neil, *Campus Critique, The Architecture of The University of Nottingham*, The Sherwood Press, Nottingham, 1998.

Fennell, J. L. I., *The Correspondence Between A. M. Kurbsky and Tsar Ivan IV of Russia, 1564-1579,* Cambridge University Press, Cambridge, 1955.

Fennell, J. L. I., *The Penguin Russian Course*, Penguin Books, Harmondsworth, 1961.

Fennell, John, 'From Professor Fennell', *Slavonica* (Nottingham), vol. 6, no. 1, December 1977, p. 15.

Gerhardie, William, *Memoirs of a Polyglot*, Robin Clark, London, 1990 (first edition, 1931).

Graham, Stephen, *Midsummer Music*, George H. Doran Company, New York, 1927.

Graham, Stephen, *Portrait of a Wonderful Scene,* Collins, London, 1964.

Herrity, Peter, *Jezik Emanuila Jankovica*, Matica Srpska, Novi Sad, 1983.

Herrity, Peter, ed., *The Bell of Freedom, Essays presented to Monica Partridge on the Occasion of her 75th Birthday*, Astra Press, Nottingham, 1990.

Herrity, Peter, *Jezička razmatranija (Studij o srbine)*, Zavod za udžbenike i nastavna sredstva, Belgrade, 1999.

Herrity, Peter, *Slovene: a comprehensive grammar*, Routledge, London, 2000.

Hill, Elizabeth, *In the Mind's Eye*, edited by Jean Stafford Smith, The Book Guild, Sussex, England, 1999.

Ignatieff, Michael, *Isaiah Berlin, A Life*, Metropolitan Books, Henry Holt and Company, New York, 1998.

Janecek, Gerald, *The Look of Russian Literature, Avant-garde visual experiments, 1900-1930*, Princeton University Press, Princeton, 1984.

Jones, Malcolm V., *Dostoyevsky: The Novel of Discord*, Paul Elek, London (Barnes and Noble, NY), 1976.

Jones, Malcolm V., ed., *New Essays on Tolstoy*, CUP, Cambridge, 1978.

Jones, Malcolm V. and Terry, Garth M., eds., *New Essays on Dostoyevsky*, CUP, Cambridge, 1983.

Jones, Malcolm V., 'La tradition de la littérature comparée dans la slavistique britannique du XX siècle (le cas de Janko Lavrine)', in Fougeron, Irina, ed., *Etudes russes - Mélanges offerts au Professeur Louis Allain*, Lille, 1996, pp. 37-43.

Jones, Malcolm V., 'Janko Lavrin, promoter of modernism and the avant-garde - a footnote', in Horst-Jürgen Gerigk, ed., *Literarische Avantgarde. Festschrift für Rudolf Neuhäuser*, Mattes Verlag, Heidelberg, 2001, pp. 73-80.

Jones, Malcolm V., 'Frank Friedeberg Seeley, 1912-2000', *Dostoevsky Studies*, New Series, vol. 5, 2001, pp. 225-30.

Jones, Malcolm V., 'Slavonic Studies in the United Kingdom since the Second World War: a personal view', in Brogi Bercoff, Giovanna, Gonneau, Pierre, Miklas,

Heinz, eds., *Beiträge zur Geschichte der Slawistik in nichtslawischen Ländern*, Verlag der Österreichischen Akademie der Wissenschaften, Vienna, 2005, pp. 267-301.

Jones, Malcolm V. and Marsh, Cynthia [published anonymously], 'Professor Monica Partridge', *The Times*, 21 April, 2008.

Kardelj, Edvard, *Reminiscences: the struggle for recognition and independence, the New Yugoslavia, 1944-1957,* translated Norris, David, Blond and Briggs, London, 1982.

Kelly's Leicestershire and Rutland Directory, [title page and verso missing, date assumed to be 1916].

Kennan, G. F., *Russia and the West under Lenin and Stalin*, Mentor, New York and Toronto, 1960, 1961.

Khlebnikov, Velimir, 'Z i ego okolitsa', in Khardziev, N., and Grits, T., eds., *Velimir Khlebnikov, neizdannye proizvedeniia*, Khudozhestvennaia literatura, Moscow, 1940, pp. 346-48.

Khlebnikov, Velimir, 'Perechen'. Azbuka uma', in Tynianov, Iu., and Stepanov, N., eds., *Sobranie proizvedenii Velimira Khlebnikova* (5 vols.), Izdatel'stvo pisatelei v Leningrade, 1928-1933, 5, pp. 207-09.

Lavrin, Ianko, *V strane vechnoi voiny: albanskie eskizy*, Tipografiia Ivanskago, Petrograd, 1916.

Lavrin, Janko, *Dostoevsky and his creation: a psychocritical study*, W. Collins & Son, London, 1920.

Lavrin, Janko, *Ibsen and his creation: a psychocritical study*, W. Collins & Son, London, 1922

Lavrin, Janko, *Nietzsche and Modern Consciousness*, W. Collins & Son, London, 1922.

Lavrin, Janko, *Tolstoy: a psychocritical study*, W. Collins & Son, London, 1924.

Lavrin, Janko, *Russian Literature*, Ernest Benn, London, 1927.

Lavrin, Janko, *Aspects of Modernism: from Wilde to Pirandello*, Nott, London, 1935.

Lavrin, Janko, *Dostoevsky, a study*, London, 1943.

Lavrin, Janko, *An Introduction to the Russian Novel*, 4th. Ed., Methuen, London, 1947

Lavrin, Janko, *A Panorama of Russian Literature*, University of London Press, London, 1973.

Lavrin, Janko, 'Difficult Beginnings', *Slavonica*, (Nottingham), vol. 6, no. 1, 1977, pp. 12-14.

Lavrin, Janko, 'Prorocheskaia dusha', Khlebnikov v vospominaniiakh sovremennikov, k 100-letiiu so dnia rozhdeniia poeta, *Literaturnoe obozrenie*, 12, 1985, pp. 97-98.

Lavrin, Janko, *Med osem in osemdeset, iz zapisnice kozmopolita*, Slovenska Matica, Ljubljana, 1987.

Lavrin, Janko, *Anton Chekhov, An Introduction to his Life and Work (Anton Čehov Uvod v Njegovo Življenje in Delo)*, Slovenska Akademija znanosti in umetnosti, Ljubljana, 2005.

Lavrin, Nora, *D. H. Lawrence, Nottingham Connections*, Astra Press, Nottingham, 1986.

Lavrin, Nora, *Slovenija, Poletje 1928, Ilustrirani dnevnik s poročnega potovanja Nore in Janka Lavrina, Vale Novak*, Ljubljana, 2004.

Lucas, H. H., 'Halls of Residence', in Wakeford, J., and Mounfield, P. R., eds., *Nottingham, Ten Years a University*, Union of Students, Nottingham, 1958, pp. 35-42.

Luker, Nicholas, *A .I. Kuprin*, Twayne Publishers, Boston, 1978.

Luker, Nicholas, *The Forgotten Visionary: Alexander Grin*, Oriental Research Partners, Newtonville, Mass., 1980.

Luker, Nicholas, *Alexander Grin*, Bradda Books, Letchworth, 1973.

Luker, Nicholas, *Fifty Years on: Gorky and his Time*, Astra Press, Nottingham, 1987.

Luker, Nicholas, ed., *From Furmanov to Sholokhov: an anthology of the classics of Socialist Realism*, Ardis, Ann Arbor, 1988.

Luker, Nicholas, *In defence of a reputation: essays on the early prose of Mikhail Artsybashev*, Astra Press, Nottingham, 1990.

Luker, Nicholas, ed., *The Short Story in Russian*, Astra Press, Nottingham, 1991.

Luker Nicholas, ed., *After the Watershed: Russian Prose 1917-1927: selected essays*, Astra Press, Nottingham, 1996.

Marsh, Cynthia, *M. A. Voloshin: artist-poet. A study of the synaesthetic aspects of his poetry*, Birmingham Slavonic Monographs, Birmingham, 1983.

Marsh, Cynthia and Rosslyn, Wendy, eds., *Russian and Yugoslav Culture in the Age of Modernism, papers published for the 75th Anniversary of the Foundation of the Department of Slavonic Studies*, University of Nottingham, Astra Press, Nottingham, 1991.

Marsh, Cynthia, *File on Gorky*, Methuen, London. 1993.

Marsh, Cynthia, 'In Memoriam: Professor Monica Agnes Partridge, 1915-2008', *BASEES Newsletter*, New Series, vol. 13, no. 1, May 2008, p. 16.

Martin, Wallace, *'The New Age' under Orage: Chapters in English Cultural History*, Manchester University Press, Manchester and New York, 1967.

Marzaduri, Marzio, 'Creazione e prima rappresentazione del dramma Janko krul' albanskaj di I. M. Zdanevic', in Magarotto, Luigi and others, eds., *Zaumnyi futurizm i dadaizm v russkoi kul'ture*, Peter Lang, Bern, etc., 1991, pp. 153-63.

Maugham, Somerset, 'Mr Harrington's Washing', *Complete Short Stories of Somerset Maugham*, Book Club Associates, London, 1951, vol. 2, pp. 864-5.

Meader, C.D., 'Russian Studies in America', *Russian Review* [Liverpool], vol. II no. ii, undated [1913?], pp. 194-196.

Meller, Helen and Mills, Jackie, *Florence Boot Hall, A Short History to mark the 70th Anniversary*, University of Nottingham, Nottingham, 1998.

Milne, Lesley, *The Master and Margarita: a comedy of victory*, Birmingham Slavonic Monographs, Birmingham, 1977.

Milne, Lesley, *Mikhail Bulgakov, Belaja gvardija*, Otto Sagner, Munich, 1983.

Milne, Lesley, *Mikhail Bulgakov, a Critical Biography*, CUP, Cambridge, etc., 1990.

Milne, Lesley, *Bulgakov: the novelist-playwright*, Harwood Academic, Luxembourg, 1995.

Mirsky, D. S., *A History of Russian Literature*, edited and abridged by Francis J. Whitfield, Routledge and Kegan Paul, London, 1949.

Modern Language Association, 'Memorandum on the Teaching of Russian' (adopted by the General Committee), *Modern Language Teaching*, xiii, 3-4, 1917 (pp. 75-85).

Moravec, Dušan, ed., *Korespondenca med Jankom Lavrinom in Antonom Slodnjakom (1951-1983)*, Slovenska Akademija znanosti in umetnosti, Ljubljana, 2002.

Moravec, Dušan, ed., *Janko Lavrin, Pisma v Domovino*, Slovenska Akademija znanosti in umetnosti, Ljubljana, 2004.

Muckle, J. Y., *British Schools in which Russian is Taught*, ATR, Nottingham, 1989.

Muckle, J. Y., *Schools, Polytechnics and Universities Where Russian is Taught, A United Kingdom List*, Bramcote Press, Nottingham, 1992.

Muckle, J. Y., 'Survey of schools, polytechnics and universities where Russian is taught', *Educational Research*, vol. 36, no. 1, Spring 1994, pp. 39-50.

Muckle, J. Y., 'Russian in the University Curriculum: A Case-study of the Impact of the First World War on Language Study in Higher Education in Britain', *History of Education*, vol. 37, no. 3, May 2008, pp. 359-81.

Muckle, James, *The Russian Language in Britain, a historical survey of learners and teachers*, Bramcote Press, Ilkeston, 2008.

Mudrova, O.V., 'Zhurnal *Slavianskii mir* (1908-1911) i voprosy kul'tury iugoslavian', *Vestnik moskovskogo universiteta*, series 10, no. 1, 1981, pp. 34-43.

Neilson, Keith, *Britain and the Last Tsar*, Clarendon Press, Oxford, 1995.

Norris, David, ed., *Miloš Crnjanjski and Modern Serbian Literature*, Astra Press, Nottingham, 1988.

Norris, David, *The Novels of Miloš Crnjanjski: an approach through time*, Astra Press, Nottingham, 1990.

Norris, David, *Teach Yourself Serbo-Croat*, Hodder and Stoughton, London, 1993.

Norris, David, *In the Wake of the Balkan Myth: questions of identity and modernity*, Macmillan, London, 1999.

Oakeshott, Michael, review of Janko Lavrin, *Nietzsche: an approach*, Methuen, *The Cambridge Review*, 1947-8, vol. 1, no. 7, pp. 450-1.

Obshchestvo slavianskogo edineniia (The Society for Slavonic Unification), *Slavianskii vopros v ego sovremennom znachenii: rechi i stat'i A. M. Aleksandrova, V. M. Bekhterova, M. M. Kovalevskogo, Ianko Lavrina, D. I. Semiza i M. P. Chubinskogo*, Obshchestvo slavianskogo edineniia, St Petersburg, 1913.

Palme, Anton, 'The Progress of Russian Studies in Germany', *Russian Review* [Liverpool], vol. 3, i, undated [1914?].

Pares, Bernard, 'Forty years on', *The Slavonic and East European Review*, vol. 18, 52, 1939, pp. 55-72.

Parnis, A. E., 'Khlebnikov: v poiskakh novogo prostranstva i o preodolenii Evropy, pamiati professora Ia. Lavrina', *in Balkanskie chteniia 2, Simpozium po strukture teksta, tezisy i materialy*, Moscow, 1992, pp. 137-43.

Partridge, Monica, 'Simon Boyanus: 1871-1952. Obituary', *The Slavonic and East European Review*, 31, 1952-53, pp. 534-56.

Partridge, Monica, 'Angliiskii iazyk iz Anglii', *Britanskii soiuznik*, British Embassy, Moscow, 1949 (weekly series of 52 lessons).

Partridge, Monica, *Serbo-Croatian: Practical Grammar and Reader*, McGraw-Hill, New York, 1964; (second, revised and improved edition, Izdavački zavod, Belgrade, 1972; third edition, Prosveta, Belgrade, 1988).

Partridge, Monica, ed., *Alexander Herzen and European Culture: Proceedings of an International Symposium*, Nottingham and London, 6-12th September 1982, Astra Press, Nottingham, 1985.

Partridge, Monica, *Alexander Herzen, 1812-1870*, Unesco, Paris, 1984.

Partridge, Monica, *Alexander Herzen: Collected Essays*, Astra Press, Nottingham, 1988, second, revised edition, 1993.

Pinto, V. de Sola, ed., *Reginald Mainwaring Hewitt 1887-1948*, Blackwell, Oxford, 1955

Popper, Karl, *Conjectures and Refutations*, Routledge and Kegan Paul, London, 1963.

Report of the Committee appointed by the Prime Minister to enquire into the position of modern languages in the educational system of Great Britain, HMSO, London, 1918. Command paper 9036 (known as the Leathes Report, after the Chairman of the Committee, Sir Stanley Leathes).

Report of the Board of Education for 1916-1917, HMSO, London, 1918.

Report on Russian and Russian Studies in British Universities, University Grants Committee, London, 1979 (chaired by Professor R. J. C. Atkinson and known as the Atkinson Report).

Review of Former Soviet and East European Studies, Higher Education Funding Council for England, 1995 (chaired by Bahram Bekhradnia and known as the HEFCE Report).

Roberts, I. W., *History of the School of Slavonic and East European Studies*, School of Slavonic and East European Studies, University of London, London, 1991.

Roosevelt, Priscilla, *Life on the Russian Country Estate, A Social and Cultural History*, Yale University Press, New Haven and London, 1995.

Rosslyn, Wendy, 'COCOA as a tool for the analysis of poetry', *Bulletin of the Association for Literary and Linguistic Computing*, 1975.

Rosslyn, Wendy, *The Prince, the Fool and the Nunnery: the religious theme in the Early Poetry of Anna Akhmatova*, Avebury, Amersham, 1984.

Rosslyn, Wendy, ed., *The Speech of Unknown Eyes: Akhmatova's Readers on her Poetry*, 2 vols., Astra Press, 1990.

Rosslyn, Wendy, *Anna Bunina (1774-1829) and the origin of women's poetry in Russia*, Edwin Mellen Press, Lewiston, Queensland, Lampeter, 1997.

Rosslyn, Wendy, *Feats of Agreeable Usefulness: translations by Russian Women 1763-1825*, Verlag F. K. Gopfert, Fichtenwalde, 2000.

Seeley, F. F. and Rapp, H., *The Gateway Russian Course*, 2 vols., Methuen, London, 1963, 1964.

Seeley, F. F., 'From Professor Seeley', *Slavonica* (Nottingham), vol. 6, no. 1, 1977, pp. 15-16.

Seeley, F. F., *Turgenev, A Reading of his Fiction*, CUP, Cambridge, 1991.

Seeley, F. F., *From the Heyday of the Superfluous Man to Chekhov, Essays on 19th-century Russian Liter*ature, Astra Press, Nottingham, 1994.

Seeley, F. F., *Saviour or Superman? Old and New Essays on Tolstoy and Dostoevsky*, Astra Press, Nottingham, 1999.

Semeonoff, Anna H., *A New Russian Grammar*, J. M. Dent and Sons, London, revised edition, 1958.

Slepchenko, Basil, 'Garantii pravil'noi otsenki uspeshnosti ekzamenuiushchikhsia' [Ensuring the correct assessment of examination candidates], *Modern Language Teaching*, vol. XIII, no. 6, Oct 1917, pp. 163-164.

Sollohub, N. S., *A Survey of Russian Teaching in British Secondary Schools*, Nuffield Foundation, London, 1967.

Spring, Derek, ed., *The Impact of Gorbachev, The First Phase, 1985-90*, Pinter Publishers, London and New York, 1991.

Stewart, John Massey, 'From Russia a hundred years ago: a letter recalled by the son of the sender', *East-West Review*, Summer, 2007, pp. 14-15.

Stone, Gerald, 'The History of Slavonic Studies in Great Britain (until the Second World War)', in Hamm, J., and Wytrzens, G., eds., *Beiträge zur Geschichte der Slawistik in nichtslawischen Ländern*, Verlag der Österreichischen Akademie der Wissenschaften, Vienna, 1985, pp. 361-98.

Terry, Garth M., *East European Languages at Literatures, II, A Subject and Name Index*, Astra Press, Nottingham, 1982. (Further volumes in the series appeared in 1985, 1988, 1991, 1994 and 1997).

The Teaching of Russian, HMSO, 1960 (chaired by Sir Noel Annan, and known as the Annan Report).

Thomas, John Heywood, 'William Neil, Warden 1953 to 1975', in Charles Watkins, ed., *A History of Hugh Stewart Hall*, The Hugh Stewart Hall Association, Nottingham, 1996, unpaginated.

Tolley, B. H. *The History of The University of Nottingham*, 2 vols., University of Nottingham Press, Nottingham, 2001.

University Grants Committee: *Report of the Sub-Committee on Oriental, Slavonic, East European and African Studies*, London, 1961 (chaired by Sir William Hayter, and known as the Hayter Report).

Wakeford, J., and Mounfield, P. R., eds., *Nottingham, Ten Years a University*, Union of Students, Nottingham, 1958.

Waterhouse, G., 'The Place of Russian', *Modern Language Teaching*, vol. XIII, nos. 7 & 8, Nov-Dec 1917, pp. 219-221.

Watts, Marjorie, *Mrs Sappho, The Life of C. A. Dawson Scott, Mother of International PEN*, Duckworth, London, 1987.

West, Daphne, *British Schools in which Russian is Taught*, ATR, Nottingham, 1983 (second edition, 1985).

Winterbottom, Derek, *Bertrand Hallward, First Vice-Chancellor of The University of Nottingham, 1948-1965, A Biography*, The University of Nottingham, Nottingham, 1995.

Wood, A. C., *A History of University College Nottingham 1881-1948*, Blackwell, Oxford, 1953.

Wooding, Norman, Cartledge, Bryan and Jones, Malcolm, *Review of Soviet and East European Studies, 1989* (chaired by Dr Norman Wooding and known as the Wooding Report).

Woolf, Virginia, *The Common Reader*, Harcourt, Brace and Co., New York, 1948.

Worthen, John, *Cold Hearts and Coronets: Lawrence, the Weekleys and the von Richthofens*, D. H. Lawrence Centre, The University of Nottingham, Nottingham, 1995.

Young, Sarah and Milne, Lesley, eds., *Dostoevsky, On the Threshold of Other Worlds*, Bramcote Press, Ilkeston, 2006.

Žitnik, Janja, 'Janko Lavrin: Slovene intellectual ambassador', *Slovene Studies*, 18, 1, 1996, pp. 3-18.

Zytaruk, George J., *D. H. Lawrence's Response to Russian Literature*, Mouton, The Hague & Paris, 1971.

INDEX

Academy Travel 81
Admoni, V.G. 117
Akhmatova, Anna 120, 124, 128
Akhvlediani, Marina 103, 137
Alekseev, M. P. 75
Amat, Jayne 8
Amirova Tamara 75, 137
Anderson, Elena 122, 137
Andrassy, Vera 90, 113, 137, 138
Andreev, Leonid 24
Andropov, Iurii 105
Anglo-Russian Literary Society 11
Anglo-Soviet Cultural and Scientific
    Agreement 57, 58, 74, 103, 116,
    119, 138
Annan, The Report 57, 58, 92
Anning, Nicholas 78, 79, 81, 88, 89,
    135
Area Studies Monitoring Group 116
Argus 25
Armstrong, Lilias, 72
Artsybashev, Mikhail 126
Aškerc, Anton 24
Association Internationale des Etudes
    Sud-Est Européennes 74
Association of Teachers of Russian 58,
    74, 85
Astra Press 86, 95, 108, 114
April, Leilani 136
Asquith, Herbert 17
Atkinson Report 92, 93, 95, 101, 102,
    105, 113, 116
Atkinson, R. J. C. 92
Attaturk, Kemal 51, 62
Avierino family 66

Babina, Galina 113, 137
Bagritsky 88
Bakhtin, N. N. 24
Barrington, E. J. 42
BBC 32, 41, 88 104
Beasley, Ina 39
Beauvoir, Simone de 65
Beckett, John 9
Beecham, Audrey 52,75
Beerbohm, Max 19
Bekhterev, V. M. 24
Bell, The, Nottingham 67
Beneš, Edvard 41
Berlin, Sir Isaiah 50, 55
Bernstein, M. D. 27

Beskrovnoe ubiistvo 26
Bilinić-Zubak, Jasna 113
Binyon, Nancy 7, 40, 106
Birmingham Chamber of Commerce 17
Birse, Arthur 48
Blok, Aleksandr 35, 36, 39, 79
Bondar, D. 16, 32
Boswell, Bruce 15
Bourget, Paul 35
Boyanus, Simon 40, 64, 72
Boyd, Alex 49
Bradshaw, Joan 92
Bradshaw, Roy 133
Bragan-Turner, Deborah 87
Branch, Michael 116
Bratanić, Maja 103, 137
Brezhnev, Leonid 71
Briggs, A. D. P. 92
Briggs, Stephanie, née Batty 8, 107,
    111, 112, 113, 114
British Association for (Soviet), Slavonic
    and East European Studies
    (BA[S]SEES) 100, 110, 116, 129
British Council, The 57, 58, 75, 77, 86,
    103, 104, 107, 108, 116, 118, 119,
    120, 138
British Universities' Association of
    Slavists (BUAS) 58, 81, 92, 99, 104,
    110, 116
Brodsky, Josip 117
Brookes, Herbert 7, 42
Brown, Mrs. 31
Browne, Mary 136
Brunger, Stephanie 120, 136
Brusar, Branko 90, 103, 137
Brusilov, General Aleksei 31
Bulavina, Iulia 86, 90, 91, 137
Bulganin, N. A. 58
Bunin, I. A. 36
Bunina, Anna 126
Burliuk, David 25, 26
Butler, John 8, 114
Bystritskaia, Elina 8, 67

Cadot, Michel 109
Calvert, Patricia 55
Cambridge Studies in Russian
    Literature 108
Campbell, Mr 40
Campbell, Sir Colin 115, 119, 128
Cankar, Ivan 24, 35

Lavrin, David 3, 7, 8, 22, 28, 38, 41, 42, 45
Lavrin, Janko 1, 3, 5, 5, 7, 8, 9, 11, 14, 18, 20, 21-45, 46, 48, 71, 73, 74, 97, 99, 100, 103, 106, 108, 109, 114, 122, 128, 129, 131, 134, 135
Lavrin, John 3, 7, 22, 30, 32, 33, 38, 41
Lavrin, Nora 3, 11, 21, 22, 31 33, 34, 38, 45
Lavrov, P. A. 24
Layton, A. R. 48
Leatherbarrow, W. J. 110
Leathes, Sir Stanley 17
Le-Dantiu, Mikhail 26, 27
Leeming, Harry 39
Leicester Technical School 14, 18
Lenin, V. I. 19, 51, 65, 66, 69, 81
Leopold, Prince, Duke of Albany 10
Lermontov, M. Iu., 24, 36, 63, 79, 80,
Leshkova, O. I. 26, 27
Lešić, Zdenko 114
Levin, Iurii 75,
Liddle, Peter 28,
Lidin, Vladimir 8, 75,
Linley, Des 111
Liverpool College of Commerce 18
Ljublianski zvon, 39
Lomax, W. (Bill) 118
Luker, Nicholas, J. L. 78, 81, 85, 89, 93, 97, 105, 108, 112, 119, 126, 127, 132, 133, 135

Maček, Dora 9, 103, 137
McCauley, Martin 129
McGrath, Natasha 131, 137
Mackinder, Sir Halford 52
McMichael, Polly 133, 136
Macmillan, Harold 59
Maiakovsky, Vladimir 25, 26, 35, 105
Major, John 118
Malherbe, François de 61
Mance, Gina 8
Mandel'stam, Osip 25
Manning, Nick 133
Mansfield, Katherine 36
Marcetić, Jovan 7, 82, 87, 90
Margaret Glen Bott Comprehensive School 103
Maričić, Steve 74, 137
Markova, Zoia 103, 137
Marsh, Cynthia, née Ball 1, 7, 8, 9, 85, 86, 89, 93, 94, 97, 101, 105, 108, 109, 112, 115, 120, 121, 124, 126, 133, 136

Martin, Wallace 35
Marušić, Marija 90, 113, 137, 138
Marzaduri, M. 27
Marx, Karl 69
Masaryk, Jan 41
Mashinsky, S. 75
Masterman, Elizabeth 7, 91
Matković, Ivan 103, 137
Matthews, W. K. 39
Maude, Aylmer 36, 37
Maugham, Somerset 11-12
Maurice Thorez Institute, Moscow 104, 119
May, Gerry 7, 8, 54, 64, 67
Mayer, Arthur 7, 56
Mayo, Peter 110
Meader, C. D. 12
Meršol, Mitja 7,
Meudon (Centre d'Etudes Russes) 81, 114
Miller, Henry 30, 39
Miller, Arthur 31
Miller, Robin Feuer 128
Mills, Christopher 78, 86, 88, 135
Milne, Lesley 8, 9, 93, 97, 109, 113, 117, 119, 125, 126, 129, 131, 132, 136
Milošević, Slobodan 121
Minto, Lord 11
Mirsky, D. S. 30, 37, 63, 64
Mitrinović, Dmitrije 36, 37
Modna ptica 39
Molière 61
Morgan, Ruth, née Fisher 7, 64, 81
Morris, Pat 87, 136
Moscow Linguistics Institute 114
Moscow Military Mission 51
Muckle, James 3, 9, 10, 85, 87, 105, 109, 111, 129
Mudrova, O. V. 24, 26
Muir, Edwin 30, 36
Müller, V. K. 72
Murjas, Jolanta 106, 136
Murphy, Lisa 136
Murry, Middleton 36

Naidenov, Nikolai 57, 79, 85, 89, 90, 101, 137
National Association for Soviet and East European Studies 58, 110
Navalnaya, Svetlana 90, 137
Neil, William 52
Nekrasov, N. A. 77
New Age, The 28, 29, 35, 36
Newiss, Joan 7, 49

Russian Language Undergraduate Study
    Committee (RLUSC) 103, 104, 107,
    119
Russkaia mysl' 117
Russo-British Chamber of Commerce 12,
    16, 17

Sakharov, Andrei 118
Sandell, Terry 7, 62, 120,
Sarkar, Sheila, née Christopherson 7, 81
Saulus, V. P. 48, 51, 57, 136
Savage, Monika 130, 138
Scammell, Michael 48, 50, 63, 69
Scarbrough Report 73, 93, 96
Scott, C. A. Dawson 30
Scott-Mitchell, Katrine 8
Seeley. F. J. B. F. 8, 47, 53, 54-70, 71,
    72, 73, 78, 80, 95, 97, 98, 99, 100,
    101, 109, 135
Seeley, Maria 8
Semeonoff, Anna 62, 79
Semyonova, Ina 75, 137
Šepčić, Višnja 113, 138
Serbian Army 28, 29
Serbian Theological College 29
Shakespeare, William 35, 36, 73
Shaw, George Bernard 35, 36
Shcherbakova, Olga 103, 137
Sheila ? (departmental secretary) 87, 136
Shestov, Lev 36
Shevelyeva, Nelli 90, 137
Shil'der, M. V. 24
Shlumukova, Irina 122, 137
Shukman, Harold 3, 7, 48, 49, 50, 52, 94
Sing, Charlotte 7, 86
Singleton, Mr 60
Sirotinin, A. N. 24
Sitwell, Edith 30
Sitwell, Osbert 30
Sitwell, Sacheverell 30
Slabe, Ksenija 113, 138
Slavianin 26
Slavianskii mir 23, 24, 26, 29, 36
Slavonic Society 52, 67, 85
Slavonica 21, 48, 57, 69, 85, 86, 90
Slepchenko, Basil 3, 10, 13, 14, 15, 16,
    18, 20, 32, 106, 129, 135
Smart, Alastair 61
Smirnova, Olga 113, 137
Smith, Gerald S. 7, 8, 9, 30, 37, 57, 78,
    79, 80, 86, 88, 89, 135
Smith, R. S. 62
Šmitran, Stevka 114
Snook, Michael 8, 133

Sobchak, Anatolii 121
Society for Slav Scientific and
    Scholarly Unification 25
Sologub, Fedor 25
Solov'ev, Vladimir 69
Solzhenitsyn, Aleksandr 75
Soviet Union of Writers 50, 75
Spellman, Eileen 52
Spengler, Oswald 36
Spring, Derek 9, 58, 79, 97, 111, 117
Sprott, W. J. H. 42
Stalin, J. V. 52, 58, 66, 75, 101
Stein, S. V. 24
Stephens, Revd C. H. 106
Stepniak-Kravchinsky, S.M. 11
Stevens, Mick 90
Stewart, Hugh 39
Stewart, John Massey 9, 39
Stolyarova, Elena 113, 137
Stone, Gerald 9, 57, 77, 78, 79, 80, 81,
    88, 130, 135
Studia Slavica Savariensia 126
Strickland, Dorothy 7, 80, 90
Stubbings, Roger, Revd. 7, 64, 81
Suez, the crisis 51, 58
Surzhina, Viktoria 75, 137
Suvorin, Mikhail 28
Swain, Adam 127, 133
Swinnerton-Dyer, Sir Peter 118
Szyszczak, Paul 8, 101, 102, 105

Taplin, Nancy, née Cunningham 7, 82
Taplin, Susan, née West 2, 8
Tate, Brian 86
Teaching Quality Assurance (TQA) 127,
    128
Terminasova, Svetlana 119
Terry, Garth, M. 22, 86, 95, 108,
Thatcher, Margaret 102, 106, 118
Thawley, Elaine, née Watkins 7
The Happy Return, Nottingham 112
Thomas, Dylan 30
Thompson, Della 7, 9, 77, 78, 62, 80. 82,
    90
Thompstone, Stuart 117, 133
Thorpe, Lewis 77
Tikhomirova, Viktoria 122
Tito, Josip Broz 74
Tolley, Brian 9
Tolstoi, L. N. 24, 33, 36, 37, 43, 63, 77,
    80, 93, 99
Tomashevskaia, Z. B. 117
Tourian, Marietta, 8, 122, 138